THE WISE SHALL INHERIT GLORY

Colleen Anderson

The Wise Shall Inherit Glory
by Colleen Anderson

Printed in the United States of America

ISBN 9781613795330

Unless otherwise indicated, Bible quotations are taken from The Holy Bible, Amplified Expanded edition. Copyright © 1987 by Zondervan Publishing House and the Lockman Foundation; and The Bible in Contemporary Language, The Message. Copyright © 2002 by Eugene H. Peterson.

Quotes from books by EW Bullinger:
   Numbers in Scripture, copyright 1967, Kregel Publishing.
   Lost Books of the Bible, copyright 1926, Alpha House.

Songs:
   From the Cross to Glory, written by Colleen Anderson and Robert Spoon. Recorded in 1973.
   The Wave, words and music written by Donny Anderson. Recorded in 1991.

www.xulonpress.com

TABLE OF CONTENTS

DEDICATION

My gratitude and appreciation to the body of Christ, to each living stone that allowed themselves to be hewn out, shaped, chiseled and formed, and set into their place and position in the walls of the eternal house of God in the Kingdom of our Wonderful Glorious Lord and Savior, Jesus the Christ! To Him be all the honor and the glory and the praise forever and forever! For without your crucified lives and the love, revelation, wisdom and knowledge imparted and expressed through your lives, gifts and ministries I would not have been able to make my contribution to the building up of the body of Christ and the spreading of His Kingdom in my generation, as well as passing on a spiritual legacy and heritage to the next.

I humbly dedicate this book to you.

And to those whom the Lord personally brought alongside me at the birthing and raising up of Living Water Ministries Fellowship and divinely connected me with, some of whom are still a part of our lives: Max and Norma Evans and their children; Tina, Rodney and children; Glenda, Jeremy and children; Frankie McGough; Gene Dillard; Joy Wood Brandstetter; Gary and Deborah Childers; The FMCI family; Jim and Jeane Hodges; Don and Cherri Crum; Rally Call; Pastors Billy and Angie Nunez; Jamie Lipe; AnneLori Rasco; Larry and Deane Diehl; and so many more, impossible to mention all, but you know who you are and God certainly does! Special mention: David and Suzy Wells; Stan and Marianne Smith; Hayseed and Mary Jeane Stevens.

I gratefully dedicate this book to you!

And to my husband, T.W. A faithful, good man who loved, challenged, encouraged and supported me in all the ways necessary, who enabled me to respond wholeheartedly to the call of God upon my life. He was a good father to our children, a loyal friend, who loved the Lord and gave liberally to the work. He went on home after a lengthy illness in 2003.

I dedicate this book to you in loving memory, Sweetheart.

Words are inadequate to express my gratitude and thankfulness for my parents, Bernie and Blanche Moore, who set such a high standard of unconditional love, integrity and faith for me and my brother, Pat Moore, and our children.

Our inheritance from their life estate was and is far greater than this world's goods! Those 'seeds' of the kingdom have continued to multiply and grow trees of righteousness, bearing fruit in every season to the glory of God our Father and the spreading of His Kingdom!

I dedicate this to you in loving memory.

It is impossible to express the depth of love and thanksgiving for the gift of my sons and daughters-in-love and grandchildren. Randy, Betty and their children, David Jordan and Shawn; Donny, Lori and their children, Lacey and James, and my great-grandson Noah; Andreas; Heath, Jamie and their children; Heather and her children. And for those added to my heart: Beverly, Tom and their children; Richard, Karen and their children; all the other wonderful spiritual children and grandchildren all God's precious ones! You are truly the Father's gifts and have brought such joy and pleasure and richness to my life and continue to do so. And to Lois and Robert Spoon, a special daughter and son. Only the Lord knows what a blessing you were and are to my life. Robert, your heart and talent and Lois's faith, love and courage and zest for life touched all of our lives and we were never the same!

Thank you all, my darlings! I lovingly dedicate this book to each of you, for it is your story too, and a part of your heritage. And to Pat and Martha, thank you for all the love and grace and help through the years. You are so precious to my heart. And to their children:

Bryan and wife Keri and children; Angie and Billy Nunez and children, what an adventure it has been! The joy, tears, love and experiences of the glory, power and grace we have shared as a family have been such a delight and blessing and strength to my soul. I love you dearly!

I dedicate this book to you as a part of your heritage as well.

And to the Church in Corpus Christi who received me as one of Jesus' sent ones and honored me. And to the special ones God the Holy Spirit joined me to, that the Kingdom might continue to increase within me and around me, and just because He loves me! He wanted to richly bless me with more sons and daughters and grandchildren! Brothers and sisters! All of you are amazing! You will never know this side of heaven the prophetic picture your lives paint of the Majesty of our living Christ and the hope and assurance of His Kingdom on earth as it is in heaven! You have ministered to me and challenged me more than you will ever know! Just to mention a few: Sonya, Charles and Maya, David, Shirley, the Fechts, the Valles, Franklands, and all the young adults, too many of you to mention by name, but you know who you are. I SO love you!

I dedicate this book to you

How comforting to know that stone upon stone, from generation to generation, the House is being built! And one day He shall bring forth the finishing capstone with loud shouts! "GRACE! GRACE TO IT!" The one new man! The bride fully adorned and laden with jewels, radiant in the beauty of her Bridegroom! The King! The church, His family! Together we will have overcome! We have His promise, the family circle will never be broken! How good He is!

Truth emerges from the generations of revelation. The cross began the process for the generations. We've come a long way, baby! What a glorious journey it has been thus far! I cannot imagine the glory that awaits us around the next 'bend'! From the cross to glory, a road paved with grace! A light goes before us, our Savior's sweet face!

FOREWORD

T his book is a testimony of love, trust, faith, truth and a witness
of the progression of maturity that comes out of intimacy with
God.

Throughout history, the Lord has had those who somehow desire
Him more than life itself. Those who will dare to follow regardless
how it looks, or feels, or what radical obedience might bring, like
ridicule, slander, rejection, etc.

Colleen is one of those whom Father has chosen to live as an
expression of radical love and obedience to Him. She has broken the
alabaster box, washed His feet with her tears, dried those precious
feet with her hair, and rejoiced the entire time.

The blessing is mine, to have walked beside this woman and
gleaned from her passion and love for Christ. These things you
cannot learn in a school. Her patience and acceptance of me were
the guiding influence that kept me searching the heart of Father, to
have what she had in her relationship to Him.

From her birth until now, she is a sign. At birth, she was delivered with her inward parts exposed and the doctors of that day did
not have the ability to deal with the situation; but God and a mother
of faith did!!! She has lived every day of her life since then by faith
and guts; honest about mistakes, transparent for all to see. Her love
for Jesus is greater each passing day...like a burning bush that is not
consumed by the fire.

Many have been touched by the fire of God through this sweet
lady. Wherever she goes, she releases that kingdom sort of love that

catches those who are looking for Him. She offends the religious, loves the sinner, and is ready and willing to go the limit for her Jesus.

As a forerunner, she is never content to accept the status quo. The next hill beckons her to action and another chance to trust the One she loves. As you read this book, you will see that she has pushed through the threshold and can be used by Father as apostle, prophet, pastor, evangelist, and teacher, according to the needs of the people. Jesus did this and He is her pattern. Oneness with Him has released the fivefold anointing to a much larger degree in Colleen than most. She does not call herself, or specifically wish to be called, any of the fivefold office titles. Colleen seeks to live as an expression of Christ, period!

Colleen has lived her life as a pioneer, creating an extraordinary map to the secret place in Christ. Be blessed, as this book tells a candid story of God's love, grace, and annointings. As Colleen puts it, "We have come a long way baby; but there is more, and the best is just over the next mountain!!!"

Max Evans
Pastor
Living Water Ministries

ENDORSEMENTS

My mom, Colleen Anderson, has been the single most influential person thus far in my personal, professional and spiritual walk with God. Cultivating a relationship with her is a divine fulfillment of a large part of my destiny, and the personal cry and longing of my heart. Our mutual longing to see and experience the "merging of the generations" has unleashed and released thus far hope unimaginable, and a glorious end-time harvest on earth that has superseded anything I have ever known! Colleen's continual display of the Father's beauty and grace, her passion and perseverance in prayer, and relentless fervor in seeing her Creator prophetically reconcile Himself to His beloved have continued to be a driving force in my pursuit of the Father's heart for myself and a lost generation. It is truly inspiring to see her life, testimony, and His Glory love be put on display through her book, *THE WISE SHALL INHERIT GLORY*.

Sonya Martinez, daughter
Founder of Blue Nation Inc.
Director of Beautiful Dream Africa

We believe in our family dwells a flame... an Olympic torch, if you will. We don't know where it began, but it first evidenced itself in our grandmother, Blanche Moore. We could see the flame dancing in her eyes as she loved unconditionally, encouraged constantly, and bravely spoke the truth in love. We know it now to be the Love and Presence of God! It is this very flame... torch ... that burns in our Aunt Colleen. This torch is passed not necessarily through physical death ... but the death that Jesus spoke of when He said, "Unless a grain of wheat falls into the ground and dies, it remain only one. But, if it dies, it multiplies." It is this type of death in which we believe this book originated in Colleen's heart. A glorious death through trials, tribulations, to reputation, and to the approval of man. Her experience of this continual glorious death to self is resurrected in the pages of this book, and it is our expectation and prayer that the seeds therein will be fruitful and multiply.

Pastors Billy and Angie Nunez
San Antonio, Texas

Colleen Anderson, priest, prophetess, psalmist, businesswoman and shepherd with the heart of a righteous mother. She has allowed God the Holy Spirit to dictate to her what will greatly help us who know Jesus to REALLY know Him and His will for our lives.

Traditionally, most of us have been taught the greater benefits of Jesus will be ours in heaven as we live a dedicated, loving life here on earth. But Colleen has discovered by intimate, consistent worship of Father God and Christ Jesus through the Holy Spirit, loving and honoring His Word, that the Wise Shall Inherit a glorious dimension of God's Glory here on earth as we are transitioning to heaven's greater glory! To be wise is to know and apply God's word with great joy, and expectancy of all His promises to be answered abundantly above what we can ask or think.

God loves all of mankind so much, and His will is that the whole earth be filled with His Glory, flooded with His Presence. As we believe His Glory is greater than our problems and the darkness, the Glory will manifest and set us free, bringing us into His marvelous Light!

Colleen shows how to believe to be wise enough to walk in this God-given heritage of glory right now, that we may be carriers of His Glory to the nations. The Glory is all He is and has. Jesus tells the eleven apostles in John 17:20-23, He gives the Glory for us to be as One with Him as He is with the Father so the world will believe God sent Him and loves them as He loves Jesus. The Apostle Paul was the very worst terrorist against the church, to wipe out the Name of Jesus. But when the Glory of God, designed to wipe out all evil, enveloped him and struck him to the ground with love and brilliance at the high noon of his evil mission, he was blinded and in fear and trembling cried out, "Lord, what will You have me do?" Immediately, he proclaimed the name of Jesus he had come to defame. The authority given him to eliminate Christians was replaced by him writing two-thirds of the New Testament.

Colleen's intimacy with God directing her, the God kind of love she has for all people motivating her, and her caution to hold to the balance of God's Word, will bring you to Glory experiences. Her transparency will encourage you to keep moving forward as God's love is so clearly revealed. Her mandate is truly from God, as you will come to know as you receive an impartation of the light, love, and power from the anointing upon the pages of this book.

David Wells, Pastor
Author of the Harrison House Classic:
"Flowing in Wealth"
and the new 'bombshell', "Jesus Was a Capitalist."

"Mom Colleen" [as so many of us know her] quickly became a predominant and influential spiritual advisor to my life over the last several years. As a pastor in the Body of Christ, Texas, the prophetic promises before me and the city in which I'm planted have ominously loomed like a distant rain cloud, longing to break out in a powerful, demonstrative way! The need for prophetic intercessors before us is ever increasing as we stand in a face-off between our God and the god of this age. Just as Deborah challenged and gave guidance to Barak, so has Mom Colleen challenged me. From a season of being "hemmed in" to a time with the "wind at my back," Mom Colleen has faithfully warred by my side to accomplish all God has for my life. The journey and adventure of her life [as told by her in this book] is a clear picture of God's redemptive grace, love, and supernatural power to equip a saint for the lifelong destiny put upon her life for over two generations and beyond. That destiny? Leave a kingdom-changing legacy for me, you the reader, and the thousands coming behind us, to accomplish the Father's perfect will in heaven and upon this earth! Mom Colleen's reward is for all of us to know and experience the Father's heart as we forerun into the future, while never forgetting the foundations built for us in history. Read this book, and get ready for a supernatural impartation of the "more" He has in store!

Pastor David Bendett
March 9, 2011

A MOTHER IN ZION! Having known Colleen Anderson only a few short years, I can truly say I have met a 21st Century Deborah. Biblical Deborah had deep faith in God. She united the people of Israel and led them to victory against the Canaanites. I have had the privilege of observing Colleen's leadership abilities as she interacts with people. I can truly say, like Deborah of old, she has a deep faith in God and the ability to unite people and teach them kingdom principles she learned through life's experiences.

Colleen 's prophetic insight is exemplified through out her book, *The Wise Shall Inherit Glory*. As the next generation of sons and daughters read this book, they will glean spiritual insight into the Kingdom of our Lord Jesus Christ and His principles that were learned and taught by this dear saint of God. Colleen is a living memorial to show that the Lord is upright and faithful to His promises; He is our Rock, and there is no unrighteousness in Him. Psalm 92:15 I highly recommend this book to be read by both young and old alike.

Nancy Brassfield
Harvest International Ministries, Inc.

True Biblical prophecy contains three basic elements: exhortation, edification and comfort. One who prophesies speaks to men for their up-building, constructive spiritual progress, encouragement, and consolation. Colleen Anderson's book, ***The Wise Shall Inherit Glory***, is filled with wisdom and prophetic insight that contain these three elements. Created by a lifetime of experience, our dear sister in the Lord has given this generation hope for the future as she relives the faithfulness of God through Christ Jesus our Lord that brings us into our final glory. "And [then] when the Chief shepherd is revealed, you will win the conqueror's crown of glory." First Peter 5:4, Amplified Bible.

Prophet Samuel L. Brassfield
Harvest International Ministries, Inc.

FROM THE CROSS TO GLORY

CHORUS:
From the Cross to Glory
A road paved with Grace
A Light goes before me
My Savior's Sweet Face

VERSES:
The Cross paid my debt
The grave buried my sin
The empty tomb my victory
A crown of life to win!

And so dear friend if you love Him
Don't walk life's road on your own
To love Him is to trust Him
And depend on Him alone

Colleen Anderson
Robert Spoon

INTRODUCTION

One of the requirements of a priest is that he could not have scabs. A scab covers an unhealed wound. One who has scabs is so overly sensitive and guarded, if you were to knowingly or unknowingly touch or 'scratch' even close to the scab, there would be an unpleasant reaction! Spiritual scabs can disqualify us from our most important ministries. That isn't to say Father God will not use us until we are fully healed.

Scars, on the other hand, left from healed wounds, are okay and keep us sensitive to help us discern the wounds in others that have not yet been healed. Our scars can provide the sensitivity and compassion toward others so that God can release His healing power through us.

2 Corinthians 1:3
Blessed be the Father of our Lord Jesus Christ, the Father of sympathy, pity and mercy and the God Who is the Source of every comfort. Who comforts [consoles and encourages] us in every trouble [calamity and afflictions] so that we may also be able to comfort, console and encourage those who are in any kind of trouble or distress, with the comfort which we ourselves are comforted by God! Hallelujah!

Each of our life stories BC [before Christ] is a mosaic of what human nature without the Spirit of Christ is capable of: Immorality, impurity, idolatry, anger, strife, rebellion, envy, drunkenness etc., etc. Galatians 5:19.

We come to the conclusion, hopefully, that we cannot save ourselves. We have no authority over the enemy of our souls, we cannot overcome in the strength of our wills, nor by human philosophy, psychology, nor any religion. "NOT BY POWER OR HUMAN STRENGTH, BUT BY MY SPIRIT," SAYS THE LORD! Zechariah 4:6. Religion is the most used 'anesthetic' to numb the conscience through ritual, discipline or self-abasement. False gods lure and hold people in the kingdom of darkness. But Jesus came! To set the captive free! "Surely He has borne our griefs [weaknesses, distresses] and carried our sorrows and pains, but He was wounded for our transgressions, bruised for our guilt and iniquities; the chastisement needful to obtain our peace and well-being was laid upon Him and with the stripes that wounded Him we are healed and made whole!" Isaiah 53:5

I pray you will not be led to see God in my story, but to see my story in God's. The evidence of His total involvement in the lives of His children to bring us to the fullness of our redemption and destiny in Him. God the Holy Spirit is the larger context and plot in which my story finds itself. When we're admitted into the family of God, we are taken seriously just as we are and given a place in His Story. None of us are the leading characters in the story of our lives. He is the Creator, Architect and Builder of His House, His Temple, His permanent dwelling place that no man has anything of which to boast! GLORY!

The Holy Spirit began to speak:
"You must hear ME, only when you receive your 'bread' directly from Me will the eyes of your heart be opened.

"You can be distracted the most by those who are the most like Me if you do not see through them to see Me!

"Your own reasoning will lead you into direct conflict with My will if you do not take up your cross daily, putting all that you are and all that you have before IT. You will fall because of the authority and power that I give you. You can only think like Me when you are in perfect union with Me." Yes, Lord.

The Holy Spirit spoke to me through Pastor Dave Roberson in 1988. He was ministering in San Angelo, TX, and had already began teaching, when he stopped and walked down the aisle toward me and called me out and began to prophesy, saying, "The Lord will not let me continue until I release this word over you." This was one of those times where the Holy Spirit makes sure there is no doubt He has spoken! The atmosphere was charged with His Presence, two or three hundred people were present, our hearts were prepared and ready to receive from the gifts and teaching anointing of Brother Dave. As he walked towards me, the anointing on him began to engulf me and the word sounded like thunder in my ears and felt like rain in my spirit, and somehow I knew God's words had already created and set in motion what was spoken, and I knew they would come to pass! Most were a puzzle to me at that time. He was preparing His house and it was necessary that now there be a personal physical house built which He would provide so another house for Himself could be built to touch the nations! Many things were prophesied that night among them. "I see a book — you will write and record the journey, the unfolding to the glory of My grace and the increase of My kingdom. I am placing a pioneering spirit upon you now!" At that moment, the power of God enveloped me and I fell out under the power.

A few months later, Nita Johnson, a prophetess, was in a conference in Abilene, TX. She called me out and spoke many things over my life: "You will bring forth the good news unto the people and it shall be a news that will break the captivity over those who are bound. I also see a book in you and it's a beautiful book, it's going to be highly anointed by the Holy Spirit through the words that will go on the pages of this book. They will have been developed through many tears and encounters and challenges, all will release an anointing that will set many free and encourage many others on their journey."

Several other 'reminders' along the way. In 2006 Max Evans prophesied, "A book is forthcoming as well as the anointing and spirit of Caleb." My Father is the Supreme Encourager!

Out of a time of fasting and prayer and meditating over the prophetic word through Dave Roberson in '88, I heard the Holy Spirit say, "Proverbs 3:35, the name of the book is *The Wise Shall Inherit Glory*."

And in that same time of seeking the Lord, He said, "And the ministry will be called Living Water Ministries Fellowship." The Word that came forth concerning the vision for the ministry was, "We would be as an oasis in the desert that would provide clear fresh water from deep wells that would refresh, revive and enable people to continue on the journey. That we would discover and re-dig the ancient wells. He said we would be cultivators and we would be cultivated. We would also be gleaners in His field, gleaning those who had fallen, gleaning from the stalk those who had been left behind and not considered worthwhile. He said some would be planted, some would be passing through, some would be sent forth as we would model the apostolic and prophetic. Needless to say, it took a while for the Holy Spirit to shake me free of some things, to tear down and then build up and impart, to prepare me not only to embrace the vision, but to walk it out as it unfolded before me. When He called and what He 'downloaded' in my spirit — talk about — "not many wise according to the flesh, nor mighty or noble, just foolish, weak and base" BUT — BUT — BUT GOD!

I earnestly pray the content of my story and my unique journey will not only end up communicating "The Wise Shall Inherit Glory" [comprehensive insight into the ways and purposes of God], but that you might be moved into another degree of glory, and the light upon your path become brighter!

2 Corinthians 3:18
And all of us, as with unveiled face, because we continued to behold in the word of God as in a mirror the glory of the Lord, are constantly being transfigured into His very own image in ever increasing splendor and from one degree of glory to another; for this comes from the Lord who is the Spirit.

Hebrews 2:9-10

But we are able to see Jesus, who was ranked lower than the angels for a little while, crowned with glory and honor because of His having suffered death, in order that by the grace [unmerited favor] of God to us sinners, He might experience death for every individual person. For it was an act worthy of God and fitting to the divine nature, that He, for Whose sake and by Whom all things have their existence, in bringing many sons into Glory!

I often felt as if I had been called forth and put on display as an affront to religious spirits. My own mind was assaulted. I had been shaken to the core of my foundation. I had been through some things! And still going through things! And change! Transition has become a 'by' word! I am so dependant upon the Holy Spirit to communicate His heart to minister to those who need encouraging, to give hope to those who think their situation maybe hopeless, or to those who think there has been so much junk and clutter and mess in their lives, too many failures and wrong choices and detours to say to them there is never too much that God can't handle, that He hasn't already made provision for. It isn't about how we start but how we finish! I can, from experience, SHOUT, "His Grace Is Sufficient!" It's never too late and it is never impossible for your Heavenly Father to work all things for your good, to turn your mistakes into miracles and the snares set by satan to entrap and destroy you, to try to interfere with your purpose and destiny, can become stepping stones to blessings you could never imagine, and that God can and will use in your life for His glory and your exaltation! And I say with boldness and confidence, God is faithful to His words, historical recorded word, and His ever-proceeding word! He watches over His words to see they come to pass and accomplish His purpose! And it is His purpose to reveal Himself, His Word and the mysteries of His Kingdom to His children, that we might know and understand what is the immeasurable and unlimited and surpassing greatness of His power in and for us who believe! That we might be rooted deep in Love, founded securely on Love!

I knew 'the Book' would be coming forth in the fullness of God's time.

Living Water Ministries Fellowship became a prophetic reality January 1, 1992, in the living room of the house He provided for us in Cross Plains, TX!

In 2003, while sitting on my front porch, my favorite place to pray and worship the Lord, the Holy Spirit came and enveloped me in the spirit and began to speak to me. It was time for me to pass the ministry to the next generation, to my spiritual son, Max, as I had taken it as far as I could take it and He wanted to extend my boundaries! More to this story later on!

It is now 2009, and the book has come to the fullness of time as well as other things! My 80th birthday fell on the 8th of 2008! How prophetic is that! So fasten your seat belts, we're going on one of those 'joy' rides that may get 'bumpy,' where anything could happen! I'm keeping mine unbuckled! I'll be doing a little flying and taking a few risks along the way!

I am so totally dependent upon the Holy Spirit for this assignment, and because He has strongly indicated it is time for the birthing. It's been almost too long in the womb. In obedience, I have begun to 'push' and the head is showing. Halle!

I know there is so much He wants to reveal of Himself and His ways. His Love and grace. His kindness as well as His severity. Much TRUTH has been hidden in religion, obscured in men's doctrines and tradition, distorted and perverted through prejudices, and we have perished for the lack of knowledge! [knowledge: 'Yada': to ascertain by 'seeing,' discern, beware, comprehend, diligence, discover, be learned, skillful, teach, have understanding]

The Lord Christ has let me know that this book will not take the usual form and may seem to not have continuity. For in sharing with you 'OUR' story, there will be prophecies, revelation, prayers, teachings, from the Holy Spirit as well as sharing parts of my journal that no one else has seen [by HIS request and my trepidation]!

Pearls of wisdom by the Spirit, a revealing of Himself, His attitudes toward His dearly loved ones, the way of His workings within us the process of the developing of our faith and the perfecting of love. The evidence He is in control and all-powerful and the nature of His unconditional love and mercy! So that we no longer perish for the lack of understanding, and "The Wise Shall Inherit Glory" Amen!

The Captain of the Host is mobilizing His army, the gathering angels are gathering! The Body of Christ is rising up all over the earth, shining brightly in the darkness! God the Holy Spirit is maturing and equipping His church! The Spirit of Grace is the Spirit of Wisdom and revelation, the Revealer of Christ Jesus to our hearts to bring us fully into our inheritance! He is the Power within His people! We are not going out of this world weak, broke, crippled and bound! We're going out in a blaze of glory! And before we go, the earth will be filled with His Glory, His manifested power! YES!

Proverbs 3:35
The Wise shall inherit glory, but shame shall be the promotion of fools.

Daniel 12:3
They that be Wise shall shine as the brightness of the firmament and they that turn many to righteousness as the stars forever and ever.

AWAKEN AND ARISE WARRIOR BRIDE

Paul's revelation of the greatness of the plan of God by which we are being built together in Christ to form His body, the church, the complicated, many-sided wisdom of God in all its infinite variety and innumerable aspects might now be made known to the angelic rulers and authorities, principalities and powers in the heavenly sphere! Ephesians 3:10

If I can fan the flame of passion or stir up our desire to move into 'Being' the church instead of 'Doing' church. If I can help us to be more aware of our true identity as the Bride of Christ, a mystery hidden from ages past, as being God's military force in the earth! The real church is a living, breathing, supernatural, heavenly new creation entity that carries and manifests the very Kingdom of God on earth! The people who KNOW their God shall do mighty exploits in His Name!

Being the Bride is not just about a wedding! This bride is a warrior, being raised up as the weapon of God in His Hand to enforce the victory accomplished at Calvary over satan and his fallen angels, being a constant reminder to all demonic powers of the triumph of Jesus Christ over all His enemies! Yes!

The church has a destiny and purpose to actually display the very glory and victory of God to the principalities, cosmic powers and evil spiritual forces in heavenly places. Ephesians 6:12

This means we are not to be postured in a spectator position, but rather an 'offensive position.' [Intercessors are offensive linemen and we need to stay in condition, beef up our faith muscles and keep well 'oiled'!] This generation is awakening to the reality of our high calling and eternal purpose as an army of God with a mandate and commission!

Paul, writing to the church at Colosse: "I am delighted at the sight of your standing shoulder to shoulder in such orderly array and the firmness and solid front and steadfastness of your faith." Colossians 2:5. This is the offensive position. The enemy cannot breach that wall or leap over it. I heard in my spirit, "My command was for my army to run through the troops and leap over their walls. Instead your ranks are easily broken through and your walls are no barrier at all. Close Ranks! Close Ranks! You have been run through and run over and the devil has stolen your goods, because the body has been disjointed, separated, divided within and without! The kingdom within is divided. The kingdom of the flesh must be conquered and you love not your lives unto death! First unity within, hating what I hate, loving what I love! If you love Me, you'll obey Me. Love the Lord your God with all your heart and soul and your brother as yourself!"

There has been a demonic curse and demonic government ruling over this planet: satan, God's enemy and ours, called 'the god of this world.' However, satan's power only resides in our ignorance. Jesus warned: "Do not be ignorant of satan's devices [strategies, deception]." When we the church are ignorant of our identity and calling as heaven's representatives and enforcers, and refuse to avail ourselves of all He has provided for our 'complete' salvation [wholeness and freedom through the power of Holy Spirit], the devil will remain in a place of power!

Jesus is clear about His mandate to rule and reign over the powers of darkness and to deliver every tribe, tongue and nation from demonic bondage! Jesus is, was, and is the pattern Son! The prototype of those born of the Spirit, that's the church, His body in the earth, His kings and priests. The mandate is still the same as in Genesis 1 and 14, Joshua 2 and 4, Matthew 10, John 14, and so on and so on! "Go take the land, subdue it, take dominion, change the culture, manifest the kingdom!"

It is time to join together, close ranks, and get out of and over 'ourselves.' Get over 'church-ianity' and get fully into CHRIST-ianity! It is time to understand Paul's teaching and instruction to the church at Corinth [1 Corinthians 3] and walk in it! I decree we will become a fully equipped army, equivalent to David's mighty men of valor, in agreement and one accord, putting up a solid front that the enemy cannot breach or break through! We must go beyond! We were not just to go through the 'gates' in '08 and camp there! It's the opening to the new place, new territory in the spirit and in the earth and we are to 'spy' out and take dominion in Jesus' Name! As the kingdoms of our heart become the kingdoms of our God, His kingdom spreads and increases upon the earth! We must continue moving with the Spirit and take whatever 'risk' He requires of us or the circumstances demand of us to come out of the old order and into the new! So many different ways to say or describe this 'season,' or 'day' or 'way.' Not new, really, it's just been hidden and concealed in religion, tradition and darkness. All things hidden will be exposed, all things concealed will be revealed. There is an unveiling and a revealing by the Spirit within us and around us. All things are being restored to their original order, and Jesus the Christ is retained in heaven until the restoration of all that God spoke by His holy prophets from the most ancient times. [Acts 3:21] We all realize our 'wineskins' must be prepared to 'hold the new wine' that is and will continue to be poured out in ever-increasing measure. And we must remember, the fruit is produced on the branches that abide vitally united to the Vine, and the wine is pressed from the fruit! I repeat! "The wine is PRESSED from the fruit!"

Mighty Warriors! You have been appointed and anointed, honored of God the Father, and given authority to subdue and take dominion. Rise up, Zion! The Glory of the Lord has risen upon you!

A BUMP IN THE ROAD!

After the Lord's admonition to get started on the book, I finished the dedication and the introduction, and came under a severe attack. I did not recognize it as such at the time. I was experiencing feelings of being overwhelmed, listless and confused. As well as seemingly endless interferences. I was bombarded with thoughts that my life and journey were really not that significant, my testimony and story interesting enough to become a book that people would want to read. I began to compare my story and life with others and gave into all of that and laid it all down.

Two months later, I began to find myself in a desert place and crying out to the Lord for a touch, a visitation from Him. I was in prayer and in the word, and I began to think about how testimonies and books had so blessed, encouraged and strengthened me on my journey. I began to thank Him and pray for those He had called and anointed to share their lives and gifts with others. The Holy Spirit began to deal with me in a powerful way, as I had not recognized the attack upon my mind and the way I was being manipulated. The Holy Spirit reminded me strongly I had been given this assignment by the Lord. Very specifically, clearly, and confirmed time after time. Was I going to obey Him or listen to the 'other' voice, the thoughts coming through my mind? His story was my story, and my story was His story!

He began to speak about the living stones, hewn, shaped and formed to fit into a strategic place in the wall of His house. No stone is without purposeful significance. He emphasized the purpose, being that through the church, the complicated, many-sided wisdom of God in all of it's infinite variety and innumerable aspects might now be made known to the angelic rulers and authorities and powers in the heavenly sphere. I began weeping and repenting. Revelation had come, as well as unbelief that I had allowed myself to be led down a path of disobedience, falling for the devil's lies! He began to talk about the progression of the glory. "The church was being released into another realm of glory! The church is in a new place, a new depth of the river! The river of grace, mercy, unconditional love, healing, power and authority, signs and wonders. We are being carried by the swift current of 'it's time! Our destination is 'the deep'! He said launch out into the 'deep' for a haul of fish no one can number'! The deep within cannot help but call out for the still deeper places! The deeper in, the more effective for the kingdom! Mysteries of the kingdom, secrets untold, prophecies of old hidden until the appointed time will unfold in the river!"

With this came a new level of energy, resolve and an anointing to complete the task with joy and expectation!

THE BEGINNING

November 8, 1928

It was time for me to make my appearance, and Daddy had taken Mother to the little clinic in the rural community of Cross Plains, where Dr. Young, from the Coleman Hospital about twenty five miles away, would come when there was an emergency or a baby to be delivered. Dad had picked up his brother-in-law, Connor Elliott, and brought him along.

The birth became very difficult and my mother was in trouble. Upon reaching into the birth canal, the doctor was shocked and Dad started weeping. The doctor quickly grabbed some sterile cloth and wrapped it around me, let Mother hold me for a while, and explained that I had been born with my intestines and some of my organs on the outside of my body! [Max said this is prophetic, my bowels have been exposed ever since!]

Talk about drama! Obviously, I survived! [no wonder I have been accused of being somewhat of a 'drama queen'!] I must continue with the story of the miracle. I am a sign and a wonder! My dad went weeping to my mother, saying that Dr. Young had not seen anything like it before and there was nothing he could do, there was no way I could live but a few hours. Mother and Dad were both Christians. Mother told the doctor he had to do what he could, that she knew I would live and not die. She had to insist. He called the surgeon at the hospital in Coleman to come. There wasn't a nurse, and for some reason they asked my Uncle Conner to help hold me!

[I was a kicking, squalling 7 lb. baby!] They had no anesthetic to give me, or thought they couldn't. Until the day he passed away, he told the story every time he saw me! What a way to start a life! The story goes that gangrene sets up rather quickly in that kind of situation. Intestines had to be cleaned out, some repairs made, and everything stuffed back through the opening in the stomach, which they had to enlarge and suture closed.

Dr. Young stayed and fed me with an eyedropper every hour through the night and next day. The family and church family were praying fervently for the bowels to move, that the plumbing would work! No bowel movement has ever been celebrated like that one! The doctor made a girdle, or truss they called it, that I had to wear for two years to prevent rupture. To everyone's amazement, I was an active, normal child, somewhat of a celebrity! For several years, the doctors would have me come to the hospital in Coleman and I would have to endure the scrutiny of any new doctor or intern, my stomach laid bare for poking and prodding while Dr. Young would describe the event and the miracle of it all!

HISTORY

My brother Pat and I grew up in a farming community between Cross Plains and Cottonwood, TX. My dad, Burnice A. Moore, better known as 'Bernie' or B.A., and my mother, Blanche Hargrove, had been raised in this community. John Anderson Moore, his widowed mother, who was native Indian, his wife, Georgia Beard, and three children, Winnie, Jesse and Lavanice, had arrived in the Marble Falls area and then moved on to this area in the late 1800s, having traveled from Tennessee in covered wagons. Dad and two brothers, James and Truman, were born in the Caddo Peak community, where they had settled on 350 acres of rich bottom land.

David Crockett Hargrove, my mother's father, had traveled with his parents, a brother and two sisters from Tennessee in covered wagons in the late 1800s. Upon arriving, they purchased land between Cross Plains and Cottonwood. Soon afterward, his father died. This left my grandfather Dave, at eleven years old, to take over the family farm and the responsibility of his mother and siblings. He later met and married Beulah Daniels Young, whose father and stepmother and several siblings had come from Alabama and lived in the Cottonwood area. Dave and Beulah married when she was fifteen. My mother was the firstborn. Her brothers were Walker, Melvin, Alvin and D.C.

After Dad and Mother married, they purchased a filling station. Yes, back then that is what they were called! Dad sold out and bought a 'filling' station in Arp, TX. It had a little house beside it that we lived in, and when I was three years old, a fire started in the garage area of the station and it and the house burned to the ground. They lost everything and Dad had no insurance. We moved back home to Cross Plains. Dad's brother, Lavanice, had a bakery there and he worked with him and worked on the farms with their parents for a while. I started first grade at Cottonwood. We were living with my mother's parents. My uncle D.C. was a senior and my first year I rode with him on his horse to school!

Then Dad got a job with an oil company, driving a truck in Wink, TX. I was almost seven years old when we moved there. We lived in a little house out on a lease, and I rode the bus to school. We finally moved into town right across the street from the Baptist church. My mother was a very good seamstress and I always had nice dresses, so I loved 'dressing up' and going to Sunday school. When I was eight years old, I responded to the invitation to accept Jesus as my Lord and Savior. When I was ten, my brother Pat Jeffery was born. It was a very difficult delivery and we almost lost them both. Mother's recovery took a while. Dad had been making payments on a 280-acre farm in Cross Plains, so they began making plans to move back home. Dad was having back problems. He had been run over by a wagon as a child and injured his back, as well suffering with migraine headaches. He felt he would not be able to endure the truck driving and oil field work he was doing.

When Pat was a year old, we moved. It was good and we were happy. I loved the school and made good friends. We had a simple lifestyle with good, hard-working, church-going people who prayed, read the Bible and did their best to live by it. They loved their families and their neighbors and fed their pastor on Sunday and tithed faithfully. Their word and a handshake was their bond. They worked from sunup until sundown five days a week [unless the 'proverbial ox' was in the ditch!] Saturday was a tub bath with soaking and scrubbing, and water heated in the teakettle! With every one taking turns, that took awhile! Everyone dressed up and drove [or rode their horse] to Cross Plains to visit with all the neighbors and relatives, eat a hamburger and buy a few staples or do some trading. The young went to the 'picture show,' which was mostly wild westerns! The movie ticket and a bag of popcorn cost us 35 cents!

Camp Bowie army training camp was in the Brownwood area, and many of the soldiers would drive over on the weekend. Some of the young men from our area who had been drafted — my uncle D.C. was one of those — would spend the weekends in Cross Plains. It was a bustling little town during those times.

Both sets of grandparents, as well as other relatives, lived a few miles apart, and often on Saturday evenings there was a gathering time for food and dominoes and music. If there wasn't 'dinner on the ground' after church on Sunday, then it was a large family dinner at one of the grandparents' houses. They grew or raised almost everything they ate, and those meals cannot be described! Those really were the 'good ole' days in so many ways. And the summers when favorite cousins would come, what fun we had! Gathering fruit from the orchard, helping clean out the hen house, weeding the garden, picking beans and peas, then the snapping and shelling, getting ready for the canning! Etc! Yea! Great fun! You do not know what you have missed! So many wonderful memories!

I cannot remember when I didn't love the Lord Jesus and love going to church. I especially loved music and worship. By twelve, I was leading the 'booster band' and singing specials. The summer revivals under the old tabernacle with the fiery evangelist and baptisms in the pond down the road or the creek! At times there would be one or two who played the guitar or 'fiddle,' who came to help my Aunt Frances Moore, who was always at the piano! I loved it! Even the hard wooden benches and the fierce blister bugs didn't discourage those Baptists and Methodists! There was a lot of shouting, amens and hand clapping! Many testimonies and tears with much thanksgiving! There was so much laughter and joy, even in the hard times. So much love and caring and giving in the midst of the depression, drought, World War II, the severe rationing and then the Korean War. Heartbreaking losses, broken and changed lives.

Worship at the Cottonwood Baptist Church was an integral part of our lives. I loved the Word and had such a desire to serve the Lord in any way available to me. The evangelist often stayed at our home, and the pastors ate with us often! I 'rededicated' my life at every revival. I seemed not to have the blessed assurance we sang about or had the revelation of the grace and the power of the blood they preached about. I hungered and thirsted for the reality of what I read in the Bible! I was always questioning them concerning certain passages of scriptures of signs and wonders and miracles, the lives and ministry of the apostles and early believers, and what I thought to be the very clear teachings of Jesus. I often challenged the pastor or teachers when their response was 'no longer considered viable' under the new covenant, or had passed away with the Lord's apostles! And they would caution me quite strongly concerning speaking in other tongues, that was surely of the devil! So! The Holy Spirit came like a mighty rushing wind, engulfed the 120 under the new covenant, baptized them in fire and power, and the first manifestation was a supernatural language, speaking in other tongues, and after all the original apostles and believers died, the devil took over???

I held those things in my heart, but followed those I loved and respected and became very 'religious' and prideful in the denomination. But the good news, the church, had come a long way from the time of the Dark Ages and the Reformation on the journey of restoration and transformation. And I am so thankful for my family and my Baptist heritage.

On with a little history:

Graduated from high school, started to business college in Abilene, and a young man I had dated in school came home from Korea with a medical discharge, shrapnel wound in the leg, with marriage in mind and with a ring. My parents liked him but did not want me to marry. I had been dating another young man for two years and I was torn about that. Ray's parents certainly did not want him to marry me because I was Baptist, they were Church of Christ, and according to their beliefs the only true church and the only ones going to heaven! I was going to hell! And they could not really have true fellowship with 'those who were lost and deceived'! This shocked me and challenged me. But Ray was so persistent and determined and started going to church with our family and answered an altar call to receive Christ and was baptized! His mother and a sister came to see us and wept and practically disowned him and told him he was going to hell and begged him to leave, Then she said a terrible thing in her grief: Now I have lost both my sons! [His brother, Eldon Auline Plumlee, a lieutenant in the Air Force, had been shot down in Europe and killed.] They were good people and loved their children, but 'religion,' false belief systems can lead us away from the true teachings of Jesus, whom we love and want to serve! I had never been exposed to anything like that, and felt great sympathy for the family. Ray was so hurt, but seemed more determined than ever, and I felt I couldn't say no. Besides, I found myself in love!

I gave up college, we married and went to ACU on the G.I. bill, and lived in an apartment on campus. A year later, I was pregnant. This was scary at first, because I had been told years before I could not have a child. So I looked at this as a gift from God and we were excited, even though it certainly wasn't the best timing and my parents were very concerned for my health. And it put a strain on the finances. Ray's dad and his mother were separated. His father, Mr. Plumlee, lived on a dairy farm with his mother not too far away and offered Ray a job on weekends. I was very naive, loved my young husband very much, but there were times I discovered he had been drinking, and we were always out of money. He always had some 'story' and would promise to stop drinking and save the money for the baby. He did really well for several months, as there was a great deal of concern for me and the obstetrician was planning for a caesarean birth. I had so much peace and was so happy about the baby, and of course there were a lot of prayers. Everything turned out well and we were the parents of a beautiful baby boy, David Randolph!

The next year, Ray decided to quit college, much to everyone's dismay. His brother-in-law got him a job in Monahans, TX in the oil field and we moved into a nice little guest house of theirs until we could find a place to rent. Ray seemed to be doing well in his job and we found a place of our own. There was a time there we were happy, and Ray cared very much for Randy, and we made friends. Then he began to not come home, and when he did he would have spent all of our money. He was fired from his job because of his drinking, and my dad had to come and move us back home. Ray went to the VA hospital for a while and convinced us he was fine. Dad bought a little house and moved it there on the farm and was making plans to put in a dairy. Ray had gone back to work for his dad, and once again that didn't work out. His dad was an alcoholic and Ray started drinking again and stayed gone on weekends. Once again, he pulled himself together and started going to church with me. Dad had the dairy going and took Ray in as a partner. It was a blessing for me to have Mother to help with Randy and it was good for all of us to be together. Pat had been drafted and was in boot camp. Mother was not doing well dealing with that. Thankfully, he did not have to serve, came home and finished college.

I found I was 'expecting' again! The doctor had said 'no more children.' So this came as a surprise and a real concern for the family. I had mixed emotions. Ray had been acting strangely and I had been protecting him because I was ashamed and embarrassed. Then he went on a binge and the truth came out. He had become addicted to drugs and alcohol while in the military. I'm sure when he returned home he planned to leave all of that behind him, but the addiction was more than he knew, and of course none of us had any idea about the drugs. His family got him back in the VA Hospital. He was discharged and he heard of a job opportunity in Portland, TX at Reynolds Metal plant. He made all kinds of promises, and convinced me to come with him. With a child and another on the way, I felt it was the only thing I could do. It was so important to me for my children to have their father. I could not accept divorce as an option. I could not give up hope. But I was losing my true self, building up walls to protect my broken heart from any more damage. I felt trapped in the love I felt for Ray, my self-esteem was crushed, fear gripped me, and I felt judged by family members for having chosen to marry him and bear his children. But my heart continued to confirm that these children were God's blessing and sign that He was with me in all the chaos, and they were the sign of His love for me. For children love unconditionally and the joy of having them in my life got me through, no matter how difficult life became. I continued compensating, stuffing things down deep. I was becoming a mess and trying to hide it from others. I did not know this person Ray was becoming. How could he choose drugs, alcohol and other women, and say he loved me? He seemed so brokenhearted and repentant and I had to give him another chance! Randy once again was pulled out of a loving environment and his school. The child in my womb had experienced anything but a peaceful environment. As we drove away, I do not know who was weeping the most: my parents, Randy or myself as I cradled with my hands the child in my womb.

We moved in with the Hart family, my dad's cousins, then into an apartment. Later we bought a little home on a G.I. loan. Randy was in first grade and having a difficult time with the move away from all that was familiar and his 'Nannie' and 'BoBo.' Eldon Ray [Donny] was delivered by caesarean section, a beautiful healthy baby boy. Mom came down and stayed a while until I recovered. Ray had done well and we all were hopeful and happy, enjoying the new baby and grateful to the Lord for His faithfulness to us. I was beginning to trust my heart to him again. Six months later, it started again. He would disappear over the weekend and spend all of our money. We would beg and borrow until the next time. I was indescribably heartbroken, hopeless, ashamed and fearful. Ray was in a lot of rage and unpredictable behavior. In the middle of one of the 'in between times,' he decided to take a course in drafting, which he had loved while in college, feeling this might be of help to him. He began working on house plans for a builder in Corpus Christi, and things were some better for only a little while. It ended one Sunday night with the children and me in the house with all the doors locked, and him outside with a shotgun. Our neighbors, who had befriended us often, called the police. Ray was arrested. Dad came and moved us back home. I was very ill, weighing 95 lbs. Randy was a wreck and Donny was only three, but he was affected as well emotionally. Because of my health, I could not nurse him and he had allergies going from formula to soy milk to goat's milk, and plagued with ear infections. We were a sad, hurting little family, grateful for the love and support of family and friends.

After a few weeks of recovering my health [body but not soul], I filed for divorce. I decided on going to the school of cosmetology in Brownwood, TX. Mother and Dad took care of the boys. It was such a loving, nurturing atmosphere for them. Upon graduating, I went to work in a salon in Cross Plains. A friend who had helped the boys and me when things were so difficult while in Corpus began to visit us. He was older, recently divorced, successful, a Christian, and very persuasive. I felt this was the answer for the boys and me.

This would mean stability, a comfortable lifestyle, and security. I was making decisions out of the shallowness of what was left of my soul. And he saw me as a trophy.

We were married at the farm by our pastor. We moved back to Corpus Christi, another uprooting and challenge for the boys. He legally adopted them. I can't forget the day the adoption was final and Randy was in the back seat and Donny was sitting on my lap. I looked back to say something to Randy and tears were pouring down his face. He seemed so very sad. I never realized the turmoil in his heart and he was unable to vocalize his pain and fear. [Ray continued to be 'lost' in his addictions for years, with very little communication and no monetary support. So there was no problem with the adoption. Years later, he met and married a very nice woman, a director at one of the rehab hospitals, and for the last fifteen years of his life he was free and it was good. He passed in '04.]

Our new life had begun. We became involved in church, Randy was enrolled in school, and things were going reasonably well. I kept reminding myself to be grateful. We moved into a nice home and Donny started to school. My husband was good to us but not affectionate or involved with the boys. A little more so with Randy, because he was older. He ignored Donny's obvious need for him to just love him and notice him. He was very meticulous, very short-tempered, and impatient. A chain smoker. We found ourselves walking around as 'on egg shells.' And he just wasn't the fathering type. No real interest in their lives, or taking any time with them, or considering my emotional need. He supported us, gave us his name but not his heart. This brought such pain to my heart after all they had been through. I tried even harder to prove myself worthy of being loved. Outwardly, I was trying very hard not to show my inward pain and turmoil. I began to have health problems and ended up having emergency surgery and a hysterectomy.

I began to be more involved with my husband in his construction business and he began to pursue something he loved even more: cars! So he opened a used car business.

My brother Pat had just graduated from Hardin Simmons and my husband invited him and his family to move here and run the car business. I was blessed they were with me, but it was tumultuous times for all of us. They stayed for a few years, then Pat had a very good job offer from Fidelity Insurance and Bonding Company and moved to San Antonio. Randy began to have more responsibility over the car business and my husband became more involved as well. I continued to try to convince myself that all was well. I sought the Lord with all my heart, but felt so powerless, so unsatisfied. I read everything I could get my hands on about the Holy Spirit, and 'the more' I just knew was available. I had no understanding of the need for inner healing, no understanding of the ravages upon my soul and self-esteem from the rejection, infidelity and abuse of my former husband, nor the soul hurts of my sons. I knew I was a long way from where I needed to be emotionally. I felt so lost!

I was always trying to earn favor, to prove myself worthy of being loved and appreciated. Because it would benefit our business, I got my real estate license. Of course, all of this left a void in Donny's life. I was just hanging on for dear life to mine, unaware of so many things I should have been, so I wasn't there often when he needed me and was just naive about many things concerning both of them and myself! I tried to be both mother and father, run our home, have every meal cooked and on time, as well as all the other things, all very driven. I would have given my life for my sons, but failed them often. And I tried to be everything for my husband. We all were struggling. He had many issues of his own and we were both doing the best we could from where we were! I knew I was to walk in forgiveness and avoid any root of bitterness, but our wounds of rejection and abandonment became deeper. Our understanding was darkened and there was very little revelation. Religious activity, serving, tithing, striving, and trying harder seemed to bring more condemnation and hopelessness. Both Randy and Donny were active in church, and had made commitments of faith in Christ. They were both such beautiful loving sons, very talented and as 'needy' as I.

My husband began to go out of town a lot on business trips and my life began to go into a tailspin. In the midst of all of this, I was crying out to God, hungry for the reality of His Presence, to know Him and the power of an overcoming life. I went to every church that I thought knew about the Holy Spirit and the love of Christ, hoping they could bring some enlightenment and healing to our lives and confirm what I read in the scriptures and believed to be true. I found the church as dysfunctional as I was, powerless. I knew there had to be more, there had to be healing somewhere. I was so rejected and hurting, and acted out on the stage of life in ways I couldn't seem to control, as in a daze.

My marriage ended after nine years. A call came from Ft. Worth. My husband, on a 'business trip,' had been in a terrible car wreck. He was very badly injured, not expected to live, and the woman who was with him was not too badly injured. They were leaving a bar at two in the morning, intoxicated, pulled out on the freeway, and hit a car of college girls coming from a ball game. All were injured, but thank God, not critically! But he was not expected to live and if he did survive, there would not be a total recovery. I stayed until they knew he would live and his family said they were going to take him home with them. He did live several more years.

Previously, I had received a phone call from two businessmen who had been suppliers for our construction business and friends through the years. They informed me that my husband had neglected the business, had some unfinished houses and some unsold, and was at the point of bankruptcy and would I please meet with them. They asked me to oversee the finishing of the houses and getting the others sold. The house we were living in was on a builder's interim loan, so I would have to sell it, and they would see to it that the boys and I had a down payment on a house and they would help me. So for the next year I did just that, and we bought a nice little house and I worked in a real estate office. Randy had graduated from high school and was attending Del Mar College and had put together a band. I knew Donny was struggling. I hoped and prayed he would be all right. I didn't know what to do. I was totally involved in making a living as well as acting out on the stage of life out of a broken spirit and lost identity, behind a defensive wall a foot thick! I was starved for love, searching for love. I stayed connected to a church, and I should have gotten an academy award for my performance! My heart was bleeding and I was dying inside. I felt like my whole life was a failure, that I had failed in every area of life.

There was talk about the 'Charismatic' renewal and signs and wonders and speaking in tongues. My antennae went up! I went to a meeting or two and submitted for prayer to receive the Holy Spirit. It was wild! This was new for everyone, but nothing succeeded with me. I felt rejected by God, and it felt like the last straw. Unbearable, and yet I couldn't give up! There had to be a 'Balm in Gilead' for my wounds. I had come to the end of my own strength. Shame, disappointment, and fears overwhelmed me! My sons were hurting and turning to the wrong things to dull the pain and mask the fear, the fatherless Baby Boomer generation, except for my father and their uncle Pat.

I was at the end of myself. I kept 'knocking' and kept 'asking,' and one day I was down on my knees with the Bible opened to Acts 2 and Matthew 7:7-11. I was reading the scriptures out loud. I then prayed again and ask to be filled with and baptized into His Holy Spirit so this hunger and thirst would be satisfied and my soul would find peace. I rose up and said, "Thank You, Lord, I believe I received." I didn't feel anything, other than a sense of peace and went about the rest of the day. That night, I got ready for bed, knelt down on my knees by the bed, prayed, got up in the bed, lay down, AND HEAVEN CAME DOWN AND GLORY FILLED MY SOUL! JESUS EMBRACED ME, HIS PRESENCE ENGULFED ME. SUCH ECSTASY BEYOND ANY EMOTION I HAD EVER EXPERIENCED. I WAS ENRAPTURED! TEARS FLOODED MY EYES. MY BODY COULD NOT ENDURE IT FOR LONG! I BEGAN TO CRY OUT! "LORD, YOU WILL HAVE TO TAKE ME ON, I CAN'T BEAR ANY MORE!" MY BODY FELT INFUSED WITH LIGHT. HE TOOK ME AS HIS OWN. I NO LONGER JUST KNEW ABOUT JESUS THE SAVIOR, I HAD EXPERIENTIAL KNOWLEDGE. HE WAS MY SAVIOR AND BAPTIZER IN HIS HOLY SPIRIT!

I FELL INTO THE MOST PEACEFUL SLEEP UNTIL MORNING.

I was never the same. My journey of enlightenment and freedom had BEGUN! The wonderful Holy Spirit had come and brought gifts! Father God loved me! Now I KNEW Christ within, my hope of glory. The same Spirit that raised Christ Jesus from the dead now lived in me!

GOD IS LOVE!

How many times throughout my life had I read, heard, spoken those three words. But to experience the substance, power, purity, beauty, and transforming reality of His Love was and is indescribable! In His timelessness, He supernaturally caused me to experience, to the degree my mortal body could stand without being consumed, "the length, breadth, depth and height of THAT LOVE and the Divine Presence and be a body wholly filled and flooded with God Himself!" Ephesians 3:16-21, as well as 1 Corinthians 13 and 14 has remained a foundational word throughout my journey. The 'honeymoon' was on the mountain top, air pristine, fragrance sweet, heavenly blue skies such a sense of freedom, peace and joy I had never known! I loved everyone, even my worst enemies. I couldn't help myself! I couldn't see denominations, ethnic differences, male or female, rich or poor. I had been given a vision of the kingdom, true 'oneness with Christ' and His body. I thought my heart would burst! The word became alive, understanding had come, the Day Star had risen in my heart, my journey to the Promised Land had truly begun! I knew I was loved, accepted in the Beloved, forgiven, chosen and purposed of God in my generation for awesome things beyond my imagination! At that time, I did not understand that this reality experience was a foretaste, a 'preview' of what the Holy Spirit would be working with us from within to accomplish, that 'this kind of Love,' all-consuming, unconditional, all-merciful Love of God expressed through His body was a goal, a mark to be reached. That 'this' love must be perfected in me, to be the motivating factor in my life.

I thought 'the honeymoon' would last forever! I had yet to understand 'the process' of restoration and the work assigned to 'THE MINISTER of THE INTERIOR' to bring about that restoration and transformation in my life!

I began my pursuit to 'know' [become intimately acquainted with Him] who my soul loved. My heart was to follow Him wherever He might lead me. An outpouring had come, sovereignly. What the Holy Spirit had downloaded had shaken the old paradigms, belief systems and concepts that had been a part of my Christian upbringing, books I had read, sermons I had heard, down to the very foundations! Not that all of it was bad or wrong, just incomplete and without power and this prisoner had been set free! Many questions had been answered, many longings fulfilled. My mortal body had been 'quickened' to new life, a veil had been 'rent'! Light had dawned and morning had come! A new day had arrived! I knew my life had purpose.

This was in the late sixties, and it was called 'the Charismatic renewal.' Without rhyme or reason to the natural mind, the Wind of the Spirit of God blew through every religious structure and denominations, into cities, streets, communities and homes in many nations. This downpour seemed to cover more territory and be more widespread than the Wales and Azusa Street revivals. Maybe it was an accumulation of those 'downpours'! There were continuing 'thunderstorms' and 'cloudbursts' and 'rainy seasons' periodically through the years, indicating a building up to "as it was in the days of Noah so shall it be!"! The flood of His manifest Presence will cover every valley and mountain top and the whole earth shall be filled with the knowledge of the Glory of God! Halle!

ON WITH THE STORY

The 'honeymoon' was beginning to transition from the mountain top to the earth's atmosphere and the beginning of the 'working out of the soul's restoration' and preparing a vessel of honor fit for the Master's use!

I was very involved in making a living for the boys and dating a great man whom I had met through a real estate sale, who was separated from his wife [not yet divorced, not very smart of me!]. He was kind, thoughtful, considerate and helped my self-esteem. I shared my encounter with the Lord and he seemed to accept it without question. He was respectful and kind to the boys and I no longer considered the fact that he had a wife and family. When he chose to go back to his wife, I knew it was the right thing. It was grievous, but without anger. Then came a time of repentance for me, and healing.

About six months later, Thomas Wilson Anderson [better known as T.W.] came into the real estate office to visit a friend. We were introduced and he began to come around and ask me to go for coffee. He was divorced, with two children. His wife had left him for his best friend. It had been pretty devastating for him and we were just going to be friends. He seemed to get along with the boys, and he definitely made me feel like a prize to go after. He was a big Scotsman, a take-charge guy, golfer, had been to Hardin Simmons on a basketball scholarship, was a natural born salesman and a Baptist, and open to my testimony. He had taken me to meet his family and I took him to meet my family in Cross Plains. He loved the country, the farm and my family. His dad had passed the year before. He had one brother, Floyd. His mother, Maggie, was still helping operate the cafe they had operated for many years, 'Andy's Coffee Cove.' We were married April 4, 1969, swearing to each other and before God, this would be our last, we were going to make this work no matter what! And we had our share of the "whats"! It was adjustment for his children as well as mine. His son and daughter were hurt, confused and angry. Mine were hurting and confused, but loving and accepting.

We had been active in a church always, and I had a group of young people, which Randy was a part of, as well as a young girl, the daughter of a family we knew who attended the church some. They became closer and although Randy was nineteen and in college and she was seventeen and out of school, her mother was definitely discouraging it, not wanting them to go out. But she would slip out to meet him and come over to our home, and she would tell some unbelievable stories, which we believed at the time because she seemed so sincere and she was very sweet.

Randy would tell me that she was begging him to get her away from them, to marry her. He was always the 'rescuer' and young love would not be denied. They ran off somewhere and were married by a justice of the peace. What ensued was not pretty. After the storm, it finally came out that she had to drop out of school and was under the care of a doctor and on medication for a mental disorder. They were trying to protect her, for there was no cure, so this was devastating news! If only they had told us up front. I understood their reluctance. Mental illness was often misunderstood as something to be ashamed of. It was a devastating illness.

Randy had such a hard time believing or accepting this, as you can imagine! Since they had come to live with Donny and me, it became evident that something was very wrong. We knew nothing about mental illness, and were shocked and brokenhearted. Then we discovered she was pregnant! All of this sent her over the edge to the hospital, where there was a meeting with the doctor who said there was no place for her to receive the treatment she needed, so he had to commit her to San Antonio. When he explained to us there was no cure, he suggested abortion. He told us and then Randy that there needed to be an annulment, because, "This cannot be a marriage, you are very young and this is very unfortunate and you will have to decide concerning the baby."

The parents took care of the divorce and made all the decisions concerning her and the situation. Randy went with them to admit her, and then he went off the deep end. He left college, went to the beach, formed a rock-and-roll band, fished for a living and tried to lose himself. He lost his identity, gave up his dreams of a college degree, and turned inward. He now was a father. A son had been born and the grandparents would raise him and would take care of his mother, who would continue to be in and out of the hospital.

It seemed on top of everything else, with so much attention turned to all Randy was going through, I just trusted that Donny would be all right. He had always been good-natured, loving, and strong, but I had no clue to what he was really feeling and what he was dealing with. There was always the age difference between them and the turmoil around our lives. They loved each other, but were not close.

Life goes on.

Some time had passed. Randy had pulled himself together, somewhat, and had come home. I was running to meetings, Dennis Bennet, Bob Buse, Kenneth Hagin and others were coming into Corpus. We gathered in buildings, Pentecostal, Catholic and Episcopal churches and in homes to experience His Presence and His power, to talk about our experiences and revelation and minister to one another through the gifts. We would excitedly discuss Catherine Kulman, Amie Semple McPherson, Oral Roberts and others, and the Lord manifesting His power and grace. I remember how hopeful and liberated we became, as one of the revelations we received was that God had come to liberate His women and bring them into their rightful place in His kingdom! To bring His order, not man's. To bring the woman to the side of man as a partner, both under the Lordship of Jesus, submitted to one another to prophetically act out the Lord's relationship with His bride the church, the body of Christ. We have come along way since that time in the process! Praise God for the women He chose to pioneer and make a way for others to follow!

There were two dear women of God whom the Holy Spirit had prepared for this time as mothers in the faith, to mentor us. Marion and

Cecelia. Marion opened her home to a group of us with a Bible study and training up in the ways of the Spirit. I for one will always be grateful for their love, wisdom and encouragement. Through their teaching gift and anointing, new wineskins were created to hold the new wine that had been poured out and brought alignment with His word.

Randy had gone into another relationship and married. He was definitely in love, but she definitely wasn't ready for settling down, and would leave for months, return, and leave again. Then she left and didn't come back. Another grievous situation, with great stress on us all. I began to share with him concerning the Holy Spirit and testify to all that was happening in our midst. I took him to Cecelia's and she ministered to him, laid hands and prophesied, and the Holy Spirit fell on Him! He began to shake from head to foot and tongues began to flow like a river! He was still at it when Cecelia and I finally got him in the truck to go home! From that time, he made every meeting with me, somewhere almost every day or evening. He loved praying for the sick and often the power of God would show up and wonderful things would happen.

There was no doubt there was a call upon his life to serve the Lord with a powerful anointing. There was a strong prophetic gift AND there was a battle raging! But he had been 'endued' with power from on High to become an overcomer and so he is and so shall it be!

I had stopped working at the real estate office and started building houses again. A few speculative and some on contract. I would build a home and we would move into it, then put it up for sale. T.W had gone into the insurance business and was doing well. Larry and Deane Diehl came to see the house that we had up for sale. They loved the floor plan and wanted to build on the golf course. She had recently been baptized in the Holy Spirit, and of course we hit it off and never stopped talking! We went to meetings together and were part of the group at Marion's home. She and Larry became friends of ours, and to this day we are still in contact. Oh yes, I contracted to build their home and we still remained friends! Throughout the years, there have been seasons when they have been such an encouragement to me and T.W., and have been used mightily for the Lord's work.

CONTINUING ON

Beverly and Richard, T.W.'s children, had moved in with us. There were certainly adjustments for us all, but it was good. Our family continued to grow! A missionary family, the Hiltons, friends of the pastor of the church we were attending, had two daughters and the oldest was fifteen and needed to live with a family in the states. We fell in love with her and Lois became a part of our family, a precious daughter and sister. She was very talented and gifted on the piano. Donny had a surfing buddy, who was also a gifted guitarist, Robert Spoon, who stayed at our house most of the time. Donny played guitar sang and played a little jazz piano. Another surfing friend, Gary Richardson, 'sort of' didn't have a home because of a broken family situation, so we fixed him a bedroom in the utility room and he moved in! With his drums! So there we were, with seven young people [a great spiritual number, and Mom and Pop make nine, another great number!]. The next thing you know, our house is 'rocking'! In more ways than one! I was loving every minute of it [well most of it]. We all were! We were extremely blessed, no kidding! They all had such beautiful hearts, great personalities, loved the Lord and were very gifted.

I was always involved in the music at the church and a worship team just sort of naturally evolved, and we began ministering at churches and different functions, and writing a few songs. We were called "The Sojourners." One of the songs Robert and I wrote became the title of the record album we did in '73, *From the Cross to Glory.* We were blessed to have an opportunity to share the gospel and the love of the Lord. T.W. was in the middle of it all, we even allowed him to sing with us occasionally! Those were wonderfully satisfying years that remain indelibly imprinted upon our hearts.

Lois and Robert fell in love and married. Gary moved out. Richard married, then Beverly. Randy was working at a car dealership and Donny graduated and enrolled in Del Mar. The economy had fallen, the bottom fell out of the housing market, I was out of business, and T.W. went to work for Great Southern Life in Houston and now WE WERE MOVING! It was heartbreaking. Our close friends, the Diehls, had been transferred to Tennessee. The changes were challenging, but God was in the midst of us and He was faithful! Donny was working at Panjo's Pizza and entering Del Mar College and refused to leave. So he and Randy roomed together and we loaded up for Houston with tears streaming down our faces!

I took a job with Marix Housing Corp., a developer and builder of Patio Homes. We rented one of the homes on their site in Katy and I became the on site sales person. After a year, a new project had begun at another location and I was moved there to work the models and do pre-construction sales and oversight. The second year, I was awarded the 'Prism award' given by the Greater Houston Builders Association for the greatest volume of sales! God blessed! I was so grateful for the fellowship with the Lord and the gift of praying in other tongues as I drove to work every morning in that Houston traffic! It was tough and challenging, a six-day week [off Sunday mornings until 1:00] and Mondays. The Lord gave me many opportunities to be a witness for Him.

We bought a home in Katy. I became a member of Evangelistic Temple, the home church of Charles and Frances Hunter, and I loved it! The Spirit of the Lord was moving mightily in our midst and I was experiencing THE WORD in ways I had longed for way back in my Baptist days. I attended the Hunter's training school and I attended every conference I could. Charles Capps, Dereck Prince, Oral Roberts, Percy Collett, Billie Brim, the Halversons, T.L. and Daisy Osborn! Then the Copelands. I was thirsty and drinking from the springs of living water! I was zealous for God and the manifestation of His Kingdom. I was in awe of Him and so grateful for the freedom I was experiencing and the empowerment of Holy Spirit! And experiencing the prophetic flow.

But all was not well on the home front!

T.W. was 'wheelin' and dealin',' doing well in his job, playing a lot of golf, gambling, and not too happy about my time spent at church. He was not interested in attending with me and began challenging me concerning my relationship and experiences with the Lord. This was extremely hurtful. Things were going well for me, business and money-wise, but I was burning out. The work I was doing would have been challenging for any man. I was feeling used and unappreciated. But T.W. was adamant about my continuing.

Randy had transferred to Houston and was doing well. Donny was struggling in Corpus, so T.W. drove down and picked him up and brought him to Houston, and he went to work managing a Panjo's Pizza Parlor. Beverly was still angry and difficult. We didn't see Richard and Karen very much.

I was determined to see every difficult situation and circumstance would in some way, under the pressure of THE MASTER'S HANDS, be tools to shape His vessels into the design He held in His mind. So I continued to pray and walk in love and grace grace grace!

He always makes a way! And HE is more than enough!

We had a family conference and the boys decided to let T.W. adopt them and take the Anderson name. I was so very happy about that, and T.W. was as well. He was good to them and was there for them both when they needed him. He fathered as best he knew and loved them. He did not have a very good relationship with his two children and seemed to try to make a difference with Randy and Donny. I bless him for that.

I had not been 'brave' enough to share with my parents the details of my experience with the Lord and baptism in the Holy Spirit. And I certainly did not use the word 'Pentecost'! They were generational Southern Baptists and really had a fear of any experience outside of their own denominational teachings and doctrines. And I don't think they considered me too 'stable' after all I had been through in my life. So, they just thought I had a typical Baptist rededication!

My dad had been suffering with lung disease for several years because of years of farming and running a dairy. I loved them so much and it broke my heart to see Dad suffer, and since I had come to 'KNOW' the Healer of our body, soul and spirit, I had this idea to encourage them to come to visit us a few days and we would take them to church with us [T.W. agreed to go], as the Hunters would be conducting the services and Daddy would be healed!

As you can tell, I was still sort of 'up in the clouds' about things. I assumed everyone would be blessed and excited to see and discover that Jesus heals today and signs and wonder can and do follow the preaching of the word! That all turned out to be the most challenging test of faith and my new commitment to Christ!

My family had always been very close, always supportive, gracious and loving. I was daddy's girl, no matter what. My mother was beautiful, strong in faith, loving, totally tireless in sacrifice.

We attended the service. Hundreds of people there. We had seats on the third row from the front. It was a powerful time of worship. The presence of God was heavy and glorious. Charles and Frances were ministering and people were getting healed, falling out under the power. They turned and waved their hand over our section and a strong wave of the Spirit swept over us and people were falling out all over the place and my dad was FURIOUS! And he demanded we leave! I was shocked! My mother was not happy either, although she didn't say anything. T.W. took us out, we got in the car, and the proverbial 'fur hit the fan'! I just kept saying, "I'm sorry, I didn't mean to hurt you, or worry you." I really couldn't get a word in sideways, and of course a flood of tears poured down my face and fear gripped my heart. As soon as we arrived home, they went upstairs and packed their bags to leave for home, a five-hour drive in the middle of the night. We were pleading with them not to go. The only thing that would change their minds would be my repentance and promise to return to my 'religion' and upbringing, and come to my senses, or else I was not to set foot in their church again and I would not be welcome at Dad's ordination service! I collapsed on the floor in shock, disbelief and total rejection. I could not turn back. They left that night.

I was in distress of soul, vulnerable to the demons of hell! Thoughts like fire burned in my head, my heart gripped in pain. I could hardly breathe, I wanted to die! The ultimate rejection! Days were spent in much prayer and crying out to the Lord, wrestlings and questionings and tender times with Jesus, and the gift of grace that enabled me to understand the depth of love my parents held for me and the fear of hell that caused them to react towards me in the way they did. My heart melted and broke for them and I purposed to only consider what they were feeling and love them and grace them through this. The Holy Spirit continued to download vision and purpose in my spirit to enable me to walk by faith and trust in His redeeming love, to continue to bring His love to perfection in me.

I knew I had to rely upon the Holy Spirit's leading to walk this out as He directed for all of this to work out to the glory of God. The way that He did just that was certainly not the way I would have chosen or expected!

HOUSTON JOURNAL

1976 through 1979

"L ord, that dream last night, seeing my name written down to be on a program to sing "Mine Eyes have Seen the Glory!" Am I to see in my lifetime the glory of the coming of the Lord? Or, will I be in music ministry singing of Your glory? "The Battle Hymn of the Republic," will I be a part of a spiritual revolution? Then in the dream I had said it had been a bad day, and then my eyes filled as YOU reminded me the good time we had just that morning, and I had to say, forgive me Lord for forgetting.

As I was driving to work I was praying and thinking about this and my mind brought up the song, "Remind me, Dear Lord," all the things, my sons, my husband, my dear family, my other children and friends, all those I hold dear that have brightened my life, are just borrowed. They're not mine at all, a gift from You! All, everything is YOURS and I have to be reminded Lord, I forget. How I wish I could recapture each joy, each blessing, that it remain 'alive' in me, but I find myself one minute in Your Presence and feeling as if I'd never forget that moment and then I'm caught up in living and circumstances and I've forgotten, until Your Spirit gently 'reminds' at another time. For I must keep my heart and mind upon the good and positive, to be thankful 'in' all things, not necessarily 'for' all things, for there are many things that are going on that I certainly am not in joy over, nor am I thankful 'for'! As You well know! But I am determined to practice 'accentuating the positive and eliminating the negative,' and strive to enter into Your rest! I know You are good and will work all things for good in our lives because we are the called and chosen according to Your purpose.

Thank You, Father!

Thank You, Lord, for directing me to the book, ***Change Me.*** Thank you for those dear ones who are so tuned in to Your spirit and are able to share Your teachings with all of us, Your children. Thank You, that You zero in on just that area in my life that needs immediate attention! Praise You, for staying on the job and performing that good work in me to cause me to will and then do what You call and ask me to do!

Lord! I say, change me, that I am always looking unto you, and submitting to Your word and trusting in Your love to redeem and restore. I am willing, Lord, open my ears and my understanding and give me wisdom and keep me on the path You have foreordained for me to walk on.

You have always held on to me, Lord, I've not always held on to YOU.

WOW! Lord! I stand amazed in Your Presence! Thank You for this past week! You really got through to my spirit! But as usual, putting into words the things of the Spirit is just not easy to do! One fact that You brought together after a series of circumstances, YOU LOVE us into loving You! Respect and fear are good things to have where You are concerned! Our 'reasonings' cannot touch the hem of the awesomeness of Your dealings with us. Thank You, Father, for the Holy Spirit, who is the spirit of revelation, the revealer of the mysteries of Your kingdom, who can and does reach beyond the natural and flood our darkened understanding with LIGHT so we can 'see.' Lord, You are SO good, so loving to us. You love us into loving You and loving others!

I did some things totally contrary to Your word. Instead of punishment or judgment, You just blessed me and loved me. You loved me through my sons, through my husband, and You broke my heart and opened my eyes and dealt with me concerning Beverly. I must apply this truth to my relationship with her, I must not hold anything against her, I must love her with your love. How can I not forgive, when through Your supreme sacrifice I stand forgiven? Forgive me my 'whining,' Lord!

I just came to talk to You, Lord. It just seems no progress is being made with Beverly. I'm finding the supreme test of Your word, "Love your enemies and those who would despitefully use you." You've shown me how easy it is to love those who love me and how that really doesn't count for much; and how hard it is to love those who don't love me and mine and yet, that's what You command! That can only be done through Your Spirit! And Lord, You know time after time I've given this to You. I know what I'm suppose to do but am unable to perform it! She is beyond a doubt the most difficult person to deal with, and Lord, You know my heart and what I've done, how I've given, turned 'the other cheek,' how I have sincerely tried all I know to try, humanly and spiritually, and it doesn't 'give'! Now, my heart is getting hardened, and it's difficult not to have an 'attitude,' if you know what I mean! I certainly am justified to feel whatever, BUT that is not what You require or what I desire. I do not want this situation to grieve Your Spirit in my life or give the enemy any ammunition! Dear Jesus, I am again laying this at Your feet! Knowing that You went through to the extreme degree of being despitefully used, rejected, that in our challenges You can supply the grace for us to overcome. Thank You, Lord, for the victory!

Two Months Later:

Wow! I know the Holy Spirit has been working mightily within me concerning Beverly! I Love Her! I just love her, can't help loving her! God's love, the Love OF God has broken through the barriers in my soul, and love for Beverly has become a natural thing, with no effort and nothing she does or doesn't do affects it! Which means my prayers and tears and obedience enabled You to do a supernatural work within MY heart and I am free to love unconditionally!

I have experienced this work of grace before, Lord. You and I know the others and the other times. I keep forgetting, if You've done it once, You will do it again!

Your spiritual laws work, Lord! As if You didn't know! Lord, I want our sons and daughters to KNOW You, to be made alive unto You! I don't want them going through the motions of religion, legalistic and dead! I want them to experience the reality of the empowerment and comfort of the Holy Spirit. Thank You, that You are hovering over all and any chaos in their lives to bring life and restoration!

HOLY HOLY HOLY are You, Lord!

Lord, You know my concerns for Randy and Donny's spiritual life. Thank You for reassuring me that they are in touch with You.

No matter how things may seem to the natural eye, Your spirit is at work within Your house! When Randy mentioned concern over 'no business,' I said, "We need to pray about it." He said, "I do, every night and morning. I haven't lost my faith in God or the awareness of His Spirit in my heart in spite of what it may look like."

Thank You, Dearest Lord Jesus, that You will continue to make Your dwelling place glorious!

When Donny said, concerning the possible purchase of the cafe in Cross Plains, "Don't push it, because we are trusting the Lord in this, if it works out then we'll know it's the Lord's will and it will be good!" Thank You, Father, for his sweet heart and tenderness and for his strength. You have blessed me beyond words with my sons. They are truly a gift from You. You know my mother's heart and how much I love them. It crushes me when they go through fiery trials and disappointments of life, but I gain strength in knowing they are Your sons first and Your Hand is upon their lives for their continual transforming and restoration! Halle!

1978

Odom's cafe is officially ours and Donny has moved to Cross Plains into his little house. Mom and Dad are so happy about this. I think Donny feels good about it and seems excited. I know this will be hard work and challenging, but Lord, he has the integrity and discipline and training for it to prosper. And of course with T.W.'s many years in the restaurant business and obviously Your hand upon it and upon Donny, it's good. Thank You for ordering our steps! Lord, may all the talents and attributes You have given Donny bring You glory. And Lord, forgive him the hidden things of the heart that grieve Your Holy Spirit and may Your Spirit ever strive with him that You might truly be Lord of his life, that all the kingdoms of his heart might become the kingdom of our God.

After returning from Sunday service at Evangelistic Temple:

Lord, I feel such desperation! These confrontations with T.W. weary me, confuse me, and I feel helpless! I am so aware of the conflict within me to stand in the midst of the 'storm' and not be blown over. I know I am accountable to You. In this 'game' of life, we must 'play by Your rules or else it's futile or ' fatal'! Your ' law of love' rules to live by are guidelines to inner peace, to change, to true happiness. I just wish, Lord, the game did not go on so long without a time out or at least more half-time entertainments! Does everyone get weary, Lord, like I do?

Well, T.W. and the boys left for Cross Plains for Mother's Day to be with the family there, and here I am having to work. BUT! What a blessing this day has been, Lord! You have seen to it that it was a very special day for me! The services at E.T. were SO beautiful and uplifting and the joy of experiencing Your Presence is beyond words! Thank You, Lord, for Your Spirit who continually strives within us to bring us into a right relationship with You, to fight and win those spiritual battles that would weigh us down and keep us from enjoying Your blessings!

Lord! You know I sometime panic when I think of the shortness of life on this earth and so much to be learned yet, and I feel so much time wasted! Dear Jesus, help me to make better use of my time, help me to put You first in all this hectic, busy world with all its demands on my time! So little we do here is eternal, and we get so caught up in just living and working!

The phone call from Randy was such a blessing! Lord, how good You are to let us see prayer being answered and Your Spirit at work!

Situation:

In attempting to plant a sign in front of a model home, I 'jumped' on the stake and hit the sharp metal bar under my instep. The pain was excruciating. I could not stand. I immediately began to pray, took authority in the name of Jesus, commanded the pain to leave, called the bones, ligaments and flesh to be restored, and the pain left completely, immediately, and no cuts, marks, bruises or soreness even later! Amazing, Lord!

Then two days later:

I've had a constant headache all week, every day, go to bed with it, wake up with it. I've taken aspirin, Darvon a few times. I prayed the same as above, declared, decreed, nothing, no relief. Praise You anyway, Lord! I know You are teaching me, training me. I just submit myself to You and give You permission to use whatever circumstance or condition You need to teach me and prepare me for service.

Lord, I had become so burdened and You are SO good to lift those burdens when we seek Your face and pray and give them to You! Randy's situation, Donny's wedding, the insurance business we're trying to buy (or the 'dealing' T.W. is trying to do, I know telling only what he wants me to know), selling our home and no place to move, the difficulties and pressures of my job, what would I do without YOU! When I asked for something from You to ease my troubled heart, I opened my Bible to Matthew and the words, "Daughter, all is well" leaped off the page and struck my heart. What more could be said? Thank You for Your presence that is SO real to my spirit, and Your love that reaches down to 'right where am' and lifts me up!

The closer I get to YOU, the less I know! I don't know, Lord, but I think that means I've made some progress!

It's becoming more natural to expect the supernatural. I'm humbled and in awe that You obviously are directing our steps, moving in our circumstances, piloting our lives, and I think maybe I'm getting out of Your way more, that I'm not blocking You with all my trying and striving and impatience. It is true, Lord, "not by might nor power but by Your Spirit," and I don't think there are any 'short-cuts'! It's always a matter of the heart, the sincere desire for change, a willingness to be obedient to Your word, giving up our so-called 'rights' and availing ourselves of all You have made available for 'overcoming ' and entering into our inheritance as sons of the Most High! Halle! I feel I'm making progress along the way to 'becoming.' "No man comes to the Father unless the Spirit draws him." Thank You for choosing me! Thank You, wonderful Holy Spirit, for hovering over the chaos of my life and drawing me to HIM. You are a Benevolent Father to all Your children.

Philippians 3:8. Yes, I count everything as loss compared to the possession of the priceless privilege [the overwhelming preciousness, the surpassing worth and supreme advantage] of knowing Christ Jesus my Lord and of progressively becoming more deeply and intimately acquainted with Him [of perceiving and recognizing and understanding Him more fully and clearly!]

Donny's marriage lasted a couple of months and he took her home to her mother! He said he was sorry, he shouldn't have gone through with it in the first place, it was a very bad mistake and it needed to be over! Thank You for his courage. Oh! Lord, grace them both and redeem and restore.

January 1979

I don't understand Your Great Love for us, Lord but I thank You with all of my heart. You have arranged for us to move to Abilene, close to my parents. The insurance deal has come through, we have sold our house and I have saved $65,000 from my time of working and T.W is opening an office and Randy will be coming and I think Pat will be buying the cafe, so the Tuckers will have a place to live and work. Donny will go to work for T.W. I know he is relieved to be out from under the cafe. It was really a challenge for one. And I don't have to work, now maybe I can follow my heart into ministry of some kind? Yea!

I fast unto You. I don't know for how long, so I'll depend on You, Holy Spirit to direct me and sustain me

ABILENE, TEXAS

Never thought we would find ourselves here! It was a perfect distance from my parents, but I knew there was more to this move than we knew at this time, and even though there were challenges I had an inner peace and joy that kept me on an even 'keel.'

One thing I have been aware of on my road of enlightenment, purpose, destiny, transformation, etc. etc.: My Father knows how to ' butter me up' so to 'slip me through the narrow, difficult gate of transition' to the 'beyond,' wherever 'that' is!

I was in prayer, asking the Lord to direct me to a Charismatic church so I could get back into the middle of things. To my surprise, I was instructed to go back to my old Baptist church in Cottonwood with Mom and Dad, become a part of that fellowship and stay until He told me it was time to move on! Holy Spirit had to really work mightily within me to bring me into compliance with that! Remember the story I shared concerning my parents and the Hunter's meeting in Houston? I was not welcome there!

My first visit home after that 'event' was on Thanksgiving. I had no idea what to expect. I was careful to avoid any conversation that might trigger anything and just loved on them and served them and we got through it. So how was this going to work and how could I bear 'going back,' how could I come under the yoke again and not be stolen from? I was in turmoil, but knew I had heard from the Lord, so I set my heart to be obedient and trust Him. The Holy Spirit pointed out prejudices, elitism, and pride. Things He wanted · to separate me from in order to separate me further 'unto' Him! "If you love Me, you'll obey Me. If you trust Me, you will make the sacrifice and with joy!" Yes, Sir!

So we drove to Cross Plains on the weekend, and on Sunday morning we began to get ready to go to church with Dad and Mom, very 'cool,' as if nothing had ever been said. And we all just 'went to church'! My dad obviously assumed this was an indication I had 'come to my senses'! But! I was now a carrier of His Presence, the barely burning wick had been fanned to a flame, and it would not go unnoticed or be of none effect! Oh, I was to continue to be amazed at His ways of dealing with His people and working His Plan!

Brother Knox Waggoner was the pastor, a friend of the family, and someone I admired and respected. There was always such a grace on him and gentleness. The people were loving and welcoming as usual, and at 'invitation' time, the Holy Spirit said go and join yourselves with this church. We went forward, and of course were received with celebration.

I met with the pastor the next day and shared my heart and testimony, all of it. And submitted to him as unto the Lord. I didn't know what to expect, tears were rolling down his face and he assured me he knew my experience was real and valid. His own revelation was outside the doctrinal boundaries of the denomination he was called to pastor! And he felt I was a 'seed' God had planted for a season in their midst to arouse a hunger and thirst for a relationship with God the Holy Spirit!

The Lord left us there a year, massaging and tenderizing my heart toward His dear loved ones. Giving me a love for His body wherever they might be in the world, at whatever level of enlightenment, in whatever denomination!

I ministered in song. I just served and loved as led by the Lord. Some began to seek me out, and there were many opportunities to share my testimony and encounter with the Lord. I was never the same, and I believe some of them were not. And the Lord had comforted my sweet parents' hearts and blessed them and blessed me. Oh! How He loves you and me! Oh! How involved He is in everything that concerns us! There is a plan in place and He is working that plan! Halle! During that time I worked with them to design an addition of classrooms and a Baptistery. It was a blessed time.

I had been enrolled by My Heavenly Father in the university of God Almighty, the Word of God as my textbook and the Holy Spirit as my teacher, counselor, revealer of truth, as well as the hidden things of the heart, and the giver of gifts that would enable me to move from strength to strength, faith to faith, and from one degree of glory to another! The Spirit of grace! He would choose the courses, the fivefold ministry gifts, apostle, prophet, evangelist, pastor and teacher. Tuition paid in full by the blood sacrifice of Jesus my Lord and Savior. The Father's desire is to bring many sons to maturity. I had questioned Him concerning Bible school, a seminary, but HE was adamant, that was not the direction I was to take.

David and Susi Wells had been sent to plant a full gospel church in Abilene, Redeeming Faith Love Fellowship. He had been an acquaintance years back, so I had visited with them on Wednesday nights and any meetings they would have. There was a continual moving of the Spirit in their midst, a precious congregation of open, hungry people. So, after being released from Cottonwood Baptist, I became a part of their fellowship. Pastor David recognized the anointing and call upon my life and the Lord used him to encourage me and allowed me to minister in the prophetic word and song, as well as share the word. This was a blessed 'season' of healing and aligning, and of course preparation for more than I could know.

One morning as I came into the sanctuary, David said, "The Lord told me to have an ordination ceremony for you. There is a Prophet coming to minister and we will officially ordain you." Thank You, Lord! I was very blessed. It was an awesome time, many words released over my life and T.W.'s that I held close to my heart. David had been a Methodist when the Holy Spirit swept him into the Charismatic renewal and he was open to however the Spirit was moving, and we had wild downpours in our midst and did a lot of 'swimming'! The Lord connected me with several who were to become a part of the next seasons of our lives.

I was very involved in the construction of our home. T.W and the boys were traveling, going different directions promoting the new products, making good commissions and all seemed well. It was good training for Randy and Donny to learn the insurance business, and I was anxious to get into our home and 'get on with my pursuit of God'!

There was such a grace upon me, an anointing to keep pressing on against the conflict and battle in my mind. I was fifty-two years old, with a lot of water under the bridge! There were deeply rooted teachings against women in pulpit ministry, divorce, etc. My own husband, though a believer was definitely not 'in the flow,' and I knew I couldn't 'call' him, only the Spirit of the Living God could draw him and 'call' him. So I felt often like a fish trying to swim upstream against the current of all of this, as well as seemingly being 'out of step' with the established church and other family members. Yet I felt constrained, compelled to trust in the Lord with all my heart and move toward the vision he continued to expand in my spirit.

One year later, after moving to Abilene, we were in our beautiful new home. I had designed a great bedroom and bath over the garage area for Donny to live. I was enjoying my freedom, visiting with Mom and Dad, and helping them, and able to spend quality time in prayer and seeking the Lord, ministering at every opportunity. About eight months later, a bombshell! T.W. informed me the men who formed the company he was connected with were in trouble with the Board of Insurance and they were out of business and he was left holding the bag'! Aside from that, the money I had worked so hard to save, he had used in the venture! And he was closing the office and would have to find another job, as well as the boys! He wanted me to sell the house we had built, which would be enough to get connected to a bank to get set up for interim financing and start building houses in Abilene! I was flat-lined, hurt, angry beyond words, devastated, betrayed! Of course he had been 'duped,' angry with himself, feeling a failure and had no sympathy or anything left for me. We were selling the house and I was going back to work! He would seek employment from insurance contacts and he had a golfing buddy who was the Budweiser distributor and they were talking about becoming partners in a restaurant! There was no discussion, except 'heated,' and no way but his. But I had a choice to make. I could not afford to hold an offence, or anger in my heart. I was responsible to God for my actions and reactions and

I determined to stay before God in prayer and submission to His word until He had done the needed work of grace in my heart for me to move forward with His peace, trusting in His faithfulness to see me through. And it came. Thank You, wonderful Holy Spirit! Once again, with man it is impossible, but with God all things are possible!

Our house sold at a good profit. Found a good buy on another house with minimum down payment and I started working with an architect designing house plans, checking out property, and T.W is working insurance leads. Randy went back to Houston to work for Charlie Thomas and Donny came to work with me. He had met a very attractive young woman with two young children while working in west Texas, and they married. The children were precious, but a ready-made family and a very insecure, possessive young woman could certainly be challenging! For all of us! But we took her into our hearts and fell in love with the children.

Donny had found his niche. He loved everything about building. He worked with all the subcontractors and learned all the trades. That was a blessed time for both of us.

I was put on staff at Victory Believers Fellowship as worship leader and Sunday morning early Bible class, as well as a part of the intercessory group. Wendel and Cathi Leech, former Methodist ministers, had also been touched in the seventies 'downpour' and had left their pastorate to start the new work. They had purchased a few acres and moved in some army barracks and were remodeling and making a sanctuary and classrooms for a church school.

There was a continuing move of the Holy Spirit in our midst. The Spirit of prophecy, salvation, baptism in water and baptism in the Holy Spirit with the evidence of speaking in other tongues, and healings! Several of us attended conferences and meetings as often as we could in the Fort Worth and Dallas areas, where the atmosphere was 'charged' with God's Presence, just caught up in a realm of glory that's difficult to describe

I and three other intercessors drove to Houston to a conference with Billie Brim and the Halversons and some others. They were laying on hands, praying and prophesying, and I was out in the Spirit with trembling and shaking for quite some time. I was in a place of timelessness. For three days I functioned in earth's atmosphere, but I was in a supernatural realm. I knew things before they happened. I saw Sunday morning service on Saturday! Everything happened just the way I saw it happen the day before! I ministered under an anointing where I could see people's needs before they spoke. All kinds of demonstrations of His power were manifesting. For the next two days, God's love was pouring out of me, people were falling all over the place, being touched by the Lord! I had experienced that infusion of love when He came and flooded my soul in '67 and immersed me into His Holy Spirit. This was different, this was empowerment for manifesting His Kingdom. I was experiencing two dimensions at the same time.

I think I was understanding. We are connectors between the glory realm and earth. Like Jacob's ladder, we become a portal for 'on earth as it is in heaven'! Wow, Lord! My mind cannot wrap around all of that. I am so humbled and grateful!

It was glorious! HE just comes! Suddenly He comes! Who can know the ways of the Lord! Who can know the Mind of the Lord? When these 'suddenlies' happen, it's so awesome, you mistakenly think you will operate in this realm or that anointing will continually be on you, but it lifts just as suddenly and you're left with just 'you' again! And you can hardly bear it. This was all training me up in the ways of the Spirit, as well as increasing my hunger and thirst and kingdom vision. I also felt as if He was qualifying me before others and validating my son-ship and calling through His manifested Presence and power. There was nothing to qualify me in the natural. Quite the opposite.

T.W. had managed to put the restaurant deal together and we called it 'The Home Place.' Financially, things had been working well. T.W. would attend church some if he didn't have a golf game, but I just did my best to stay in peace with all of that. Donny and I were busy, we had bought a piece of property to do a small development of patio homes, as well as some larger homes in the country club area. God was blessing, life was full.

Lacey Dawn Anderson was born July 30, 1982. An easy birth and a perfect, beautiful baby girl! Thank You, Lord. I treasure every opportunity to baby sit. Give Donny strength, he is so tender and has so much love. Protect them all, Dear Jesus.

In '84-'85, an economic disaster! The oil market fell, drilling shut down, businesses were closing, the housing market fell, bankruptcies all over the place. There were no mortgage loans being made, period. We had two large homes just completed and two smaller homes for sale. We had paid down on a piece of land for a development. So all of that was in jeopardy.

The loan on the restaurant was with a bank where T.W.'s partner did business, and they were under investigation by the banking commission and all the loans and notes were called in. Since there were no loans available anywhere else, they called a foreclosure on our restaurant! I was praying every way I knew to pray, I worshiped, declared, decreed, stayed in the word and hung in and trusted God. But that ball just kept rolling! "I have told you these things, so that in ME you may have perfect peace and confidence. In the world you have tribulation and trials and distress and frustration; but be of good cheer, take courage, be confident, undaunted! For I have overcome the world. I have deprived it of power to harm you and have conquered it for you!" WOW, Lord! Your word is indeed a light unto my path, a hope for the future. I receive Your peace and trust You. We are Yours.

A call from Mom. She was on the way from Cross Plains, bringing Dad to the hospital. We got him checked in and his doctor came and examined him. Dad began to share with us an experience with the Lord. The Lord had told him in four days HE was going to take him home! We made the decision that only what was necessary to keep him comfortable would be done. Each of us, his children and grandchildren, all had opportunity to love on him, bless him and thank him for the awesome dad he had been, the example he had set before us all of faith, integrity and unconditional love. God began to heal him before he left. Just a few hours after he was brought in, he began to breathe without difficulty and the pain seemed to leave. He sat up in the bed and talked with us. We all cried together, and shared stories and laughed! We had a wonderful two days! Dad looked and acted like a miracle had happened. I could not believe he was dying. Pastor Knox stayed with us, close friends came by and some stayed.

The grief of Daddy leaving us was softened by God's healing grace upon him, and His loving Presence upon us all. On the third day, he just closed his eyes as if to take a nap and at the dawning of the fourth day he took his flight! The evening before, I had stayed with him and I sensed angels in the room. There was such a holy presence, I fell to my knees by the bed, just worshipping and praying in tongues. I caught myself and quickly stood up and looked at Dad in fear, and the Lord said, "Daughter, have no fear, he understands and sees it all now!" Such release and healing came into my soul as I laid down beside him and wept, as I marveled at the Father's love for His family and the assurance we have in Christ Jesus. This parting was just temporary! Praise His Name forever!

In '85, we were forced into bankruptcy, the restaurant was closed, the bank foreclosed on the houses except one, we moved into it on the interim loan, and I would continue to work to get it and the others sold. Of course, the bank would not lose any money, only Donny and I. We always paid the subs as we went and waited until the houses sold to get our profit. So no one was hurt really in the end except us. But in the midst of this, a miracle of God, I got a cost plus contract to build a very large house out on a ranch, which kept us working for another year-and-a-half until something opened up for Donny. I sold the house we were in and took a small house in trade and we moved into it. T.W. left for Corpus to stay with his mother and went to work for Humana Insurance Co.

Randy lost his job and moved back to Abilene. A precious young woman, Betty, who had been working for him soon followed him, and some time later they were married. He went to work in San Angelo as manager of the Chevrolet used car lot. Then he, Donny and Pat opened a used car business in Abilene that lasted for a couple of years.

Donny and Rita had joined our worship team at Victory and the children had enrolled in the school.

There was an awesome anointing and presence of God upon us and the fellowship. The Holy Spirit was moving upon His people. The Spirit of prophecy was flowing. We were being impacted in His Presence, salvations, baptisms and healings. There was a supernatural peace upon me, and intimate times with the Lord brought vision and expectation for the days ahead. The Holy Spirit called our worship 'Judah.' Randy joined with us and a precious couple we had connected with from Pastor Wells' church, Stan and Marriane Smith, had joined us as well. There was such an anointing upon each member of the worship team and the manifest Presence of the Lord so graced us!

T.W. came home. He seemed humbled and contrite. I told him I was totally surrendering to God and the ministry He had called me to, whatever it looked like and wherever it took me, and that he could make our living, for I was not working any longer, we would live on what he made. Tears were pouring down my face and love was pouring from my heart. I knew there would be many benefits as well as challenges. He agreed.

The Lord sent David Wells by with a word for him concerning his life and walk with the Lord. And the call of God upon my life was his call as well, and how I needed him to stand with me and support me. I was very much encouraged. I also knew in my spirit I was being moved along by a current of God's river along a predetermined route and no 'rapids, falls, boulders or dams' could stop the flow of the river. The river was in me and every member of His body and the river was GOD ALMIGHTY! YES!

One month later:

Harold 'Hayseed' Stevens, a very anointed, on fire evangelist whom we had met through Pastor Wells, and the Lord had connected our hearts, came to hold a revival at our church. He had been in pro football and in 'the world' big time. He had a Baptist praying wife and mother interceding for him, and one day driving down the highway in his big Cadillac, he had an encounter with Jesus Christ as His manifest Presence filled the car, baptized him into the Holy Spirit and took ownership and called him to preach the gospel of the kingdom!

It was a glorious time. The anointing upon the worship team was awesome! There was a powerful anointing upon Hayseed, like fire! People were not just falling out in the Spirit, the fire of God was throwing them across the room! The power hit Donny when Hayseed laid his hands on him and prophesied. It threw him all the way across the room! He was baptized into Holy Spirit and was out under the power! T.W was prayed for and touched in a special way. Randy had an awesome experience, much prophecy and ministry. I was blown away! Unspeakably blessed! Some things had come to a 'fullness of times' and God had moved gloriously! I was in the river over my 'head' again, crying, "Lord! Let the River carry me, Dearest Lord Jesus. Cause the current of 'it's time' to carry me where You want to take me, where I need to be, and sweep my precious husband, sons, daughters and grandchildren into the current with me and do what will bring You the greatest glory! Cause the Spirit of Wisdom and Revelation to rest increasingly upon Your people, move us to reach into, lay hold of, receive all You have provided and made available to us to 'Be' — Become sons of God, the harvest of the seeds sown by earth's travail!"

"But what of that? For consider that the sufferings of this present time, this present life are not worth being compared with the glory that is about to be revealed to us and in us and for us and conferred on us! For even the whole creation waits expectantly and longs earnestly for God's sons to be made known, for the revealing, the disclosing of their son-ship!" O, Glory!

Wendel and Cathi had ask me to help them build a house on property close to the church. It was a blessing for them as well as for me, and really helped with our finances. The Lord proved so faithful to meet our needs. We had literally been stripped of home ownership. I had gone from Cadillac to a 'very used ' Oldsmobile. and not knowing if there would be enough gasoline to get to where I needed to go! There were offerings stuck in my hand, checks in the mail ("The Lord told me to send you this."). This was a season in my life I had never experienced. For years I delighted in sowing, giving, serving, and this was very humbling! He was continuing to bring me into my true identity and dependency upon Him. We can certainly have a lot of blind spots, and when the Holy Spirit begins to address those and open our eyes, it can be shocking and painful! But so liberating!

An outpouring of the Spirit with miracles and healings hit Bob Tilton's church in Fort Worth and we made several trips down there. Victory made arrangements for a satellite dish and screen where we could participate in their services. Those were exciting healing times for all of us. There were some ministers in these outpourings who didn't have the character to sustain the new wine, and there were disappointments and destruction. But there were many others who continued to stay in the river and move forward, who faced the fire and persevered, who had received revelation and vision and would become the fathers and mothers, apostles and prophets. evangelists, and pastors/ teachers for the equipping of the end-time saints. Yes, Father God, Your Glory shall fill this earth!

I was asked to lead or pastor a house church of about fifteen people. Those were blessed days as the Spirit of prophecy rested upon us, building up His body. This progressed to a rented space at the YMCA and baptisms took place in the pool! I had the awesome privilege of baptizing Betty. The fellowship moved into a rented building and we held services there for about a year. Precious people, and the Lord blessed mightily. He was continuing to 'train me up' and then move me on.

The worship team, Judah, was continuing in prophetic worship and God was moving in our lives and ministry.

Brother Hayseed and Mary Jeane had planted a church in Weatherford, TX. "Living Way Ministries Fellowship." He asked us to become their worship team. So for two-and-a-half years, we traveled by van and cars to Weatherford every week. It was an awesome privilege and God richly blessed all of us in so many ways. There was always a prophetic flow, and one song Donny wrote always blessed Hayseed so much, because he had such a heart for Israel. "I'm a son of David, I'm a seed of Abraham." And Judah's theme song became "The Mighty One of Israel." I will always be grateful for the heart of that ministry, the expression of love, the freedom and atmosphere Hayseed provided for the Holy Spirit to be in charge. There were 'deposits' made into all of our lives. Thank you, Hayseed, Mary Jeane and the wonderful family! Hayseed had a call to Africa and God connected him to Desmond TuTu, as well as to Israel and Prime Minister Began. He was involved in drilling one of the first deep oil wells in Israel. He was on airplanes so much, and in '03 after arriving home from Israel, as he stood by the fence greeting a neighbor, a blood clot hit his heart, and he was gone instantly. God just 'took' him! Earth's loss. Heaven's gain! He was definitely a carrier of the glory.

T.W was struggling, doing a lot of traveling, selling insurance. He received a job offer from Humana to open an office in Abilene and insisted I get an insurance license and become an agent for Humana to help us get back on our feet financially. After much prayer, I felt the peace of the Lord upon it and finally agreed on one condition: every penny I earned would go into a savings account. Getting an insurance license proved to be a bit of a challenge! And then having to drive to Dallas alone to take the test, once again relying upon the wonderful Holy Spirit and His gifts to supply the needed grace and wisdom to get it done! And HE came through in miraculous ways. Passed it the first time!

JUST AS I AM, 1-3-87

During a time in His Presence and intercession, the Lord began to speak to me in the song, "Just as I am without one plea, but that Your Blood was shed for me." (L.M. Woodworth, Charlotte Elliott, 1789-1871, William B. Bradbury, 1816-1868)

Father God tells us to come boldly to the throne of grace to receive mercy and find grace to help in time of need. Hebrews 4:16 and Ephesians 3:12. That we may have boldness and access and confidence. Hebrews 10:19. Having boldness to enter into the Holy of Holies to come into His Presence.

We approach the throne, we go to Him without one plea, only through the Blood! We have no merit of our own. We all come the same way, from the highest to the lowest, by the Blood! My request, my petitions will not be granted because of 'deeds of righteousness' that I have done, but because of the Blood and the Covenant and my faith in the Blood and the finished work of the cross and His word.

I must come to God, entering into His Presence, not because I feel worthy in myself, because I prayed two hours that day or I visited the sick or I gave from my lack or I drove to Weatherford every week to minister. Not because of my works or my obedience. For nothing I 'do' earns me favor, I already have favor! All the blessings of Abraham are already mine in the covenant. The privileges of a 'son' are already mine! Grace has already been extended to me! I must learn to receive from My Father because of the Blood! Because He is Lord God, Covenant Making, Covenant Keeping God, and by faith in the Blood of Jesus and faith in the Word, everything is already mine! There is no way we can be good enough or do enough to 'earn' anything! It is all by faith and because the Blood HAS been applied to the mercy seat and God no longer deals with us in judgment or wrath. It was all laid upon JESUS! So the Blood continually cleanses us from all sin and everything that does not conform in word and deed or thought to God's will! As the Holy Spirit shines the light of Christ upon the sin in our lives and we repent and turn away from that sin, we have 1 John 1:9 as an anchor for our soul and a sword with which to slay that old dragon, the devil, the accuser of the brethren! "Therefore, there is therefore no condemnation for those who are in Christ Jesus [here lies the 'kicker'!] who live and walk NOT after the dictates of the flesh [our carnal nature, but after the new nature] but after the dictates of the Spirit! Romans 8:1. Paul says, in Romans 6:11, "Reckon [Greek; logizomai: take inventory, conclude, esteem, suppose, impute and think on] ourselves 'dead' to sin' but alive unto Christ." We must avoid coming under the control and bondage of condemnation, and our sin separates us from intimacy with Jesus and our Father. One of the most damaging things the enemy can do, I believe, is get us to focus on all that's wrong with us, our failures. Paul said: "forgetting those things that are in the past or behind me, I press on toward the goal of the high calling of God in Christ Jesus ..." We must come to know the truth as it is in Christ Jesus and Him crucified. For I have been crucified with Christ, [in Him I have shared His crucifixion] it is no longer I who live, but Christ [the Messiah, anointed one] lives in me; and the life I now live in the body I live by faith [reliance on and complete trust] in the Son of God who loved me and gave Himself up for me!" Glory Hallelujah! Jesus said: "The spirit is willing but the flesh is weak." So He ratified the new covenant with His own Blood and took our weakness and gave us His strength. His Name and all that He had became ours and all we did not have became His! This grace is not a license to indulge the flesh, NO! It releases us into His Agape [all-merciful, unconditional Love]! And that Love compels and constrains us to return that Love to Him through loving others, ourselves, and becoming a servant to the body of Christ and following Him wherever He leads us!

The sin nature cannot be 'reformed.' Reckon it dead! It will always come under temptation, just from living in the world. Satan is god of this world and he has a kingdom of darkness where business is conducted by despots, powers, master spirits, who are world rulers of this present darkness, and the spirit forces or demons of wickedness in the heavenly supernatural sphere. Jesus said: "Satan, the thief comes to steal, kill and destroy BUT I came that you might have life more abundantly!"

As long as we are in this earthly tabernacle, God has to make provision to deal with sin because He cannot look upon or tolerate sin in any form. Sin is sin. The greatest is the sin of unbelief, of rejecting Christ and His sacrifice. There are no degrees with God. Only man judges the degrees of right and wrong. The provision was the perfect sacrifice, Jesus, who paid the penalty once and for all for all sin and iniquity, sickness, disease and poverty. Failure to fulfill all the law resulted in the curses and brought death, BUT Jesus became a curse, He fulfilled all the requirements of the old covenant and replaced it with the new covenant of life and blessing and grace and favor with God the Father and purchased our freedom! Our sins are not covered, they are blotted out! And in the depths of the sea of God's forgetfulness! This is the liberty! Whom the Son has set free is free indeed! There is no more sacrifice to be made, HE was IT! Upon receiving Him into our lives and accepting Him as our substitute, our Savior, redeemer and King, we instantly are partakers of His Divine Nature! In the mind of Almighty God, I am already transformed into the image of His Dear Son, who was perfect, without sin!

So, what happens to the inherent sin nature, while we are in the process of 'BEING' changed little by little by the word and the power of the Holy Spirit that so mightily works within us? What happens to all the 'deeds' of the flesh? We do not focus on them! We declare the Blood sufficient! We fully cooperate with 'The Minister of the Interior,' as He brings conviction and we do battle with the Word and we follow the 'instruction manual' for our soul's restoration! Through Faith and Patience we inherit the promises! We develop a lifestyle of walking in love, and walking in the Spirit, trusting the wonderful Holy Spirit to empower us, to lead us into all truth, to reveal the mysteries of the Kingdom, and to truly make us one with Christ and with each of our brothers and sisters in the faith.

Religion has kept us so bound and fearful, discouraged and ashamed, so in strife and striving. Or else deceived us into believing it is the church and the rituals that save and protect us. When all the time God is crying out, "Your sins are blotted out, don't focus on them, focus on ME! My Word is anointed and I watch over it to prosper it in the thing wherein I send it. It will divide asunder and separate the spirit and the soul and make them distinct so you discern what is good and what is evil so you can make choices to choose the good and then walk in it through My bountiful supply of grace and in the power of My Spirit. Little by little but absolutely, you will be changed from glory to glory, for you are MY workmanship, it is I who works in you both to will and then do of My good pleasure. See yourself as I see you, in My Son, the Christ, whole and perfect, and come boldly by faith in the Blood, the finished work of the Cross, just as you are without one plea but that My Blood was shed for thee, not of works, lest you should have anything to boast about, But all of GRACE and all of ME!"

Thank You, Lord

8/7/87 PROPHECY THROUGH NITA JOHNSON, GIVEN AT CHURCH ON THE ROCK

Tongues, then Interpretation:

*G*od wants you to know He's putting the pieces of the puzzle together. You have had like a great big jigsaw puzzle, and slowly but surely you have been putting the pieces together, but it seemed like the closer you got to the completion of the picture, there were pieces missing that you couldn't find and you didn't know how to find them and you started seeking God because it brought such confusion to you as to where the missing pieces were and to why they were missing. God wants you to know that God will bring forth the pieces supernaturally. And yet a season, and the season is short, I believe that within one year you're going to see a transformation take place in you and in your ministry and in all God has called you to do. You see, those missing pieces were the pieces of the call that you didn't know or understand. I don't see you in a stationary place right now, I see you moving about. God is going to cause you to move about and the women that bear the Good News will be of a great host, the scripture says, and so you will bear the Good News unto the people and it shall be a news that will break the captivity over those who are bound. I see you going from place to place for the next season and bringing freedom to the captives! I also see a book in you and it's a beautiful book! It's going to be highly anointed

84

by the Holy Spirit through the words that will go on the pages of this book. They have been developed through many tears. Those tears will go into bringing forth the anointing that will set many free and manifest His kingdom, Sayeth the Lord!

So know that it hasn't all been for nothing! But God is yet to do a great and wonderful thing. So plant your feet where God has put you for the season and allow yourself to become strong. Get into the word like you've never been before, and into His Presence in a greater dimension than ever before.

I see a storm coming! You don't need another storm, I know that, but you're strong enough to bear this one, I want to tell you right now! During the storm, God's going to bring forth a new revelation and in that new revelation, just like Job went through the storm and at the end of that storm, God revealed something to Job about himself that just set him in awe, just set him in awe! And it brought forth a new thing in Job's life and that's what's going to happen. This storm is going to bring forth an anointing that is going to be so powerful in your life, that as you stand to minister the word, I see the tears flowing and I see the people being healed in their seats and I see the souls coming into the church to be saved.

So where it seems the mantle of favor has been lifted, God wants you to know that it's going to be intact, and He is going to move on your behalf on behalf of His church.

Then Jerry Stroup, the Pastor:

You are as Miriam and you've come all through the storms, all through the bondage, and you're free! You are going to be leading the saints in worship and praise and dancing before the Lord in great celebration and great victory! They are going to follow you and they are going to have a great sound and a great shout and a great praise to the Lord in the camp!

THIS PROPHECY FROM THE LORD CAME TO RANDY SIX DAYS PRIOR TO BETTY'S WRECK!

9-1-87

"*M*any *years ago, I, your GOD, gave you a vision. You were on top of a mighty white steed overlooking a valley of perversion and division. You had a bloody sword in your hand! You had crossed over into the land of promise. You have a warrior spirit within you, My Spirit of battle, of glory, of valor and success from which you cannot depart! You have channeled it in other ways, into things of the flesh and nothing there ever stays. You think you are down. I will lift you up! You think you are low. I will place you up high! Greater indeed is He that is within you, which is I the Lord, than he that is in the world! Even now you are doubting that this is Me and do not understand the spiritual gift I have given you! The devil is a liar! Would the devil tell you something that would exalt you, would he tell you the real truth about your true identity? No! No! No! He has come to steal, kill and destroy you. But whatever he raises up, I will not allow to stand. I will knock it down with one sweep of My Hand! Your heart I know, and within you I GLOW!*

"*It is now time for the basics of My Word to apply, YOU AND YOURS SHALL LIVE AND NOT DIE! All that seems to be lost shall be gained and only the glory of the Lord shall remain! And only the victories in the spirit will count and continue. The failures of the flesh of the past, no one in the future will remember! If you will just commit that you and your house will serve the Lord, I will open doors, solve each and every problem, and be your rear guard!*

"I will eliminate problems before they occur, and every attack from the enemy, I will be there to deter!"

Betty left on a trip to Mexico a few days later, and before she left, Randy was led to write down the scripture, Psalm 118:17, "You and yours shall live and not die to declare the mighty works of God," and stick it in her purse. Betty was not aware of this.

Randy had called me concerning the word of the Lord and His instructions to plant the scripture in her purse. He was uneasy about her going. We prayed and declared the word over her.

On September 7th at 9:30 p.m., we received a call from Oscar, Betty's brother, in Monterrey, Mexico.

9-7-87 BETTY'S CAR WRECK

At nine-thirty in the morning, on the seventh of September, 1987, Randy received a call from Oscar, Betty's brother. She and her sister, Tina, had been in an accident, hit by an eighteen-wheeler! Betty was driving and sustained numerous skull fractures, ruptured spleen, broken hip and pelvis, broken facial bones and was not expected to live, in fact had been pronounced dead at the scene! Tina had only bruises and a broken shoulder. The emergency doctors told them, with the kind of skull fractures that had occurred, people normally died instantly! She had undergone emergency surgery to stop the internal bleeding and remove the spleen, but nothing else could be done until she was more stable. She had been unconscious since the accident, and the doctors did not give them much hope. Our imaginations could not have prepared us for the reality of her broken and bruised body!

The stress was almost unbearable, and in our natural selves, we could not stand. But God All-knowing, All-seeing had prepared us all beforehand. Unknown to us at the time, His strength and Word would not fail us as we remembered His word to Randy and His instructions. We had been given the Word of the Lord to stand on and we chose to believe His report! He had spoken and He had instructed it be written that it be established that the devil could not take her life! His peace would not leave us and His sweet Presence would fill us and surround us!

We immediately called for intercessors from all areas and they in turn called others. Randy and I began to make our plans to go and seek the Lord's direction and wisdom. We left the next morning, wrapped supernaturally in His peace and strength! We both knew that we were totally dependent upon the promises of God. The lack of power, strength or wisdom in ourselves seemed to be emphasized, and we were so aware that nothing in ourselves could be allowed to interfere or hinder following the instructions and directions of the Holy Spirit if satan was to be totally defeated and God to receive all the glory!

The eleven-hour trip was spent praying in the Spirit, listening to tapes and sharing and boasting in the Lord. Worship and singing, praying and interceding! Sometime the car would be filled with the cloud of glory! At times we could feel a holy heaviness upon us, and at the same time a sense of floating. The Lord spoke to my heart and said the prayers of the body were bearing us up and pushing against the powers of darkness, and we were to walk in the authority and take what had already been won! I looked up and tears were rolling down Randy's face, and he could see two angels up in front of the car! Halle!

About this time, we were stopped by a highway patrol out of San Antonio and he walked up to the car and said he had clocked us at eighty and could he please see Randy's drivers license? As he was handing him the license, the young man's face took on a puzzled look and he did not even look at the license. He mumbled something about slowing down and walked back to his car! We laughed, thinking the glory around the car dazzled him!

We drove in and went immediately to the hospital. The only air-conditioned areas were ICU and surgery! The waiting rooms were not clean and there were armed soldiers stationed in several areas. It was not comfortable or safe feeling. When we saw her, it was evening of the second day and she was beginning to show signs of regaining consciousness. Oscar, who spoke English, said according to the surgeon, those with the injuries she had suffered usually died at the scene, and if she regained consciousness there would most probably be loss of speech, memory, hearing and vision! It was difficult to determine anything else at that point. When we walked in and bent over her to speak to her, she began to open her eyes and she said, "You came, both of you came!" She was coherent, alert, knew everyone and what was going on, and had not a problem with speech! Everyone was amazed! The miracles were continuing!

Randy and I prayed in the spirit continually, which no one paid very much attention to! It was as if we were only empty vessels for the compassion and love of the Lord to pour out upon Betty. A miracle was worked in Randy, as he hates hospitals and had expressed his concern several times about his being able to deal with all of it. I watched in awe as he tirelessly and sacrificially, with supernatural strength, dealt with all of it and with tenderhearted mercies of our Lord pouring from him to Betty and to her family. Everywhere we went, a soldier would follow and Oscar would caution Randy to be careful, that they looked for excuses to harass or even arrest! The heat, not understanding the language, and Betty's struggles and pain created an atmosphere that required a constant dependency upon God and hearing from the Holy Spirit and relying upon His grace! We were amazed at our endurance and the grace to meet and deal with every situation! Randy was without sleep for thirty-six hours. He mentioned several times he was walking totally by the spirit, as if he was outside of himself!

The next evening, Betty's parents took us out to their house to sleep and get some rest. We were in a large room with two beds. About one or two in the morning, Randy woke me up saying, "Mother, the Lord has been speaking to me and given me a vision! I need to repeat it to you as a witness and to establish it!" He was weeping and awash with the Spirit, and the Presence of the Lord was so heavy around us. He lay on the bed, so overwhelmed in the anointing he began to cry out, "Lord, I cannot stand this anymore, it is more than my body can take! I'll go where You send me, I will do what You tell me to do! I will destroy the works of the devil!" He was just enveloped in the spirit and I just quietly prayed. After a while, he went back to bed, but I knew the Father was ministering to him most of the night. In the morning, he was 'glowing' like a heavy sunburn, and very weepy still. I recalled the prophetic word the Lord had spoken to him, 'your heart I know and within you I glow!' It was a marvel! He had not had much sleep but was refreshed, and a strong aura of authority was around him. We walked out into the yard and he began to tell me of the vision and some of the things he and the Lord had talked about.

The vision: He was at the scene of the accident and Betty was raised up and healed. Suddenly Randy was standing on top of the wrecked car and a funnel of intense light from heaven came down over him and hundreds of people were standing around and receiving their healing. Oscar was standing by the car and Randy asked him if he wanted to be saved and delivered, and he said yes. The light over Randy covered Oscar and lifted him up beside Randy on top of the car! Then he saw this beggar, lame and dirty, coming up the road, walking in the ditch, and the Lord asked him, "Are you willing to minister to this kind?" And Randy put his arms around him. After ministering a long time, he was exhausted and he saw this van or recreational vehicle drive up and several men get out and say, 'We are missionaries going into the interior of Mexico, do you need help?" Later on, he got into the vehicle with them. The vision ended. Then the Lord asked him if he would be willing to go to the scene of the accident and proclaim, "The Lord Jesus Christ is God over Mexico!" He agreed to do that. Then the Lord said, "Betty made a choice and the devil took his opportunity, but this will be to My Glory and his plans will not succeed!" Then He said to him the Spirit of wisdom, revelation and might would rest upon him and his delight would be in obeying God and he would minister to the downtrodden of the earth and the breath of his mouth would slay the enemy! At that point, I remembered in 1980, while in intercession for Randy, the Lord had spoken the word 'root' to me so clearly, I was stunned and then Isaiah 11:1, "Out of the old root a new branch will bear fruit and the Spirit of the Lord shall rest upon him." At that time, I had marked this verse in the margin of my Bible and dated it, which I quickly opened and showed to him. We both marveled at what all of this could mean! The Lord also told him that He would instruct him in all things concerning Betty. When the pressures were great and there was a crisis, he was to pull himself aside and seek the Lord and inquire and worship Him and He would give him wisdom! And He did just that! Time and again! As we both determined to walk by the spirit, to deny our flesh and our natural emotions to rule us and let Him flow out from us, we saw time after time little miracles, big miracles, God was sovereign over all and in us! Amen!

We returned to the hospital. They had taken her out of ICU and put her in a room with two extra beds, so we were able to stay around the clock. This was so important for her continual recovery. We had to be 'on our toes' at all times! Time after time, we saw the word and prayer overcome pain, fear and obstacles! They could not keep Betty sedated enough to keep her comfortable because of the head injuries, and there were terrible times between injections that prayer and the word took dominion over the pain and peace came and sleep came!

Praise His Name! Every word of faith spoken was challenged, but no weapon formed ever really prospered and every injury continued to heal and treatment and procedures took place as needed and condition warranted. There was progress above normal! We noticed how quickly the cuts and contusions were healing, and there was no redness or swelling. She stayed alert and knew everything that was going on and cooperated in every way, and the doctors and nurses always acted surprised and pleased! Of course, we had to interpret most things through facial expressions and actions, unless Oscar or a cousin of theirs came by who spoke English! We knew that the prayers and intercession of the faithful ones at home was a power source and we were there as conductors for the prayers and the word to manifest in Betty and the whole situation, and of course, we had to hold the ground that was taken. The demonic activity and oppression were indescribable! The warfare was continuous on every front! We took turns sleeping so one of us was on guard at all times. The gift of faith rested upon us in such a dimension of grace we had never experienced! We held tightly to the Word, the victory had already been won!

Every doctor and nurse who attended Betty did so with great tenderness, compassion and care. The devil had tried to take her life and attempted to finish Randy off as well. There was such a battle raging for their lives in many areas! But God has established His throne in the heavens and He rules over all! And He has chosen His dwelling place in the earth to be within His children! And His sons and daughters to rule with Him! We knew our authority and the power of the word and we used it with success. The standard of the Lord had been raised up within Randy and it was like a rod that could not be broken, maybe bent slightly at the tremendous pressure, but never broken and never stayed bent for long! Wonderful Holy Spirit made Himself known as the Comforter, the Strengthener, the Enabler and the Power so many times in the anointing that we could hardly stand, with water coursing down our faces! How humble we felt, how totally dependent upon Him it made us! How conscious we became of the fact that Christ within is truly the anchor of our soul. When you're in darkness, you have no well to draw from if your only source is yourself! How shallow and powerless the natural realm, and how weak this mortal body! How frightening to be without the true knowledge of God and His indwelling Presence! Betty's courage and endurance could only have come from the power and grace of God that rested upon her to see her through!

There was a righteous anger within us at the devil's work! I say righteous anger because man's anger lashes out of the flesh in physical attack. But this anger poured out in pure love and compassion. Randy and I said to each other several times, we felt like we were outside looking in at all of this! For what operated in us and through us toward Betty and her family was God revealing Himself to them. I believe the true love of God is the higher power that releases the healing flow. I thought about the story of Matthew 14, when Jesus heard about the beheading of John, how angry He was at the devil! He must have been grieving, but He did not retaliate and attack the people. No! He launched His own attack and let His compassion and love flow and heal all manner of sickness and disease, and destroyed the works of satan. And for one man, John, thousands were released from satan's captivity! Halle!

At that point, as I was sharing with Randy what the Lord was sharing with me, he stood up right there and shouted out, "This evil you have done, satan, will cost you plenty! Multiplied thousands will exalt the Name of Jesus through our family!"

Each day and night brought its own challenges for each of us, such as the discipline of choosing God's way and word, when our emotions and frustrations and the stress would for a few moments rule. But we knew that we could not afford to let our feelings or the flesh get in the way of our being available to God the Holy Spirit for the anointing to deal with the situations that confronted us.

Some time later Betty was moved to a private hospital that was more comfortable. The move was very hard on her because of her hip and pelvis. And Randy was the only one who could handle her with less pain. There was a particular time she had to be taken to x-ray. He had gotten her onto the table just fine, but the intern attempted to place a pillow at her side and hurt her and she began crying out in such pain. We stayed right by her side, praying as they wheeled her to x-ray. And stayed right outside the door, walking and praying! Randy came down the hall to where I was and said, "Listen to this song of the spirit!" He was singing a beautiful melody, that sounded like Hebrew, and then very boldly began to dance as he sang! Thankfully there was no one around! When they brought her out, she was smiling, in no pain, and they were able to get her back onto the bed with no pain! We ask if they had given her a shot or pain medications, and they said no, that it was amazing, she had fallen asleep on the table! We had to be bold and could not afford to be intimidated. We prayed in tongues at all times and praised God loudly and that song and dance brought a victory!

The next day in the afternoon, she was having a particularly hard time and seemed to be getting weaker and going in and out. Finally we convinced someone to get the doctor and they finally discovered her blood pressure was dangerously low and there was not enough blood to get a test! So they began to make arrangements for a blood transfusion. While we were waiting, we were battling, singing and worshipping and celebrating Betty's life, and the presence of the Lord so filled that room that we both fell to our knees beside the bed, weeping and praying. I looked up at Betty and her arm was straight up in the air! She kept it up for the longest time! They had made the statement when they discovered her blood count so low that they did not know how she could hold her eyelids open! I thought that I would help her keep her arm up, but decided not to touch her, God's Presence was so strong on her! The Holy Spirit told Randy to stand on Mark 16, and lay hands on her, which we did from the top of her head to her toes. He then instructed us to stand on 1 Peter 5, and anoint her with oil. This we did all over her body, and then we began to sing, "This is Holy Ground," and it truly was! We had taken that ground for God and His Presence had filled us and filled that room! Betty was strengthened and refreshed, amazingly so, before she even received the transfusions!

Late that evening, a terrible pain hit her head and she was crying and passed out! We could not arouse her or get a response. I stayed with her while Randy went to find someone. This was a Saturday and very few were on the floor. And no one there could speak English! Finally, after a considerable time had passed, an intern came and took vital signs and they left. We did not see anyone else for quite some time, and by that time she had come to and ask what had happened! I wish I could say we did not panic, realizing immediately the devil's smoke after the wonderful experience a few hours before, but fear gripped me for a few minutes and I thought my own heart would stop beating! Randy hung in there and did not give any ground! The anointing upon him was amazing! A new doctor had come by and said her ears had to be cleaned out, as there was glass in them! They were going to try to repair her hip as well. They felt the danger was passed for the head fractures. Because they had waited so long, the surgery was not totality successful and her hip did not heal properly.

We continued to have to deal with Betty's family. They were insensitive to Betty. There was much agitation and strife between all of them, and Betty would be exhausted. We were so concerned and Randy would try to stand up for her and help them understand this was harmful to her recovery. But that just created more hostility toward him. It was just a very challenging situation and frustrating for us. Of course, they had no understanding of the spiritual aspect of any of this or why we were even there, and seemed to resent us rather than appreciate us. We did try to understand and tried not to take it personally.

Over two weeks had passed and I had to return home to Abilene, and of course take the car. We had assurance from Papa Oscar, Mama Tina and sister that Randy would be taken care of. They would see that he had transportation, food, and would take turns staying with Betty so he could get out and rest. That did not happen! With both of us there guarding each other and praying in agreement, almost everything that tried to operate did not for long! They did not show up for three days! He was stranded, facing an openly hostile attitude, and it was very stressful for Betty. And the situation became more difficult for him. After ten days of dealing with all of this, he called me and was so drained, putting out so much without much rest. He said he had to have some help or he could not hold up and keep Betty going. I told him I would come some way and I would call people to intercede and he was to call me the next day. It was around noon when he called and he sounded so refreshed and up. He shared that the night before, he had soared to new heights with God! He had been in the cleft of the Rock with the Lord and had been strengthened, revived and he was fine, I did not need to come!

As had been the pattern since the beginning, after every victory and a time of refreshing there was another challenge around the corner! There were issues that came up concerning further procedures and treatment. Once again, Tina and relatives went against Randy and what he felt was the best for Betty. She chose to agree with them instead of him, which later proved to be wrong, so she had to endure the result of that with more stress and another three days in the hospital! It was an uphill piece of business. When she entered into the negative flow of confusion with her family, she took herself out of the divine flow. After much prayer, I felt led to speak with her concerning this on the phone, and prayed with her. Her will and independence were very strong even in the weakness of her body, and of course Randy was hurt and frustrated, not for himself but for her safety, protection and peace of mind.

At last she was discharged from the hospital and she was taken to their home with a hospital bed. After a week, she asked Randy to get her out of there and back to Abilene. He called us, and T.W and I went after them. It was a very difficult trip for her and I knew I would have to stay with them some and be available for whatever was needed to take care of her, not knowing how long her recovery might take. She could not walk as yet. We certainly had a testimony of our Lord's Omnipresence and Omnipotence! Power and Grace!

LETTER TO MY FATHER GOD, FROM MY MOTHER HEART TO HIS MOTHER HEART

The strongest of strong love on the earth is a mother's love for her child or children. From the moment of conception onward, the very nature of that love is protecting, shielding, and giving, always expecting the best, blind to imperfections and faults. The giving of life, giving birth from your own body, produces the strongest emotional ties known to mankind. The greatest pain to the soul is when that child is hurting or in pain. The old saying, "A mother or father can handle any trauma or pain to themselves, but if their child is in danger or pain, the anguish is almost unbearable." So, no matter how old the children become, when they hurt, you hurt. And when there is emotional trauma or upheaval, a mother will tend to feel responsible somehow or to blame, and in the fierceness of her love, she has failed. In all the strength of natural mother love, it was not enough to shield them from pain and failure that accompanies living and experiencing life for themselves. For some it is easier to break free from those emotional ties. Certain situations and circumstances influence these emotions differently, such as a shared father/mother responsibility, a home that provides a healthy balance and stability for parents and child, or the contrast of a single parent home. In many situations, we truly have suffered and perished for lack of wisdom and understanding. Obviously and absolutely, God's ways are always the best and His words and commands are not grievous!

They bring blessings, joy, fulfillment and peace in our lives and relationships.

Will we always seek our own way, Father? Why can't we immediately do what You say and follow Your instructions and walk in Your abundant life? How it must grieve you, Lord! How You must suffer over our rebellious ways and our pain and suffering! I can only measure your heart by my own, knowing that YOU are the totality of man, that my 'mother heart' originated in YOU, that You literally gave us birth. YOU were our Father/Mother before our earthly father! So, how emotionally and forever strong are Your ties to Your children! How could I ever think YOU would give up or ever love Your children any less, or ever see us except through eyes of love that never see the faults or failures and the mess! For I am Yours and your life is in me and You cannot cease loving me! So, with Your great Love and Your mother heart and the wisdom of a Father, You will never, never relax Your hold upon us! You certainly are able to keep that which we have committed unto You. Just as my children are bone of my bone and flesh of my flesh, even so we are of YOU! So, I must believe that You surely understand and forgive my sins against my children, because You know that natural love, no matter how strong or fierce, will always fall short, will do or say or respond wrongly from the sheer emotion of it. I am so aware of the inability to love perfectly, to be all my family needs and deserves. You surely know that I long for YOUR love to be perfected in me, for I know Your love will always bring peace and drive out all fears, as well as creating a perfect environment for You to work! You know how much I love them, and yet I have gotten in Your way many times and I know I have hurt them. Who will deliver me from my natural [unredeemed, unhealed] soul-ish emotions? Praise God! I know You will! And I do know, Dearest Lord, that they are your sons even more than mine and You are mighty to save, deliver and heal. How can I doubt Your faithfulness? My strong feelings that I have to try to 'fix it,' to make it right, to straighten it out, is really lack of faith in You and comprehending how perfect is Your love. Teach me, Lord, to walk by the Spirit toward my loved ones in mercy, unconditional love and wisdom. How can I lay down my natural love for Your supernatural love? I cannot, You will have to work it in me.

I could not have lived, Father, had I not known that You only see the true heart and know that Your children, in ignorance and in trauma of soul, were out of step and fellowship with YOU, and not because they willed it. I will not waver, Lord. As for me and my house, we will serve You! I stand against all doubt and unbelief, all fear and all confusion. I apply the Blood to the doorpost of every dwelling and release the blessing of peace, health and prosperity over every member of my household! I loose the Word to the renewing of each of our minds to bring us into alignment with Your will and purpose for each of our lives! I declare that I will not go down to Egypt for help and lean on the arm of the flesh. For I will say of YOU, YOU are our shield, our buckler, our deliverer! In You I put my trust, and I shall not be ashamed. All my household is under the covering and protection of the Mighty One of Israel, and no calamity, destruction, sickness nor poverty shall come nigh or overtake our dwelling! You will rebuke the devourer for our sakes. You have opened the windows of heaven above us and You are releasing blessings that we can hardly contain, and You are supplying all of our needs. We are recipients of the blessings of Abraham!

Glory, Glory! My inner self rises up in exaltation and adoration and thanksgiving, manifesting in joyous songs of praise and the clapping of my hands and the dancing of my feet! Continue to teach me and lead me into the higher realms of the Spirit. A touch, a taste is not enough! I will not be satisfied until my triune being is in harmony with and in agreement with the Trinity. You said to me through Your prophet that "I would be satisfied in my house." I cannot be satisfied until my sons and daughters, my household, are in fellowship with You and in Your will. And until my own house, Your abode, is wholly Your domain to move freely about with no closed off rooms. A house flooded with light! Selah.

DIVINE ENCOUNTER

12-7-87

Sitting in my chair, having set myself to pray and intercede, after a very difficult week of pressure, challenges and just hurting from disappointments. I had 'willed' myself to worship and love on the Lord. I was doing that and praying in the spirit when I became conscious of the stiffness and pain in my neck and head, and I began to say with a great release of faith and putting my hands on my shoulders and neck, "I am God's property, I am His possession and I command and demand this spirit of arthritis to leave me. I will not be hindered, interfered with because of this condition. I will not tolerate this." As I was declaring this, I began to be engulfed by the Holy Spirit and my words were no longer just coming out of my mouth, but were manifesting in my heart. My motives became pure, it was no longer for my comfort or benefit but a surrender to His perfect will for me, for my body was for Him and I belonged to Him. The anointing became heavier until I was 'weighted' down and I was 'out' of myself and was enveloped in a intense blue light! Indescribable! Something lifted off me, out and off my neck and up through my head and I could only lay back in my chair in this light-ness. My whole body was light, and yet so heavy I could not move! I was weeping and began to lift my hands up to worship Jesus, and I knew I was healed and that something else was taking place. I was overwhelmed with the joy of it, and I was in and out of intercession, all different kinds of tongues and travail with great weeping! I began to feel heaviness in my arms and hands as if they were not mine. I was out in the spirit and yet conscious of what was happening.

[It is very difficult to express the emotions and experiences of the spirit. It is always so glorious and holy!]

I knew this was a baptism for service, a call to specific ministry, and all the intercession was birthing destiny. The eye of my spirit was drawn to my hands. They were mine, but they were His. I could not lift them, they were so heavy, so I gently crossed them in my lap. I was weeping and saying the name of Jesus over and over. Such love filled me, the ecstasy of being in the Divine Presence, I could hardly bear it! But I did not want to leave Him. I kept seeing His hands, strong and soft and gentle. I loved His hands. I felt Him touch my lips and something happened, I can't explain. After this, I felt a tingling in my feet and I thought, yes, my feet needed to be anointed! My whole body felt 'alive' unto Him! I don't know how long I lay there, basking in all of this surrendering and yielding and loving Jesus. For a long time I held my own hands in reverence hardly daring to move them, it still felt like they didn't belong to me. I remember thinking that there was no watch on my wrist, but I saw a watch on a chain around my neck, and wondered what that could mean. [Later I understood the Holy Sprit was pointing out my need to wait upon Him and watch for His timing.]

Then I went into a dream state. The intercession and great crying had stopped, just a gentle trickle of water down my face and a great peace settled down upon me. The heaviness had lifted and I felt I was floating! I was wearing a beautiful, flowing white dress. Great love was coming out of me. I was praying for many people, laying hands on them and saying these words: "Jesus, this is a member of Your body, a part of You, You can't have a part of Your body crippled, sick, out of joint, out of divine order! Heal them Lord!" I saw my son, Donny, and others I didn't recognize, worshipping, and my son, Randy, standing beside me. And off in the distance, I saw my husband, T.W., standing in a mist or fog.

It was late afternoon when I awakened. I will never be the same.

PROPHECY THROUGH
PASTOR DAVE ROBERSON

2-19-88

B rother Dave Roberson was holding a meeting in Abilene. The atmosphere was heavy with the Presence of the Lord and the Holy Spirit was ministering to His people in many different ways. Randy had brought Betty to the meeting to be healed. She had not been able to walk since the accident, and he carried her in his arms into the church. Betty was very reluctant, but Randy was determined. During the meeting, Brother Dave came over to her. He had not seen Randy carry her in. He reached his hand out to her and began to minister to her and then he said, "Rise and walk in the name of Jesus." She stood up, and with Randy's help began to walk down a short distance to the front, and then a few more steps across the front. The church was praising God and it was awesome. Randy and I were weeping and rejoicing! She made great progress in her recovery, although the bones did not come fully into alignment.

Then Brother Dave called me out and began to prophesy, and it seemed the anointing upon him was increasing. People were falling out all over the place!

"Transition — Oh the change! The change that's working in you! It's nothing that you've seen before, I say! The earnest desire that's been resident in your heart, know you not it's been ME? Sayeth the Spirit of the Lord. Moving in you, moving upon you in the night

*times, moving upon you in the day times, and what is about to rise
upon the inside of you is bigger than anything you've ever walked
in before! Oh, your hand is on the doorknob at this time! For I AM
pulling you through this door! And the anointing that you will walk
in will be different than anything you have ever seen, My daughter.
For even as you have craved the supernatural creative power, this
day, the manifestation will began to come forth and flow through
your hands as never before."*

He grabbed my hands, and it was like electricity was going
through me, I had been trying to stand during this time and suddenly
I was thrown backward to the floor!

He continued: *"You have received the true phenomena of healing
and the working of miracles, which is coming forth in seed form this
moment, that is what is happening now!"*

I treasure all of the words of the Lord given to me through the
years through the 'GIFT'S ' Jesus gave to His church, and have
warred with these words as they brought vision, identification,
encouragement, and confirmation. And with them always came the
'Grace,' the power and anointing to bring them to fulfillment in their
time. I have walked in and experienced the fulfillment of many, and
some in small measure. I know that prophets' words at times are an
invitation, not a guarantee! God speaks prophetically to invite us
to more fully cooperate with the Holy Spirit in faith and obedience
as we pray to release the manifestation of the things prophesied.
But I discovered throughout my journey, there is a fullness of time
for the fullness of the measure of all God has spoken and foreordained. One day we will be served a glorious sit-down, full course
dinner in the KINGDOM of our God! But for now, we have only
had 'tasting parties,' a full meal here and there, a 'sampler buffet' if
you will, a 'preview' of that which is to come! We ain't seen nothing
yet! We have only touched the hem of His Glory. The levels we
have reached in faith, love, joy, peace, righteousness, power and the
manifestation of His Kingdom and ONENESS with FATHER, SON
and HOLY SPIRIT are a plateau that God the Holy Spirit is about to
'explode' out from under us, and leave us suspended in the Glory of
His Presence and manifested Power! Yes! Halle!

I believe that for numerous called 'out' and called 'up' saints, it has come to 'A fullness of time.' they are the 'Mothers and Fathers, the revealed' matured sons, the equippers 'of the end-time harvesters' for the Great Day of the Lord!

MAY YOUR NAME BE EXALTED, OH LORD GOD!

Dream Encounter

5/15/88

There was this handsome, strong man, beautiful in countenance, beautiful mouth, perfect teeth that kept a smile, almost to the point of laughter. A smile of joy, of delight, of approval upon His lips. Gentle eyes, deep pools of dark blue [I think], transparent and twinkling. A glow of happiness upon His face! He was standing very close to me, inviting me to come into His arms

I knew He was my betrothed [I would never use that word; this was no ordinary dream, this was another realm and Jesus was visiting me!] I was unsure of His love for me. I behaved in ways to test that love. I exposed my very self openly so He would see 'me' and the deceitfulness of my heart and the ways I felt I had betrayed Him. He never reacted. His expression never changed. He never showed disappointment or disapproval, never a shadow of turning came upon His face! Still deep within me, I could not yield to Him or trust Him totally. It seemed the way I felt about myself and my life was holding me back. I could not quite believe HE loved me so completely. Then He said: "I'm taking care of the papers, the license, and we are going to the wedding." He picked me up in His arms and began to walk. All the while I was looking into His Face that held such a love I could not comprehend! We had gone quite a distance and these thoughts were going through my mind: "How much farther is it? He is so strong, His steps have not faltered nor His arms slackened. He is not wearied or tired, the support of His arms are still holding me firmly and securely! This is amazing!" Love for Him engulfed me and my thoughts were that I had offered no resistance when He had suddenly picked me up, and it felt quite a natural thing to be going to a wedding with Him, but still I could not entirely release my whole self to Him. I yearned to, strained to, but something held me back and THEN! Like heaven opened up, I began to experience within my being His true, loving heart! His unconditional love! I knew He really did approve of me, accepted me, loved 'ME,' just as I am! And for that instant my whole self melted into Him in the most holy spiritual union, indescribable! His love for me broke through and burst into my soul! I believed He loved 'me' and He believed I was a perfect bride for Him! It was glorious and I did not want it to end. I woke up under an anointing that did not lift for quite some time.

To record the sensations and deep emotions of the encounter, I was reluctant to even try. I felt I would tarnish it, knowing it would be impossible to describe such a supernatural happening with a natural vocabulary. But I knew I must, that it would anchor me and might encourage others.

Obviously, all the past relationships that had caused such wounds of rejection, dealing deep blows to my self-esteem, had kept me from fully trusting Christ's love for me, and there was no way I could move forward into what He had purposed for me and the precious ones He wanted to love, touch and heal through me, without a deeper revelation of His unconditional love.

Song of Songs, Chapter 5 and Chapter 8:5. The Message

"I was sound asleep, but in my dreams I was wide awake; Oh! Listen! It's the sound of my lover knocking, calling!

Look! Listen! there's my Lover! Do you see Him coming? Vaulting the mountains, leaping the hills. My lover is like a gazelle, graceful like a young stag, virile. Look at him there, on tiptoe at the gate, all ears, all eyes, ready! My lover has arrived and he's speaking to me!"

"Get up, my dear friend, fair and beautiful lover — come to Me! Look around you; winter is over, the winter rains are over, gone! Spring flowers are in blossom all over. The whole world's a choir — and singing! Spring warblers are filling the forest with sweet arpeggios; Lilacs are exuberantly purple and perfumed and cherry trees fragrant with blossoms. Get up, dear friend, my fair and beautiful lover — come with Me! Come, my shy and modest dove — leave your seclusion and come out into the open! Let me see your face, let me hear your voice. For your voice is soothing and your face is ravishing."

Answer: "Then you must protect me from the foxes, foxes on the prowl, foxes who would like nothing better than to get into our flowering garden.

"My lover is mine, and I am His. Nightly he strolls in our garden, delighting in the flowers until dawn breathes its light and night slips away.

"Turn to me, dear lover, come like a gazelle. Leap like a wild stag on delectable mountains!"

"Who is this I see coming up from the wilderness, arm in arm with her lover?"

He said: "I found you under the apricot tree, and woke you up to love!"

I know it is difficult for some men to relate to Christ as the Groom, the lover of their soul, and see themselves as the bride of Christ. I pray you will be able to 'see' from a spiritual, heavenly perspective, and not from the natural realm. And consider Jesus' prayer before His crucifixion:

"... That they all may be one, just as You, Father, are in Me and I am in You, that they may be one in Us, so that the world may believe that You have sent Me. I have given to them the glory and honor which You have given Me, that they may be one even as We are one; I in them and You in Me, in order that they may become one and perfectly united that the world may know and recognize that

You sent Me and You have loved them even as You have loved Me." John 17:21-23

In Ephesians 5, he speaks of the marriage covenant and how wives are to love their husbands and husbands are to love their wives. And then in verse 32: "This mystery is very great, but I speak concerning the relation of Christ and the church, His sons." In the Spirit there is no gender.

It would be beneficial to study the Psalms and David's relationship to the Lord and the intimacy they shared. And the special intimacy John the Apostle had with Jesus. And King Solomon in the Song of Songs. Christ and His bride, the church.

I know that Jesus reveals Himself to each of us, male or female, in very beautiful, profound ways. It is His great desire that His sons and daughters have experiential knowledge of the length, depth, breadth and height of His love for us, that we might be a body wholly filled with God Himself.

The secret place is in the oneness with Christ. He who dwells in the 'secret place' of the Most High shall abide under the shadow of the Almighty. Psalm 91.

THE GLORIOUS END-TIME CHURCH

In 1988, I was sitting before the Lord with His Word before me and fellowshipping with HIM when a vision began to form. I saw a great majestic eagle, with wings outstretched, covering the globe of the earth from wing tip to wing tip! Within myself, I began to feel her strength and determination, as if nothing could stop her flight. Her eyes were intently focused, her face set like flint, her posture and position exuding power and authority. Her wings were trembling in the wind, as if poised for purposeful flight.

I felt the desire and unction of Holy Spirit to pick up my pen and write:

The Glorious End-time Church!

Like a bird out of prison
The great eagle has risen
And her wings are covering the earth!

In majestic and lofty splendor
With great grace she will render
Justice over all the earth!

She is soaring to new heights
Bathed in Glorious Light
Protected by a mantle of Truth

Great strength and great power
Will testify to the hour
It is time for the King's Return!

This great bird of prey
Has been hidden away
Concealed in the cleft of the Rock

Renewing her strength
Defining her purpose
As the satanic host laughed and mocked!
The mysteries of the Kingdom she'll unlock!

Now she is poised for Flight
With the final victory in sight
Carried on the current of the WIND

As she yields to the WIND's Power
She becomes stronger by the hour
For the task that lies ahead!

Her destiny etched in the set of her brow,
Not man nor beast
Can stop her now!

She is destined for the Throne!
Higher than she has ever flown!
This to be her Last!

She must snatch her Prey
Before the end of the Day
And while it is yet still Light!

With her face to the SON
Her race almost Run
Like the sound of a Trumpet she cries aloud!

The Spirit and the Bride say Come!
Whosoever Will — Let Them Come!
And take freely of the Water of Life!

As I meditated on the vision and the word, a few days later the Holy Spirit began to share with me some exciting revelation out of the scriptures that increased my faith and vision for the days ahead, for the position and glory of the end-time 'many-membered' body of Christ! He was continuing to deal with the old escapism mentality of the Scofield generation!

He spoke: Ezekiel Chapter 1:10 and Revelation 4:6-8. It was as if the Finger of the Lord was on key words. I felt as if these scriptures encompassed the Alpha and Omega of Creator God, the Glory of God the Son, Creation, His plan of redemption and His Church! The Beginning and The End!

I share this with you, not as a complete revelation, nor addressing each detail of the vision, but to encourage us in the progression of · transformation, of God's unfolding plan, and to discern the 'times.'

I believe the Spirit is saying the eagle represents the third day church in the fourth dimension of Ezekiel's river. [chapter 47]

In Ezekiel's vision, there were four living creatures. Each of the living creatures each had four faces. In John's vision, the same four living creatures now each had but one of the four faces!

"The likeness of their faces, they each had the face of a man facing out to the south; the face of a lion to the right facing east; the face of an ox to the left facing west; the face of an eagle to the back facing north."

Four is the number of completion, divine perfection, and His creative works! It also marks division, as it is the first number that can be divided.

The fourth book of the Bible is Numbers, in Hebrew called 'B'Midbar.' It relates to the wilderness of earth, and our pilgrimage through it.

Cherubim in scripture have to do with creation, always. They are seen in connection with guarding, atonement, and they are seen on the mercy seat. In Revelation they announce the 'Coming One' when all the kingdoms of the world become the kingdom of our God!

The four faces picture, first of all, God's creation in general. Secondly, Jesus, Son of God, Son of man. Thirdly, the believer, and fourthly, the church, the corporate son. In their unfolding revelation through time and eternity, of purpose and destiny!

Four-sided 'cube,' completed prophecy.

The Holy of Holies a perfect 'cube'!

The New Jerusalem coming down from heaven, 'four square'!

The First Face: Man

Adam, the first man. Deceived by the ancient serpent, "as sin came into the world through one man and as a result of sin, death spread to all men. How much more surely will those who receive God's overflowing grace and free gift of righteousness [putting them into right standing with Himself] reign as kings in life through the ONE MAN JESUS CHRIST! Just as by one man's disobedience the many were constituted 'sinners,' so by ONE MAN's obedience many will be made righteous!" In Romans 5, He is called 'the last Adam.'

The 'first' [law if first mention] born pattern Son, bringing many sons into glory!

In the Middle Ages there were drawings that depicted these four signs as the four Gospels, representing Jesus.

Matthew presenting Jesus in His humanity, Mark presenting Him as the Lion, Luke presenting Him as the Servant, and John presenting Him as the Eagle.

Second face: The Lion

King of the animal kingdom, majestic, noble, fearless. Facing right to the east.

Jesus called 'The Lion of the tribe of Judah.'

Ascended and seated on the Right Hand of God the Father as King of Kings and Lord of Lords!

Born in the east, entered the gates of the city of Jerusalem from the east, riding on the colt of a donkey!

Will return in clouds of glory in the eastern sky!

Given all power and authority over all the powers of the enemy!

Third face: Ox

Most powerful of domesticated animals.

Father God referred to Jesus as "MY Servant."

He put on the servant's towel and washed the feet of the disciples, a supreme example of humility. He was the Word of Life, the Word demonstrated in the flesh.

Jesus said, "Take My yoke upon you and learn of me, for I am meek and lowly."

He was presented as 'the burden bearer.'

Fourth face: Eagle

Most powerful and majestic of birds.

Air supremacy, connection between earth and the heavens, type of deity, symbol of the prophetic flow of the Spirit, and most often represents Freedom!

Jesus, from the heights of heaven's glory to earth. The Spirit of God Almighty overshadowed a virgin called Mary. Rejected Messiah, lived the Word, fulfilling all of the law's demands, preached the gospel of the kingdom, manifested and demonstrated the power of it, endured the cross, raised from the dead, released the Holy Spirit upon the earth, established His Kingdom, merging heaven and earth, and took His flight of freedom. When He ascended on high, He took captivity captive and led a train of vanquished foes and bestowed gifts upon men! Now seated on the right hand of the Father as the Mercy Seat, ever interceding for us. Now He calls, "Come fearlessly, confidently and boldly to the throne of God's grace, of His unmerited favor and receive mercy for your failures, and find grace to help in good time for every need!" Glory!

The Four Faces as representing the individual Believer, the Church.

Man:
The new creation man born again of the Spirit.
Being transformed into the image of the Son of God.
Heaven is God's home; earth, man's home.
The Blood of Jesus redeems us back to God's original plan and command. Adam, the man and the woman, mankind, walked and talked with their creator, communed and fellowshipped with Him. God said: "Let us give them dominion over the earth. They will be the new temple of God My dwelling place in the earth, a temple not made with human hands. Through the Seed, bringing many sons into glory!"

Lion:
As born anew by His Spirit, buried with Him in baptism, we have been clothed with power from on high;
The violent take it by force. They shall tread on serpents and scorpions and over all the power of the enemy.
The righteous are as bold as a Lion!
Greater works than these shall you do, for I go to my Father.
Overcomers through our testimony and the Blood of the Lamb!
You shall reign as kings in the earth!

Ox:
Bearing one another's burdens.
Wearing His yoke we plow, we tread out the grain.
Present your bodies as a living sacrifice, which is your reasonable service.
We have been made priests unto our God, serving in His house.

Eagle:
We are spirit, we have a soul and we live in a body. We are not bound to earth.
Strong in His might and the power of His Spirit, we do battle in the heavenlies!
Given supremacy over earth and the heavens.

We are told to 'yield' to the Holy Spirit, to strive to enter into His 'rest.'

Positioned in heavenly places in Christ Jesus!

"But to those who wait for the Lord, who expect, look for, and hope in Him, shall change and renew their strength and power; they shall lift their wings and mount up [close to God] as eagles [mount up to the sun]; they shall run and not be weary, they shall walk and not faint or become tired!" Isaiah 40:31

I believe the Holy Spirit showed me the eagle as symbolic or a type of an end-time church. A generation, a company of believers, having progressed to the fourth stage on the earth, having come to the revelation of the immeasurable, unlimited greatness of His power in and for us who believe, mature sons, perfected in and by love. Jesus ruling and reigning in His house, revealed in His multi-faceted many-membered Body! The Glorious Church! Taking her liberty, walking in love, walking in the Spirit. Taking dominion, changing the culture, walking in power and demonstration of the Kingdom! Powerful in her kingly, priestly anointing! I believe that generation is in the earth now!

This end-time church will rise to meet Him in the air, so shall we ever be with the Lord!

The cherubim that appear in Ezekiel 1 is the 'forth telling'! The same creatures appearing in Revelation 4:7, the 'fulfilling,' the reality! They are themselves around the throne of God, full of eyes, now eternal like their God, crying Holy! Holy! Is The Lord God Almighty!

I want to share some interesting facts and inherent characteristics of Eagles and make a few applications.

Are you an Eagle?

1. The Eagle has a voracious appetite.

"I have prepared a table before you in the presence of your enemies."

"I Am the Bread of life, take and eat."

"He has filled our mouth with good things so our youth is renewed as the Eagle."

2. The Eagle hides himself in the cleft of a high rock and rubs and beats off the old beak and talons and pulls out the damaged feathers and then waits until he is renewed. [The Rock will offend and tear, then heal]!

"Do not conform to this world system, but be ye transformed by the renewing of your mind."

The other Eagles gather around and protect the one injured that is being restored and renewed in the cleft of the Rock. They are fiercely protective of their own!

"Love the Lord your God will all your heart and soul and your brother as you love yourself."

3. She goes to a high point on the rock to launch her flight and to survey the area.

"Without vision the people perish." We soar on the wings of the Spirit, 'seeing' from a heavenly perspective, seeing with the eyes of our spirit and hearing with the ears of our spirit. Ascending into His Presence through worship, praise and prayer, to develop intimacy and fellowship.

"Come up here and I will show you things to come!" He is our Maker, our Father and Friend who sticks closer than a brother. Messiah, the Rock of our Salvation! We are His beloved, who recline at the table with Him, leaning upon His breast to hear His heart beat!

4. The Eagle is very alert, discerning and very difficult to fool, the most difficult to trap or catch in a snare. He has tunnel vision and sees afar off.

"Do not be ignorant of satan's devices, he goes about as a roaring lion seeking whom he may devour. Resist him and he will flee from you. Become wise as a serpent but gentle as a dove."

5. When the Eagle takes his flight, he yields to the wind current, letting the wind carry him. He rests as he flies, for he is riding the current and the longer he flies, because he is not using his own resources

or energy, the stronger he becomes, and he goes after his largest prey after he has flown a while!

Halle! Flowing or yielding to the Wind [Holy Spirit] is entering into the 'rest' of the Spirit. Ceasing from our own labors and entering into His.

There is no 'burn out' in the Spirit. We have become dependant upon Christ and His Anointing and following the leading of His Spirit, moving with the Wind or current as He wills, in His will through the power of His grace. Whom the Son has set free is free indeed!

The Wind of prophecy at our back, and the refreshing Wind of promise gently blowing upon our face! Oh! Yes!

This Glorious Church with the Characteristics of God, the Great Eagle, will be full of His Glory, radiating His Love, stewards of His Grace and Power, snatching its prey and soaring away under the very nose of satan and his demons!

Exodus 19:4 "... I bore you on eagles' wings and brought you out!"

Deuteronomy 32:11 "As an eagle that stirs up her nest, that flutters over her young, HE spread abroad HIS wings and HE took them, HE bore them on HIS pinions!"

Psalm 91:1-4 "He who dwells in the secret place of the Most High shall remain stable and fixed under the shadow of the Almighty. Whose power no foe can withstand. I will say of the Lord, He is my Refuge and my Fortress, my God; on Him I lean and in Him I confidently trust! For then He will deliver me from the snare of the fowler and from the deadly pestilence. Then He will cover me with His pinions and under His wings shall I trust and find refuge: His truth and His faithfulness are a shield and a buckler!"

There is a great turning away from the hype and entertainment, from fleshy ministries, religion, with great longings after only His Presence, just Him. We're being brought to a place of awe and reverential fear of the Lord. I believe we are in the Time of Autumn, the Time of Tabernacles, of Harvest. The Church must be ready to receive and disciple. This sovereign move will not only be upon flesh in physical healings, but a mighty display of His love and mercy and goodness! In contrast to the world's system of evil and injustices and religious systems of bondage, He will reveal His goodness! He caused His goodness to pass before Moses, and Moses worshipped Him and said, "Show me Your Glory." His Glory is His goodness, His purity, His love and compassion. Paul had a revelation also of His goodness. He said, "His love compels me, constrains me to follow Him!" Moses said, "If Your Presence does not go with us, we cannot go on! Is it not in Your going with us that we are distinguished as Your people, from all other peoples? Show us Your Glory!" And God said, "I will make all my goodness pass before you and I will proclaim My Name. The Lord!"

Psalm 31:19. David said, "Oh how great is Your goodness which You have laid up for those who fear and worship You, goodness You have wrought for those who trust and take refuge in You before men!" Oh, Love the Lord, all you His saints! Be strong and let your heart take courage, all you who wait and hope in the Lord! You shall mount up with wings as Eagles! Amen!

I must needs go a little further in the revelation.

Now, back to Ezekiel 1. He said: "Beside the four creatures were wheels, a wheel within a wheel, the rims high and with eyes all around and everywhere the creatures went, the wheels went." Once again, the eternal glory of God's throne and creation. God is all-seeing, all-knowing, ever-present. Omniscient, omnipresent and omnipotent God! This also depicts Creation with 'Circles' and 'Cycles.' He is the Alpha and the Omega, the Beginning and the End. All things began in Him and return to Him! He is the Author and the Finisher of our faith! All things were created by Him and for Him and for His pleasure they were created! Creating is His nature.

We have Christ the Son in God the Father and the Holy Spirit. The Three in One! There is One faith, One Spirit and One baptism. One Blood, one Father of us all. Jesus said in His prayer to the Father before His passion, "I pray, Father, that they may be one, even as we are One." A wheel within a wheel!

He said: "They had four wings and they were touching. Everyone to his other side, the wings were touching." Once again, signifying the interdependence upon one another. Community. The corporate son. As I meditated upon these 'wheels,' these 'circles,' I began to see as looking through a microscope! Circles! Circles! Cells! Moving independently yet touching, supporting, working together. I mean, God is into circles! Wheels! He is the Hub, the Center. Everything radiates out from Him! Cells! Never-ending cycle of eternity. Our bodies are made up of living 'cells.' As members collectively of the body of the Lord Jesus Christ, we are living 'cells,' organisms, connected, interconnected by One Spirit, a part of One Body, multiplying all over the face of the earth! Wow! Yes!

I want to share with you something very interesting. I don't know if you have read the "Lost Books of the Bible." Some of them are mentioned in the scriptures. We have Enoch referred to in scripture, so Enoch was considered to have been a reputable prophet of God. A favored son.

In the eleventh chapter of Enoch, he talks about the 'circles of creation'! The angel carried Enoch on a journey through the Heavenlies.

"The men took me up and led me to the fourth heaven and showed me all the successive goings and all the rays of the light of the sun and the moon, and I measured their goings and compared their light, its circle and the wheels on which it goes like a wind's wheel, of the earth inside the sun's wheel going past with marvelous speed, and day and night with no rest!"

He speaks of the sun's wheel and of the earth inside the sun's wheel. "The sun is a great creation whose circuit, or circle is 28 years, and begins again from the beginning."

Then in Enoch 16, he goes on and talks about the solar circle, the lunar circle and the great circle containing 528 years.

I just share this bit of information to bring some confirmation and give you some 'food for thought'!

One last thing. I have mentioned Ezekiel 47, concerning the river of God and the progression of our journey. This is certainly not a complete revelation of this passage, just leaving with you some points to ponder.

The waters issued out from under the threshold of the temple toward the east from the right side. When Jesus hung on the cross, the sword pierced His right side, blood and water gushed forth! The new birth experience by the Blood, confirmed by the baptismal waters. The birth of the church, His bride, His kingdom now in the earth! Verse 4: "Again he measured a thousand cubits and caused me to pass through the waters, waters that were ankle-deep." The starting point: Stepping into the River of God the Holy Spirit, who is the revealer of the Word. Who will now lead us into all truth and our inheritance in Christ Jesus! The Spirit of Grace that empowers us for the journey. [Going from First Fruits now to Pentecost, the baptism into the Spirit!]

"Again he measured a thousand cubits and caused me to pass through waters that reached to the knees." Intimacy, worship, prayer, moving from the faith that brought us into Christ, into the river now, into the 'light' and full surrender to the Lord, Master of the House.

"Again he measured a thousand cubits and caused me to pass through the waters that reached to the loins." Moving from faith to strength now. Our loins are now girded about with the belt of Truth that covers the 'loins,' a most important piece of our armor. The center of our strength and defense and power!

"And afterward he measured a thousand cubits and it was a river that I could not pass through, for the waters had risen, waters to swim in, a river that could not be passed over or through!" Having progressed from faith to faith, strength to strength, glory to glory! The SEED of Christ within having come to full stature! The FOURTH dimension! Unable to touch bottom, water over our 'heads,' our natural reasoning, abilities, gifting. No longer leaning unto our own understanding, but leaning, trusting fully in Him. In the secret place of the Most High, under His wings! Filled with and immersed in

His Glory! Experiencing the fullest measure of His love for us, the fullest measure of His power that is within us, enabling Him to carry out His purpose and do superabundantly above all that we dare ask or think, beyond our highest prayer, desires, thoughts, hopes and dreams!

Jesus: "Marvel not at what you see me do, for greater works than these you will do!"

The river of God flowing throughout the land, and everything lived wherever the river flowed!

Lift up your heads, Oh ye gates! The King of Glory is coming through!

CROSS PLAINS, TX

The Unfolding Vision

After these divine 'encounters' and spiritual experiences, my love for Christ and sensitivity to His Spirit within me increased, as well as a new passion and love for the body of Christ.

I was in a state of 'awe' most of the time, constantly in prayer and worship and in the word, traveling to meetings where I knew the 'river' was flowing. I was so filled with gratitude that He continued to bring healing to my body and soul, dealing with religious spirits, and revealing mysteries of the kingdom to my heart!

Through a close friend, Peggy Woodson, I became acquainted with the founders of Beulah Ministries in Raleigh, NC, and Roselea invited me to be one of the speakers as well as minister in song at their yearly women's conference. I had just finished recording a new album with a song I had written, "I'll Still be Standing When the Storm Passes Over." And it just so happened, the conference title was, "When the Storm Passes Over"! I was honored and made the commitment to be there. Larry and Deane would drive me, and Deane would assist me. Then I found this lump in my breast! You might know! I could not get in with a specialist in Abilene for a month, and everyone was so concerned and my sister-in-law made an appointment for me with one in San Antonio. They did a lumpectomy, determined it was benign [I just knew that it was, but everyone was relieved], and I was supposed to be in North Carolina in four days and it was over a two-day drive! I knew I was supposed to be at that conference and family members were not happy with me that I would not cancel! The doctor loaded me down with pain medication and bandages and we drove back to Cross Plains and spent the night, then got on the road the next morning. There was grace, but it was challenging! The conference was awesome. Hundreds of precious women were so blessed of the Lord. He showed off mightily and many were never the same!

In '88, through the prophetic word and other divine encounters, the Lord began to bring more clarity and vision for the next season of our lives. I knew He had been preparing me for a specific assignment. He kept sending me to Joshua Chapter 1, concerning this next 'crossing over' the 'Jordan.' I definitely had not passed 'this' way before! New spiritual territories and new 'giants.' He kept emphasizing, "be courageous and do not fear for I AM with you." So I continued to follow His leading with fear and trembling!

I began to hear, "Go and look for a piece of land to build a house in Cross Plains!" Now, I knew this was surely from the devil to get me off course and interfere with God's plans for the next place of ministry! Cross Plains was my home town, the place of my birth and where I graduated from school, and I certainly did not want to move back there, no never! Jesus! Even You could do very little in Your home town!

And remember, I was selling insurance, we had taken bankruptcy, renting a house, driving a '79 Olds and no money in the bank. T.W. was working and paying our expenses and I had managed to put three thousand in a savings account! No credit, just getting by!

Once again, when the Father begins to 'woo' us and draw us to Himself through the Blessed Spirit of Grace with such tender love, and then gently but firmly remind us Whose we are and the wonderful gifts and anointing He mantles us with to bless His people and continue the works He began, we can never resist His love or His call. We can only go forth with joy and trembling!

A call came from Mother. She was not feeling well. She had been having some heart problems, had been on high blood pressure medication for years. I called her heart doctor, picked her up and took her to the hospital. I called Pat and he drove in from San Antonio. It happened to be his birthday, and not one he wanted to celebrate under those circumstances ever again! They checked her in, the doctor came by and put her on some medication and said he needed to keep her a few days. The next day in the afternoon, she was having difficulty breathing and pain in her arm. The nurse kept taking electrocardiograms and saying every thing looked fine. I knew better! The Holy Spirit had alerted me and I started doing battle. I went to the nurses' station and VERY insistently said, "If you do not call her doctor, I will make so much noise in this hospital, and if I call him you will not like it!" They got on the phone and I prayed in tongues, I prayed the promises and not under my breath! The doctor came quickly, the nurse came into the room with him, and he checked Mother and shouted, "Get me a wheelchair and call the operating room, NOW!" He made an incision in the clavicle area and injected some kind of medication and eventually put in a stint. She recovered and lived another seven years. We were SO thankful, we were just not ready at all to let her go!

After Mom's recovery, in faith we began to drive to Cross Plains, looking for property on weekends and staying with Mother. There was this beautiful acreage across the road and down from our home place, full of oak trees and a hilltop building site that was prime property. My Dad as well as my brother even a few years back had tried to acquire it. No way it could be purchased. But with everything we looked into for six months, I kept going back to 'the Richardson place.' I felt so strongly that was the place the Lord wanted! So one day I called and took the plunge. "Mr. Richardson, we want to buy your property and build a house on it." Very quiet on the other end, then "I believe I'll just sell it to you! I'll have my daughter call you." That was it. Okay, Lord! Now what? After the good news, fear struck! This will certainly have to be a miracle attributable only to YOU, LORD! During the six months I had managed to put another $2,000 in savings, for a total of $5,000.

A couple of days passed, then his daughter, Sharon called. "Dad said you all wanted to purchase our land. My husband and I agreed with Dad to sell it to you. My husband will be in touch after we have had a chance to talk about it!"

We were praying, I was fasting and experiencing such peace, knowing the Father had this all worked out. He knew what we had and didn't have, and this was His plan OR it wasn't! The next day, they called and simply said, "This is the deal. The land is on an assumable G.I. loan, no qualifying and we would like $5,000 down and we'll pay the closing cost!" I tried to stay cool and calm, and in a controlled voice responded, "That's great, we'll take it." They would have their lawyer draw up the papers and would be back in touch! Needless to say, I had one of those Holy Ghost jumping, running 'fits,' shouting and crying, and of course on the phone to report the news! My Mother, T.W., as well as others couldn't believe it. Thirty days later, we closed!

For the next year, we worked and saved. Business was good and there was some provision coming in from ministry. I was working on house plans and we would go out to the property and stake off a building site. Many of our friends came and walked the borders and prayed. We staked the corners with scriptures and cleansed the land. A year later, we had saved $20,000 dollars and were ready to begin. During this time, on trips back and forth, I would stop at an abandoned Methodist church, and each time I was so stirred about acquiring it. The dimensions were almost the same as the plans I had, and it was tall enough for a story and a half. It was still sturdy and floors still good. So I began to make contacts and checked with a lawyer. I found the last surviving deacon and the charter, which gave them the right to sell or dispose of it and any proceeds go to the cemetery. So we made the purchase. We began making plans to move it to the property. As the movers got it onto the road leading up to the building site, we had a visitor, a very irate former member who accused us of taking the building without permission, and they demanded we return it! Now mind you, this old building had been vacant for years, in disrepair out in pastureland, used by vagrants and kids. Talk had been for years that someone was going to burn it down! We thought everyone would be delighted it was being salvaged and restored! Not so! This man found someone else to help him harass us. They contacted the *Abilene News,* and the next thing you know, our names and a very distorted story were on the news! We had taken a 'landmark'! We called our lawyer, he called a meeting with the man who was creating such an uproar, and I made the decision to let them have it back. They could move it at their own expense! What an experience. What was that all about, Lord? I thought I knew I had heard from You! I paid a carpenter getting it ready to be moved and paid the movers, so $2,000 down the drain! Sometime later, it burned to the ground. It was hard for me not have a degree of satisfaction over that!

We hired a local contractor and began to build on the site. Six months later, we had it 'dried' in, and we were out of money! But we were working hard and business was good and we were confident that on a 'pay as you go plan,' we would within a year at least get the downstairs finished so we could move in. Then T.W. had a heart attack! Quadruple bypass surgery! He was critical for several days in Intensive Care. Billy and Angie had been alerted in the spirit the day of the attack that this would be a battle for his life and had made calls and they had prayer going. Many were praying. The Lord had people stationed everywhere! One of the nurses, a Christian young man who radiated the love of Jesus, who attended him, came up to me in the parking lot and began to share with me that Holy Spirit had given T.W. as an assignment to him and he was to watch over him, lay hands and pray over him at every opportunity! I stayed with him day and night. After a week in ICU, he developed a staph infection in his abdomen, where he had so many shots. Randy and Donny came to visit [they were both living in Corpus Christi now] and because of their jobs, could not really stay and help very much. Beverly and Richard just didn't come at all, which made it very difficult for me. After two weeks, I developed clots in my legs and was in great pain and had to have a painful procedure. Lois and Luke drove in from Arkansas and took over for a week! When Lois stepped in, it was 'take over time'! Such a blessing! I recovered in that week and was ready to see this through. T.W. had been given so many medications, he was having extreme hallucinations for days. Finally after thirty-one days, we were home. Then to rehab, and two months later he started to work some. Soon after this, Humana Insurance, the company we worked for, closed their offices in Abilene very unexpectedly, without prior notice and suddenly we were out of a job!

So! What now, Lord? It seemed we were always going from one cross [whoops] crisis to another! I suppose there is no other way to experience the Glory and the brightness of the morning of HIS

Rising, to show Himself mighty on our behalf and to convince us that with man it is impossible but with God all things are possible! Faith works through Love and both must come to perfection in us. Faith pleases God. Faith is the substance of things hoped for, the evidence of things not yet seen. Amen, Lord! I will strive to enter into the rest of God and wait to see what only You can do, knowing You are doing a very necessary work within us to enable us to come into mature son-ship, that You may receive ALL the Glory! And we will be lifted up in You!

During this time, we received the surprising news that Betty and Randy were expecting a baby! And then the news it would be a boy! I was quickly reminded of a prophetic word spoken over Betty a few years back concerning this, at a time when that seemed impossible! And I remember the awe that came over me as I seemed to 'know,' this was the main reason satan had tried to destroy Betty's life, to prevent this one from being brought into the earth! Who will he be, Lord? What have You foreordained for him in his generation? Then my mind quickly went to Isaiah 11:1-5, a scripture the Father had spoken to me years ago out of a time of being in His Presence and intercession for Randy! I had thought at the time it was just for Randy and would be his destiny. Now I knew the Holy Spirit was saying Randy's son was 'the branch' out of the root or loin of Randy that would come into this earth with those attributes, gifting and anointing to be a part of a generation that would be 'world changers' in a great end-time move of God! It would have already been 'downloaded' as a part of his DNA before he was ever in his mother's womb, that no man could boast and only the Lord Jesus Christ would receive all the glory! What vision that brought! What hope and faith that instilled in me! What joy!

Almost another year passed, and needless to say, once again we were in 'NEED OF A MIRACLE, FATHER'! Faith was tested fighting hopelessness, and everything else that comes from satan in times like these. But I stood toe-to-toe with my sword drawn, and worshipped and danced and leaned upon the proven faithfulness of God and His Word! There was no way we could pay our bills and save up enough to apply to the work on the house and there it sat, dried in, no siding and just a shell. T.W. had gone to Corpus

Christ and was working with the boys in the senior market with new products until he could get established and work as an independent broker in our area.

One of those 'suddenlies'! OH, Our Heavenly Father already had His solution ready to come forth in His time! A call from Larry and Deane Diehl. Remember them from Corpus Christi? Deane speaking: "Colleen, both Larry and I had dreams last night with the same instructions from the Lord. I was very reluctant to tell Larry my dream. Well, over breakfast Larry said, 'I had a dream last night and the Lord spoke to me very clearly and it's pretty challenging. He said we were to give Colleen and T.W. enough money to finish their house so they can get moved in.' I began to weep, and said, 'Larry, that was my dream too!' Larry wants to talk to you about it!"

Larry said they were compelled to obey the Lord and here is what I needed to do: Get a cost sheet worked up to completely finish the house, complete the downstairs with all amenities so we could move in. I was weeping and saying, "I can't do this, only the Lord knows when if ever we could pay you back!" Larry said, "The Lord did not say anything about that, but if you ever can pay it back, it will be without interest. But if we never get it back from you, that's the Lord's business, all things come from Him. And we are taking a two-week vacation and coming to help you on cabinets and trim and whatever and bring you a check. So start ordering the material and contact your carpenter!"

I was melted and poured out. Blown away. We were talking close to $50,000!

A week later, they arrived. We met at Mother's, as our plan was to stay with her so we would not be driving back and forth and we could stay 'on the job'! We had salvaged a lot of material from a hundred-year-old house in Rising Star, one-by-twelve planks, some old ornate doors, and Deane and I cleaned, pulled tacks and nails and stained all of those planks to use on walls, cleaned and sanded doors, and trimmed windows. Larry almost completed the cabinets and did much of the trim. It was an unforgettable experience! Mother served us awesome meals, three times a day. Every inch of that house was saturated with prayer and worship. People came by for ministry and one friend of mine with a beautiful voice would stand on the balcony and sing and prophesy at the top of her voice as well as all around the property! Randy and Donny would come from out of town and trim trees, clear out brush and haul stuff to the dump. We knew they really came to visit 'Nannie' and pig out on the awesome meals she served, and the love and encouragement she lavished upon them! No matter, we got a lot of work out of them. They earned their blessings!

Two weeks, and Larry and Deane were gone. I continued to stay with Mother and work. T.W. was home working in our region, but still had not recovered his strength and refused to follow the doctor's instructions about life changes, so he wasn't regaining his strength very fast. He was really unable to do very much to help, but did what he could. I began a search for a 'handyman' who could work with me, and hired Gene Dillard. He had worked much of his life in the oil fields, had suffered heatstroke, divorced, did odd jobs and just bummed around and fished, among 'other' things!

He and I installed one-by-six pine plank flooring on all of the downstairs, sixteen hundred square feet! We finished up a lot of trim work and a lot of painting. During this time, I would get phone calls and be praying for people, and speaking in tongues. People were coming and going and Gene, after about two months, began to take his hat off and bow his head while this was going on. I never 'witnessed' to him, but our life and ministry and love of Jesus were all around him and if he worked there, he couldn't escape! God had a plan!

Barbara Wintrouble had been coming to our area to minister in a small community, Grosvenor, TX. Whenever possible, I always attended her meetings. During a meeting on April 5th in '91, after praying for intercessors and impartation of fresh anointing, at the end of the service I was walking out and she called out to me and said, "You are a leader among women! God called you a leader among women! Many things and many voices have risen up against you to interfere and stop you, but soon you will have a clearer vision of what you are to do. You must walk in the call and the anointing, for you are a leader among women!"

Then there was another gathering on June 7th in '91. During the meeting, she called me out and began to prophesy, "There are those close to you who do not understand the call upon your life. Some will come to know, others will never understand. You must cease to be affected by this, you have been troubled and you've tried to make them see, but you must go on, you have a prophetic ministry as well as pastoral, walk in it!"

These words were so timely and came at me as the voice of Father God, which gave me the strength and vision to press on.

In November of '91, we were in our home God the Father had provided for us, according to His Word! We didn't have a porch, used concrete block for steps, and the upstairs was closed off, but we were in and it was awesome and beautiful! To God be the Glory!

Soon after we were in, I was sitting in the living room resting one day, and Gene came driving fast up the road, got out and ran in the door, trembling! "I didn't drive here! Something or someone got a hold of me and my car just drove out here! I don't know why I'm here, but I need something, I need help! I need God!"

Well! We had a Pentecost downpour! He got born again, Jesus baptized him in the Holy Spirit and he was speaking in tongues and lying in the floor! He was never the same. God the Holy Spirit delivered him from alcohol, tobacco, even fishing all the time! He completely surrendered to Christ! He has been a part of LWM since that time, an awesome intercessor and lover of Christ's Church, a Good Samaritan all over the community, was T.W.'s caregiver for several years, and is my brother and friend.

VISITATION AND PROPHECY FROM THE LORD GIVEN TO RANDY

April 1989

*R*andy, I Am the Lord Your God, your son is of ME. Just as you are. His name shall be David Jordan Caleb. He shall be mighty in My strength. My gifts will manifest daily in his life. When he is born, he will come into this world pure and unspoiled. His mother's spirit is very powerful and that is no accident, because the mother's spirit affects the son. It is important that you, as head of your house, provide an environment that will retain the unspoiled condition of the newborn.

The human infant is small in the flesh but the spirit is great. The spirit never sleeps and is always receiving. Randy, control what his spirit receives from the moment it enters this world. You wonder why you do not see cripples walk out of wheelchairs? If you will feed this newborn spirit a diet of My word, you will see that and much more!

Your family is blessed with much revelation knowledge. This knowledge that has taken all of you years to accumulate may be passed on to this newborn child in a short time. However, you must not allow anything of the devil to pass into the child's eyes or ears. It is so simple. When the flesh is young and weak, again I remind you, do not underestimate the strength of the spirit in the newborn child. It is so easy for them to receive when the flesh is weak and helpless.

Read and study My Word concerning King David. His greatest feat was performed as a young child. Why? Because his spirit and faith was strong and his love was pure. The eyes and ears are pathways that are traveled by sight and sound. A newborn child has these pathways just as an adult does. Randy, you can control the traffic on these pathways.

My grace and My mercy are sufficient for you. I will provide you the strength you need to perform what I have asked of you. The devil is becoming more active, therefore like a flood I will raise up men to control and defeat him. I will return for a glorious, wealthy, righteous church! You have the opportunity to groom a newborn child to take a great part in this final chapter of earth's history. Randy, the devil tried to kill your mother to prevent you and your brother's birth. I did not allow it! Then the devil tried to kill your wife to prevent your son's birth. Ha! He tried the same thing again! Again, I did not allow it!

An unforgiving heart is a barrier that blocks my mighty power. All of you must truly forgive everyone who has hurt you. And do not hesitate even one hour! Do not try to forgive in the mind, but truly forgive from the heart! That will eliminate the barriers and allow My power to start to change people, things, circumstances and places. I can cast off the harness of satan and replace it with My traces! Be strong in My word and protect yourself against the wiles of the devil! Be gentle in business dealings but also be wise as a serpent. Have the mind of Christ, use His Name and His word with authority in prayer and supplication concerning business dealings

Clarify and frame your vision, hold on to it. For without vision the people perish! Your heart's desires that I place within you can be and should be your vision. Define your vision! Make it specific and real according to My word! Speak it out, get into agreement one with another! There is power in prayer! Don't just think it! Say it! You are the seed of Abraham and heir to His blessings. Believe that you receive and so shall it be!

David Jordan Anderson arrived by caesarian birth on August 8, 1989.

We felt this was somewhat of a miracle because of the surgeries and injuries from Betty's miraculous survival of the accident in '87. There was doubt she would be able to have children, or so the doctors indicated. The pregnancy was very much a surprise to them both. Randy was forty, and Betty was dealing with fear and concerns. When Randy received this word from the Lord, he was so blessed and grateful. He came to Cross Plains while we were working on the house and shared this with me. I was unspeakably blessed and excited! In '84, an intercessor, Sharon Gray, had prophesied to Betty she would have a son!

Betty thought 'Caleb' was a little too much, but the three names are so prophetic and have to do with his call and destiny, although they are not registered in earth they are registered in heaven!

8-8-91 JOURNAL

Today, Brother David Wells called to speak to T.W. He was not at home, so he began to talk with me. I had asked about a time when I could visit with them and receive some prayer and ministry. I wanted to open myself up, become very vulnerable and transparent. I trusted them to hear from the Lord and minister to me. I so wanted to handle the seemingly never-ending challenges with T.W. better than I felt I was. I wanted so much to keep moving forward, for him to become more Christ-centered so he wouldn't be so 'self'-centered and demanding.

My heart just gets so crushed, Lord, no matter what I do. I am just so imperfect, Lord. You have shown so much grace to me, You have touched me so deeply with Your love and Presence and I have so much love to share with him, but he treats me like an enemy, rude and demanding. I know it's spirits, but I also know there is deliverance, You are the Deliverer! But unless he surrenders to you and breaks before You, then he will never know the blessings You purposed for him. We both will be stolen from. Father, he is so sure of his salvation, and that he has received Your Holy Spirit! I am continually under attack, not only from him but then the battle in my mind to keep from losing heart, to keep my mind on Your word, and to believe and not quit!

I shared with David my frustrations and concerns. He was aware of T.W.'s lack of real interest in what was obvious to everyone else, the Lord's hand upon my life, our life, and the supernatural happenings going on around our life for years. He just wasn't on the same page for some reason. There was no revelation. He said it was like he was encased behind a wall, hardened. And when he would talk with him, he listened, agreed, but really didn't hear. I then shared with him my problem with what he does or doesn't do that has consequences which involve me always, and I pay along with him, over and over. I ask, does what I believe, my prayers and what I do, enable God to cover and protect me regardless? Obviously it had not, for all these years the consequences of his actions and disobedience to the Lord, I pay right along with him and for the most part, much more! But, because of my faith and relationship with the Lord and obedience to His word, I have increased! In faith, in the fruit of the Spirit, wisdom and revelation! The Lord's plans were not affected. He had not changed His mind, and this intense battle and the struggles were preparing me and I believe, T.W. as well, for a greater glory. If I could stay the course, satan would be defeated and the weapons he had been using against me would not accomplish their purpose!

David is so kind and loving, he began to talk to me about faith, resting, not carrying the weight of all this, to go on with God and put it all in His Hands, forgetting the past, telling me the story of him and Susie and their struggles. Then it was as if every word was now, "If you will do this," and "If you would do that," "If I stayed in that heavenly place with the Lord, everything would line up, T. W. would come on," if I, if I! I began to 'feel ' responsible, the old accusing voice; it's your fault, if you measured up, if you did more, if you did this, things would change! I could not bear it! David could probably feel my restrained quietness. He said, "Now I'm not talking about striving, I'm talking about decision." I felt the tears coming. I managed to end the conversation quickly. When I hung up, I broke and wept and wept. I thought my heart would finish breaking. Why, Lord, am I responsible? Why is it up to me? Why am I always made to feel as if I am the one responsible, which seems to leave everyone else off the hook? And I'm the fall guy! Why am I reacting like this, Father? Is there no earthly, godly husband/wife relationship for me, Lord? No true 'partnering' companionship with an earthly mate! Is our relationship the one? My heart cannot be divided? I cried loudly in tongues until I was wrung out.

I pray, Dearest Lord, that some of that was travail and the desert place I have been in for these few months, of not feeling Your Presence, no prophetic flow, no' unction' of Your Spirit, and that any barriers in my soul were broken through. That You have dealt with the thoughts of backing off, trying to convince myself it really isn't that important, that I've already experienced more of You and the reality of Your kingdom than many in my generation, and maybe I've just been deceived. It would be much easier not to 'buck the tide,' so to speak. The thing is, Lord, my only times of true joy and freedom and being my true self is in Your Presence. In worship and ministry. Right now, I don't know where I am, or what to do next. I am undone, I am feeling insecure and inferior. Please help me be free! I don't want to pretend, to project, to perform. I just want to be 'me,' who You see me to be!

I don't know how to express what is going on in me, it is too deep. If You aren't my Protector, my Shield and my Savior, then I am lost and without hope. For I myself have nothing more to give, to say, to try, to do, if everything falls, it falls! I will not accept responsibility for anything else or anyone else and I don't know what to be responsible for! This conversation today with David, if You can use it, Lord, to Your glory and for Your purpose, I submit it to You. Here I am, just as I am, where I am, wherever that is. I love You, Lord.

The darkest hour is just before dawn! I do not know why I never remember that when I am in the dark! In November, the visitation of the Lord and the revealing of His purpose for the move, and more pieces added to the 'puzzle' of the prophesies in the '80s, a clearer picture began to form, along with the increase of His kingdom within me! No one can love us like the Lord! His love never fails!

*Open my eyes that I might behold wondrous things out of Your Law
    of Love
Make me understand the way of Your precepts and raise me up and
    strengthen me according to the promises of your Word
Remove from me the way of falsehood and unfaithfulness to You and
    impart Your law to me*

Teach me, O Lord, the way of Your statutes and give me understanding that I may keep them

Incline my eyes away from beholding vanity and restore me to vigorous life and health in Your ways

Establish Your Word and confirm Your promises to me and let Your mercy and loving kindness come to me!

Thank You, Father!

THE BEGINNING

Vision and birth of Living Water Ministries Fellowship

November 1991

I celebrated my sixty-third birthday on November the eighth. A week later, T.W. was out of town. I had been lying on the sofa, just praying and worshipping the Lord, concerned about the years 'flying' by, when I was enveloped in His Presence and words began to form before me. Ezekiel 37 was 'scrolling' down before me and at the same time I was reading the words, Jesus would interpret them and direct them to me. His words: "It is I who have brought you out in the Spirit of the Lord and set you down in the midst of this valley for it is full of dry bones. It has come to a fullness of time and I am moving in the earth upon a people in this hour in ways you and they have never seen nor experienced and yes, I have and will continue to 'put you on display' so to speak, as an affront to religious spirits. But more as a light that shines in the darkness that will light My Way for My church in the coming days. I Am calling forth an innumerable company that will confound many and bring great increase to My Kingdom and release My Glory!" I began to grieve at the darkness and the lifelessness and the seeming captivity the people were in. Then He said: "Will you love them for Me? Will you prophesy to these dry bones in the power of my Name?" I was overwhelmed with tears and the preciousness of His Presence, crying out, "Yes, Lord! Whatever You want me to do!" I was seeing people in all walks of life. At one point I saw people in rags, dirty, bent over, and He said, "Will you wrap your arms around, love and prophesy over these?" Then the words on the scroll changed and it became Nehemiah Chapter 2, then it became Chapter 4. His words as these verses were scrolling down before my eyes: "There will be intense warfare, just remember angels will be contending in the heavenly realm as you will be contending in earth's realm. I am not sending you into enemy territory on this strategic assignment unprepared or ill equipped. I haven't brought you this far not to take you through. Everything you need will be there when you need it, wisdom, revelation and ever-expanding vision and the Spirit of Grace to empower you. And My Word shall lead you! As you have 'worn many hats' in the world that enabled you to fulfill the requirements and demands of the seasons and circumstances, even so, the ministry gifts I give to My church for the equipping and building up of My dwelling place will be mantles that will provide the anointing to serve and minister to My people as the situation requires. I will send others to stand by your side to work side-by-side with you and you shall prophetically demonstrate the transformation and the turning 'right side up' of my church as I turn some things and some people 'upside down'! I Am restoring order and bringing alignment with My kingdom and I am restoring the tabernacle of David. I will bring a spiritual son to stand by your side. He will be My prophet and you shall model the apostolic and prophetic. This house is a gift to you to be a gift to my church. There will be a birthing here for a greater work that will touch the nations! Do not number the people, little is much when I AM in it! You are a seed, the ministry will be a seed, that will produce a greater harvest than you will be able to see or know!" I was under an anointing for days in a 'daze' and in great reverential fear of the Lord!

A week later, He sent me to Fort Worth to a meeting held by Barbara Wintrouble. She wasn't feeling well that evening and she sat in a chair and ministered. During the meeting, she pointed me out, called me up and I knelt down by her side and she laid her hand on me and began to prophesy to me out of Ezekiel 37 and Nehemiah 2 and 4! I thought I would faint out of sheer AWE! Lord, you continue to amaze me! At all the divine connection, orchestrations, confirmations and the glory of the unfolding of Your plans! WOW!

For the next few weeks, I was fasting and praying in the Spirit. Without a doubt, Living Water Ministries Fellowship would become a reality. I had been 'tagged' and set in place. I poured over THE WORD and all the prophetic words of the past, as well as Ezekiel 37 and Nehemiah 2 and 4. During this time HE added Ezekiel 47:1-12!

I cannot describe to you the mental and emotional attacks that came. The wrestling with my flesh! The inadequacies, the battle of the mind! Knowing the affect this would have on my mother and other family members and the attacks that would come from some of the people in the community, as well as some of the established churches in the area. Nehemiah 4 gave me a pretty clear picture! And the Holy Spirit's constant reminder of Ephesians 6: "our battle, this spiritual war, is not against flesh and blood, [contending only with physical opponents,] but against the despotisms, the powers, the master spirits who are the world rulers of this present darkness, against the spiritual forces [demons] of wickedness in the supernatural realm!" You can have a clear mental picture and knowledge of possibilities, but until you face and experience the reality, you really 'know' very little! And I don't think I could have been any more prepared than I was. You just can't prepare for that kind of experience in advance. It is most certainly a 'walk of faith, a walk of the Spirit, and walk of love'! Our 'weapons' in this battle are mighty to the destruction of satan's strongholds! The people of Cross Plains and Cottonwood and all the surrounding area were and are a loving, giving community and with great churches, pastors and humble believers who love the Lord Jesus and love one another! And any 'attitude's or 'opinions' they held and may have expressed towards me and the ministry at that time, were not any different than those I held and expressed years back against any church or group that operated in revelation outside the 'box' of my denomination or the understanding I had at that time. Every 'cell' of His body in the earth is important to the health of the whole body. One by the Spirit and one through the Blood! Walls are crumbling! Revelation is increasing! Love will TRIUMPH! Oh! How beautiful is the Body of Christ in the earth, displaying His nature, beauty, power and glory as they are on the journey of fulfilling their purpose and destinies in God, as He is supernaturally bringing His kingdom on earth as it is in heaven!

What an adventure! And not without 'perils'! [A picture suddenly came into my mind of an old 'silent film' in the twenties, "The Perils of Pauline." She was lying on a railroad track, tied up, and a train was coming and she was screaming wildly for her knight in shining armor to rescue her!] The 'perils' of Colleen! HA! By no means do I or would I compare my trials and distresses to the great number who have gone through so much more for 'THE WAY.' I love what Paul said: "the indignities have dignified me."

On January 1, 1992, LWMF became a prophetic reality. Ten people gathered at our home and we covenanted together to begin a fellowship. I had prepared a statement of faith and shared fully the Lord's word and His heart according to the revelation He had given me up to that time.

We gathered every Sunday morning and each brought a covered dish for our meal and fellowship afterward. It was a time of worship, prayer, ministry and sharing. Joe and Mary would help me with worship. Joy and others would serve. Thursday evenings would be worship, testimonies and prayer. From the beginning, the Spirit of Prophecy flowed like a river! Several would flow in the giftings. The Holy Spirit encouraging His people, loving on His people, healing His people. HE is always so good! Oftentimes, I would prophesy several minutes, and in rhyme! He was blowing His Breath upon our dry bones and we were being resurrected to new life. He wanted to make sure we had no doubt it was by His Spirit! Those were such wonderful, precious times together, no one had any agenda but to be in His Presence, worship Him and hear from Him and receive from Him. Each week more gathered, twenty, thirty-five ... All that came through the door were precious, hungry-for-more-of-God people! Some remained through the years because God purposed it. Others were sent to plant other ministries and to work in His vineyard in other places. The house would fill up! The Holy Spirit had led me in the designing of the house, and the only inside walls downstairs were those enclosing the master bedroom and bath. The rest was all an open flow.

I began to have further understanding that the Father would go to any lengths, move mountains, supernaturally provide a beautiful home in the country to save, heal and restore even one of His children! So great is His Love for each of us!

About six months later, T.W had a call from his brother, Floyd, who lived in Corpus Christi. Their mother had been in a nursing home for several years, and in attempting to lift her from one bed to another, they dropped her and she was injured. We did not know that Floyd had filed a lawsuit against them. It had been over a year and there wasn't much communication between them, so we had no idea what was going on. The call was to inform us we would be receiving a check for $140,000! As our part!

Talk about rejoicing! We were blown away! Three days later, the cashier's check arrived! We sat down at the table and made a list of all we owed. We paid off all of our debts and wrote out a check to Larry and Deane for the full amount they had given us to finish the house! Then we began to make plans to finish the upstairs and get the wraparound porch built and some stairs, a gravel road constructed leading up to the house, as well as the storeroom and carport. And I gave Donny my '79 Olds for a beach car and bought a Suburban! Wow! We were some happy campers! So were the ones we owed money to! We finished the upstairs, Donny and Heath came and hung the sheet rock, taped and floated. It was a very hard job, and Donny developed a hernia and later had to have surgery! We all worked very hard to save as much as we could, and paid cash for everything.

By the end of '92, our beautiful home was complete and it became a great blessing to all of our family, as well as Living Water Fellowship and to all the friends of the ministry. When Apostles Jim and Jeane Hodges would come to minister, or Dr. Don and Cherrie Crum and many others, I would always tell them before they left that I did not wash the sheets for a few days until I had slept on them, to give every opportunity for a transfer of anointing! They were appalled, of course!

There were many challenges those first few years. Mother was always so good to me and loved me dearly, but she could not hide the fact she was uncomfortable and 'embarrassed.' I know it was out of concern for me and fear for me. She could not understand because of her deep roots in the interpretation of the scriptures according to Baptist doctrine. I've said before, I treasure my Baptist heritage, their love for Christ and His word and hearts of 'community.' Individually and corporately we are in 'the process' of restoration and transformation. A woman preacher with no 'seminary training,' pastoring a congregation, forsaking her Baptist heritage, teaching a baptism in the Holy Spirit with the evidence of speaking in other tongues, prophesying, healing the sick and casting out devils! And coming back where everyone knew her! It was an affront to the religious mind. Some whom I had known all of my life made an effort to avoid meeting me on the street. Many kept their distance. All kinds of stories were circulating. We were labeled a 'cult.' If I had not gone through the extremely hot fires of rejection and abandonment of the past, I don't believe I could have endured. I encouraged myself continually in the word of the Lord and with fasting and much prayer. Those the Lord had brought around me were great support, as well as understanding 'seeds' of past revivals and Pentecostal experiences had been 'sown ' in the land and God was increasing the harvest from those seeds sown! The greatest encouragement was the Lord's manifested Presence!

During this time, Rita had taken the children and left again! They had gone through this several times and it was so hurtful for the children, as well as devastating for Donny. But this time, because of the circumstances, Donny said "no more." So there was a divorce with great pain and heartache for him and the children. Those were hard, difficult times. All we could do was pray and walk it out with His help. HIS Name is Redeemer and Restorer.

Our home in the country became a gathering place for our families during holidays, and Mom's place the overflow. Those blessed times are etched in our memory. Our children and grandchildren and Robert, Lois and Luke would drive in from Arkansas, Pat, Martha and their family from San Antonio, and relatives and friends anywhere in the area! The guys would bring their guitars and music, laughter and tears, cooking and enjoying great meals together with much thanksgiving! Lots of deer and bird hunting and games would be the order of the day, every day!

In '94, the Holy Spirit began to indicate it was now time for a larger meeting place for the church to gather. And once again, as with the house He arranged for us to have, He would provide, for with man it would once again be impossible and we would continue to see the Lord confirm and validate this was His vision, His agenda, and He was working His plan! These times have their challenges, but are so exciting and glorious and faith-building in their unfolding! As we press on to lay hold of all God has prepared for us to 'lay hold of,' to apprehend that for which we have been 'apprehended'! Bless His Holy Name Forever!

He continued to deal with me concerning old 'religious' mind-sets, ways of 'doing' church and 'becoming' the church! Also, for the need to come into alignment with His divine order concerning the structure of this company of people who were a part of His church. He continued to root up, tear down and dismantle most things I had ever known about 'having' church or 'doing church,' not only from my Baptist days but what I had experienced in some of the new churches springing up. I just knew HE was doing a NEW thing, not new really, just restoring things back to His original plan and purpose. Dealing with motives, performance, and ritual. Turning our hearts back to Him. Teaching us how to be led by His Spirit. Most times, the 'pendulum' has to swing all the way to the other side before it can come back to the center!

He began to talk to me about 'Apostolic relational oversight'! [What does that look like, Lord?] Up until the late '70s, I knew very little about apostles or prophets, except what I knew from the scriptures. All I had experienced, as far as I knew, up until Jesus baptized me into the Holy Spirit, was pastor and evangelist, then experiences with ministers with the prophetic gift. He was in the process of uniting His body in the earth. He showed me a 'map' with dots on it and said He was the original 'net-work-er'! (He continues to remind me to 'connect the dots,' follow the 'thread' of where HE'S been, so I'll have a better picture of where HE is going!). I continued to pray for the prophet that He was to bring alongside me, and this 'team work' we would be doing. This was not to be a 'one man show.' I knew there were to be elders with specific gift-ings to carry out administration. Now mind you, this was way out there for me, as well as everyone else. I definitely had no 'point of reference.' I had not been this way before. In fact, I was beginning to understand what 'pioneering' was all about. I hadn't a clue what I was doing or where all of this was taking me. I knew my PAPA was full of surprises and He loved to surprise His children! How awesome is wonderful God the Holy Spirit, who is the Revealer of the mysteries of the kingdom, revealer of secrets, and the One who leads us into all truth, and gives us such marvelous gifts! How unspeakably honored and privileged we are to be called the sons of the Most High God!

I began to drive, look and check out places that had possibilities. There was this very nice building on Highway 36, on half of a corner block built ten years before by an oil drilling company for offices. I knew they had moved on and someone was renting the building. I researched the owners and made a call. Yes, it had been for sale, was rented at the present time, but they would like to sell it. I made an appointment to look and knew the moment I walked in, this was it! Perfect setup, and with a small kitchen. All that would have to be done was remove all the partitions between the offices, which left one large open area for a sanctuary, build a platform and baptistery, decorate, and buy chairs!

I knew the young man renting the building acted a little nervous, and found out later that his rental contract had an option-to-purchase clause.

I need to tell you that at this time, the church had saved $5,000 from tithes and offerings. The Lord had said from the beginning I was there to serve the people and follow Him, and until He told me differently I was not to take a salary. I could accept personal gifts, but that was all! From '92, T.W. began to prosper in his business. He worked hard, tithed faithfully, and fully supported me in every way.

I received a call from the owners of the property that the renter was unable to exercise his option and they wanted to sell! We had been, of course, standing in faith and praying. I knew that this was 'it,' and all I had to do was wait for Father to work His plan in His time! I had firsthand experience! I was excited about how He was going to do it this time! Also, the Lord had told me what we were to offer. The conversation went something like this:

"What are you asking for the property?"

"We bought it in a bankruptcy situation for $160,000 and we'll sell it to you for $150,000."

"I appreciate that, but we are a congregation brought together by the Lord to plant a church and this is our offer, $135,000. We pay $5,000 down and you carry the note for ten years and you pay all closing costs, we will pay for title search."

"What! No way we will do that. Goodbye!"

About six months later, a call came. "Uh uh, Mrs. Anderson, are you all still interested in the property?"

"Yes, sir. What do you have in mind?"

"Well, we'll go with you on the deal, just like you said."

"That's great, we thank you, and the Lord thanks you!"

"I will call the title company and have them draw up the papers and I'll give you a call."

"That's Great! God bless you!"

[I had another 'spell' running through the house, dancing and praising the Lord and making phone calls!] Just a reminder, the purchase of our home property was with $5,000. The number of grace and ministry gifts!

Two months later, we closed! And began the work on the renovation. Everyone worked on the project every spare minute, spiritually cleaning house and grounds and saturating the building with great worship and prayer! T.W. and Terry found some nice folding chairs for us. Donny gave us his piano. We purchased a P.A. system and a couple of the men who played guitars helped me with worship! A blessed beginning! Thank God! He never leaves us at our beginning, but is always positioning, repositioning and perfecting!

The Lord sent a young woman, Frankie McGough, who began to come and worship with us soon after we started meeting in our home. Our hearts connected immediately. We had awesome powerful times, experiencing prophetic prayer. The Holy Spirit definitely took us places in the Spirit we had never been. We just uninhibitedly went with God, in acting out prophetically, and at times building displays of what we were 'seeing' in the spirit as we were praying We knew we were hearing from God, but had not seen or heard anything quite like this. We did find validation in the scriptures, and later on as we were connected with other ministries. We always kept the doors locked to be certain no one walked in on us! The Lord continued to add some awesome women to the intercessors team, as well as some awesome men! God took us to the nations, to the streets, to the region, revealed secrets and mysteries, continued to heal us, and illuminated our darkened understanding, renewed our minds and set us free to love and worship Him and follow Him into battle!

We were experiencing His manifest Presence in our midst. People were getting delivered, baptized in the Holy Spirit, experiencing a touch from the Lord, and falling out under the power. Then some people heard of all that was going on and the word going around was, I was handing out pills and causing people to act 'funny' and pass out!

I tried to have contact with some local pastors, attending their meetings. They were polite and respectful until one of them refused to attend any longer if I was there. [He is a precious brother and I love him] So, rather than be a party to offence, I gracefully stepped out. There was just a 'whole lot of shaking going on everywhere'! Our challenges were to keep our eyes upon HIM and be obedient to His word in every situation. It was not easy.

I was active in the southern Gospel Music Association during that time, participating in some of the conventions, and I would invite some of the gospel groups to come and minister at LWM. We would have large crowds and that broke a little ice! Mother would come and enjoyed that very much.

In '95, we were having a conference with AnneLori Rasco, a Messianic Jewish woman whom I had met a few years back in meetings in Abilene.

Our hearts connected. She was a friend to the ministry and to me. Through her grew a greater understanding of the church's roots in Abraham and 'the one new man' in Christ, Jew and Gentile [those outside the old covenant], now one under the New Covenant! She was and is a very anointed teacher and prophetess, living in Beth Sheva, Israel. The Presence of the Lord was heavy upon us. The building was full and I was standing at the front with AnneLori and the Holy Spirit said, "See that young, white-haired man in the back row? I'm bringing him alongside you. He is My prophet, he doesn't know, and you won't tell him until I tell you to!" Wow!

I didn't say anything to anyone, and on the way to Fort Worth, taking her to catch her flight the next day, we were both 'high' on the meeting and time in the Lord's Presence. Out of the blue, AnneLori said, "Oh, yes! Did you see or speak to that young white-haired man seated in the back row? He and his family will be coming and he'll be standing alongside you!" I'm glad T.W. was driving! I just don't handle these things calmly, as you may have guessed by now! It's all just so awesome! So, what do I do now, Lord?

Well, I was rejoicing and praying and seeking the Lord the next two days, and finally felt I had the Lord's leading. The young man's name was Max Evans and with his wife, Norma, had just taken the pastorate of a small Methodist church in town. I gave him a call and asked if they would be willing to meet with me. Of course, they were gracious and a little curious. They shared briefly with me some history and Max's conversion and encounter with Christ, and the baptism in Holy Spirit and speaking in other tongues. They had been serving under a pastor in Brownwood before they accepted the church here, and had attended the conference at LWM simply to check us out, because he had heard some of the 'talk'! So any thoughts they had or questions were answered during the meetings.

I shared the story, the encounters, vision and assignment and that He was going to bring 'someone' alongside me, and together we would model the apostolic and prophetic. I told him what the Lord had spoken to me at the meeting, and of course the confirmation from AnneLori. I encouraged them to wait on the Lord for a sure confirmation to their hearts. I believed He would make it very clear in a dream or vision that there would be no doubt. I knew they would need a strong anchor to hold them steady to stay the course in this earthshaking transitioning as we moved forward. How wise is the Lord! Here is this tall, good-looking cowboy, not a drugstore cowboy, a real one! A horseman. He had worked ranches, done it all and more! A man's man, straight as an arrow, no mincing of words. He had been worldly and his marriage was in the healing process. He had a precious wife, whom I loved immediately, and two beautiful daughters I had yet to meet. No question it would REALLY have to be God to position them in a newly planted church with the commission and assignment on it that we had, as well as submitting to a sixty-five-year-old [I certainly didn't look it or act it, of course!] woman pastor, whom only God Himself would qualify! But the man God would pick would have been prepared beforehand and as always, God had a plan and we got to be a part of that plan. With all the glorious happenings as well as fiery testing!

The amazing thing was, neither one of them 'flinched' or 'batted' an eye during our conversation! They sort of sat on the edge of their seats, but kept eye contact. [I didn't know if they were in that position so they could 'bolt' at any moment, or not!] I knew their hearts were stirred and did not doubt this was all the Lord's doing. We prayed and they said they would be back in touch.

I think it was about ten days later, Max called. He had received a very clear vision from the Lord and they wanted to come and visit.

VISION AND PROPHECY 1992

While in worship and intercession:

I n the spirit, like an inner vision, I saw a rushing river that seemed dammed up, unable to flow. The dam or wall that was holding it back was constructed of stones all different sizes and shapes. As I looked, I saw there were areas in the dam where stones were missing and there was a trickle of water flowing through, and then there were areas where the wall was almost gone and the water was flowing freely and swiftly. Words began to appear on the stones, written in black: unforgiveness, resentment, doubt, fear, ignorance, condemnation, men's traditions, prejudice, racism, spiritual blindness, anger, rebellion, adultery, lust, fornication, self-centeredness. I began to feel and see the pressure building up against the dam, and I knew it was giving way to the rushing waters of the river! Then the Lord began to speak: *"My servants, My messengers, My people who are in covenant with Me are a people robbed, plundered and snared in holes and in houses of bondages. They have followed their own ways and moved in the shallow stream of self-effort, sitting in the glow of their self-made fires, and they have had grief and torment and failure after failure. Who will restore them? Because they are precious in My sight and honored, and because I love them, I will give men and women in exchange for their lives! For they are My witnesses, My servants whom I have chosen that they might know Me, and understand that I AM HE, for I give drink from the Rock in the wilderness and rivers in the desert to give drink to My people,*

My chosen, the people I formed for Myself that they might be to the Praise of My Glory and the Honor of My Name! My Word is a Big Yes in the earth! Have I not said and will I not do it? The flow of My Spirit is building! Who can stand against Me? All power in heaven and earth has been given to ME to impart to you to overcome and destroy the works of darkness, and it shall be so!"

WORD OF THE LORD, MAY 11, 1993

Out of a time of prayer and seeking the Lord:

"*I have spoken and shall I not do it? Why do you think you are being quickened to certain scriptures such as 'follow those who through Faith and Patience inherit the promises'? And things I have spoken in the past, concerning the boys, keep crowding out the other voices in your head? It is so that you can be strengthened to hold on and endure with patience and so see the fulfillment of what your heart has cried out to see, and for which you have continually petitioned Me! Believe! My daughter, trust Me, and you will see that what I have spoken will come to pass indeed!*

"You are experiencing heartache and pain because of what you see and what you hear that seems to contradict all I have said and all you have prayed and believed! For the very grievous of situations are only opportunities for ME to display MY grace and glory! They are Mine, too, you see. And I know how hard it is to stop mothering, and you will be a mother always. You can relax in that, it's all right, for you have to be what I have made you to be! All plans of the devil to stop and prevent you from fulfilling your purpose and destiny and finding your life in Me did not succeed! Isn't that more proof for you to hold on and continue to believe for the increase of blessings for them and their seed?

*"For truly, I AM GREATER IN YOU AND GREATER IN THOSE
YOU BORE THAN he THAT IS IN THE WORLD! And they are MY
sons and they have MY Heart right down to the core!*

*"I know you have prayed and wept before ME what seems to you
an eternity, but I AM not in time, my child, and it's only a short while
to Me and I will have My Way with what is Mine. Trust and see!*

*"Now, your grandchildren are MY grandchildren too, in a
sense, but remember, I have no grandchildren or step-children, for
I AM Father to all and I AM still Omnipotent, Omnipresent and
Omniscient over all MY family!*

*"Don't ask at this time about T.W. You do what I tell you to do
in all things. And what I have for him is between him and ME, but
all thing are in the palm of MY HANDS! So rest and believe! Keep
your spirit stirred, use all at your disposal to keep yourself going
and pressing on and do not look back! And remember, you must do
as you have advised others, gather the 'manna' every day and the
'meat' together now, and drink deeply at the spring, for you are
going to need great strength and wisdom that only comes from Me,
and I will supply liberally! I will hold nothing back from you that
you need. Be sure to keep coming and keep coming to ME!"*

Lord, forgive me, I thank You for Your tender mercies that 'bring
me to my senses' and into agreement with Your word.

CROSS PLAINS JOURNAL

11/19/93

Oh, Lord, I feel as though I'm being 'UNRAVELED' ... again! I pray that You are the One holding the end of the string, and that someday You will get to the center of ME and things will be straightened and in order! And 'darkened' understanding will become fully illuminated, and the shocking, difficult situations and challenges will not cause a 'fly apart' or 'unraveling.' It feels as though I'm 'stuck' in the outer edge of the 'wilderness' when I thought I had crossed over the 'Jordan' and was making my way deeper into Your Rest! But this conflict in me, this 'dual personality' — flesh and spirit! Yes, the Spirit prevailing over the flesh — only after the FIGHT! I get discouraged and disappointed in me! I am frustrated at time being wasted, taken for granted, used up for things that have no lasting value, things that entertain and serve the 'flesh.' I know You gave us all things to enjoy. You know I'm not being 'religious' about this, it is a matter of the heart that concerns me. I am separated and consecrated unto You in my heart and in my strongest desires, but it seems my life is not lined up with that! Why can't I gather to me and hold to me everything You have taught me? All the ways of You I have learned? Why can't I walk consistently in all of it? Why am I not able to DO and KEEP doing in pureness of heart, what I believe is part of my purpose in You in the earth? WHERE is the Place of Rest?! WHEN is the Place of Rest?!

I thought I had walked with You. Pardon me, You had walked with me through the death of 'self-centeredness,' 'self-conscious-ness,' the death of 'self,' and yes, I understand it has to be 'killed daily.' [Paul: "I die daily."] And of course, Jesus, I have been changed! You have worked mightily within me. I am a new cre-ation man. I am not disappointed in You! I just am not satisfied with mediocre, with half-hearted ways, with things unfinished, cluttered or undone. It's discouraging to come this far, and it seems finally I am 'somewhere,' to find I am 'nowhere' — again!

I throw myself on the mercy of the court! Father! I plead the Blood! I have no case to argue! All the frustrations with T.W. and our children's challenges and heartbreak, and I feel so torn and hopeless, tempted to give up and give in and now 'locked up' myself! Again! As You have said this week, "the violent take it by force!" And then I ask again, where is the Rest? How do I get and stay in the Most Holy Place, in communion, in Your Presence, leaning, trusting! Loving all and treating all with Your Grace! I feel as though I have only presumed myself to be or saw myself to be something I am really not. Father, I've said so many times, I understand Elisha desiring the double anointing! He recognized his weakness and inabilities, that there is no power but Your power to change anything, and he was not reticent in asking for everything You had to give him! You said You have given us all things pertaining to life and godliness! Give me a willing heart. [I thought I had one fully willing and surrendered — but something is wrong!], that I might do your will, walk in Your ways. Give me understanding and wisdom, that Your Truth and the Truth concerning You might be known. Give me what You know I need, to be able to do what You have called me to do! To walk in the ever-unfolding vision of my destiny in You. Thank You, Lord, that You won't let me waste the rest of the time You have allotted me. Forgive me, Lord, for being lazy and careless and undisciplined. Lord, here I am, please help me understand where I am and give me hope for what is beyond this 'gate' I must press through. Take me on through and establish me. I am striving to enter into 'Rest' for Your Name's sake! I understand this 'dissatisfaction' and driving 'need' will be a catalyst to propel me forward.

Give me contentment if there is 'no more.' But please, Holy Father, pull me on through to the other side of NOW if there is more, to quite this Rest-Less-Ness within me. I am Yours

On the first day of December, I received a book I had felt led to order, ***Secrets of the Most Holy Place***! Most of my questions were answered through the book. Some key words were even the very same! Holy Spirit, YOU are Amazing! Thank You.

Prophetic word released over LWM Fellowship through Colleen, December 15th, 1993

"Oh, My children, My people, My family! Do not listen to the accuser and walk in condemnation and be crippled by guilt! Run to Me and receive the grace that's been purchased for you through the sacrifice of My Son. And walk free! Walk in freedom! The moment you truly repent and accept my love and forgiveness, your failures will become steppingstones UP! You have been coming right along within the boundaries of My eternal purposes for you. You are moving along the path of progress! As you embrace My Ways and receive My instructions and follow the leading of My Spirit, you will experience a dimension of the supernatural you cannot imagine!

I cannot allow you to stay where you are. I know the process of transformation and preparation has been hard and difficult at times, and has taken paths you did not expect or understand. And yes, everything you have identified with, everything of your own making, old ways of doing and thinking and believing and being has been shaken to the ground! Yes, you have been tossed to and fro, dashed to the shore by waves of adversity, heartache, pain, disappointments and discouragements! At times, your mortal body went to the limits of emotion. And I, your Father, bottled each tear as My heart was gripped by your fears and doubts and pain!

"Now some of you are as the son who took himself out of the Father's house, took the Father's provision and struck out on your own! And the thief caught up to you and beat you up and robbed you and left you for dead! I am the Good Samaritan who pours in the oil and the wine, who raises the dead to life again! I AM the God of all comfort! I Am the Good Shepherd who leaves the ninety and nine

and goes in search of the one who has wandered and then carries him on My shoulder until he never wants to leave Me or wander off again!

"*You are bone of My bone and flesh of My flesh. My blood flows in your veins. You are destined for greatness and glory! You are destined for completeness at the Lord's return, and you will put off the mortal and will no longer be limited and your warfare will cease. But until then, you must fight the good fight of faith. You must enforce the victory won at Calvary where you are, in the sphere of authority you have been given. Your time on earth has been appointed and each of you has been anointed and is being equipped to carry out My purpose for your generation and your place in time! You are on schedule! My schedule!*

"*So lift up your heads, strengthen your weak knees, raise your trembling hands and rejoice!*

The accuser has been cast out, he cannot accuse you to Me, he cannot get past the Heavenly Intercessor, the Mercy Seat Jesus! That old serpent can only accuse you to your face and deceive you if you allow it, so that you do his work for him. He knows authority has been given to you and he has to go through man to carry out his evil intent! So do not indulge your flesh or be swayed by his influence, which is contrary to My redeeming Love. BE wiser than your enemy by becoming as wise as your Teacher!

"*So believe and know there is a work going on in you and around you. I have set the seasons, and to every season there is a purpose. Lawlessness is increasing, and I have warned you that in this world you will have tribulation, and injustices will cover the earth, but I also said to be of good cheer, for I have overcome it for you!*

"*The Wind of My Spirit is increasing in intensity and will purify the polluted air and the stale atmosphere. And I bring the rain of refreshing and there will be a quickening, and a gentle breeze will cause some of the smallest burning wicks to be fanned to a great flame! And many will become emptied vessels to be filled with My power to destroy the works of darkness!*

"*So my friends, My dearly loved ones, take up your cross daily and follow Me. My sheep hear My voice!*

"Be enforcers of Love. Be enforcers of Truth. Be enforcers of Peace! As you draw from Me all that you will need. Come and let us break bread together, and I will share the very mysteries of the kingdom with you, and I will tell you of things to come and I will take from the Father and give it to you, for all that the Father has is mine! And I will cause you to reign on high and you shall possess the promises, and blessings shall overtake you!"

Thank You, Lord.

May of '94:

A frantic call came from Lois: Diagnosed with breast cancer! The thing she feared the most, because her mother had died with breast cancer! The surgeons wanted to do surgery by the end of the week, could I come? I flew into Little Rock the next day.

JESUS! Let us reason together! My heart is breaking and I must stay strong for Lois, Robert, Luke, and our family! We need Your faith, the faith of God, and an abundant supply of grace!

The dread name of cancer has now come so close. Lois. Thousands of prayers, proclamations, petitions on her behalf, bombarding heaven. Yet she has had to go through it all. Biopsy, double mastectomies, lymph nodes, now chemotherapy! In my seeking You, I found some leaven tucked away in my words, Lord. "She has been so 'good' all of her life, faithful in all Your ways of compassion, love, generosity, serving You and Your church joyfully, worshipping You with the talent and anointing You gave her, etc, etc. Now, Lord, why haven't the prayers and faith stopped this thing?" The deep thought behind this reasoning with You: She doesn't deserve this because of 'her' goodness and 'righteous ways,' she should not be suffering and going through this fire! The authority of Your Name and the New Covenant Blood should have produced a miracle!

Oh! Lord! I know good works never bought anything! Not any works of righteousness that we have done, but it is all by grace through faith that we are saved and made whole! I plead this cause on mercy alone, and the precious Blood of Christ according to Your perfect will and foreknowledge, and I worship You for Lois's life!

Thank You for pointing out my error. My intercession will be different! Yes, we do know You are not the author of sickness and disease. All good things come from You and it is the devil who comes to steal, kill and destroy, and You came that we might have life and have it more abundantly! Lois has been so strong in faith, yet I am wondering if the 'fear' she voiced many times is a stronghold here? Show me how to deal with this in the spirit, Father. You came to this earth to destroy the works of darkness and You have given to us authority in Your Name. How are we missing it? Why isn't this working? Or working for some and not others?

The thing is, Lord, Your Presence unquestionably surrounds us all. Your involvement in so many situations surrounding it all is very evident! I am, we are, so grateful! At the same time, it made it harder to understand why the biggest mountain before Lois did not move! If You could send people, arrange circumstances, envelope us in Your Presence, give Lois an anointing of joy before the surgery, fill me with supernatural wisdom and strength and enable me to meet the demands of the situation, etc., etc.! You certainly were recognized as being "the fourth man in the fire." But Lois got burned! Physically marred and emotionally scarred! Where was Your best? As Your word was stood upon, Your principles applied, Your instructions followed ... it wasn't stopped. The anointing that fell upon her the night before the biopsy, the anointing with oil and prayer of the elders, and the sensation of heat and power that went through her caused her and all of us to expect a 'good' report. The shock that came at the report, having to accept the findings and submit to the radical surgery and chemo — each of us is dealing with many questions, under attack in so many areas. We only have one choice. To fall upon the Rock, to trust You as never before and walk this out as You supply the strength. We trust You with Lois's life and recovery, and that in all of this and with all of us, may Your Name be glorified!

Cheryl went to Benny Hinn's meeting, was touched by Your power, felt it in her body, knew she was healed, knew the doctors would find the pituitary tumor gone, and walked in faith. The symptoms were strong, the x-rays revealed the progression, it had to be removed. So, she had to summit to surgery she had to go through the trauma and the pain. And the prognosis not very good.

Over and over this scenario is played out on life's screen! The phone call yesterday from a person I had never met, who had been told about me, wanted counseling. Her situation had ended in death for a young man, 36 years old, Spirit-filled believer, involved in church, faith-filled, fully expecting him to live and not die — he died. She is coming next week for ministry! With these questions in my own mind, on one hand I absolutely KNOW, and on the other hand I feel spiritually disoriented! I have to trust that somehow You can get through this shaky vessel and pour her out a drink of hope and encouragement and direction. I know I have nothing to give her, and although I do not understand all things, I do know You. Amen

Oh, Lord always in the midst of heartbreaking situations, Donny's visit was such a blessing! He seemed different, happy. He told me about this young woman, Lori, who works in the office in the same building where he works. " Mom, she is gorgeous, classy, very competent, and kind of 'old fashioned,' and we kind of hit it off. I've just never been with anyone like her." When I jumped in and said, "Oh Donny, she is really your type, she is really what your heart yearns for, she sounds perfect for you! She is an answer to prayer!" Of course, you know Donny, he doesn't like to get in too serious of a conversation for very long, 'gotta keep the emotions in check! Oh, Father, thank you! I know You are redeeming and bringing restoration! He has built up a lot of walls to deal with, the pain he has gone through just to survive and keep going. I believe those walls will began to crumble and his heart will be mended. I just know Father, it is Donny's time and You will bless him greatly! I pray for Lori that You will bless her and bring restoration as well, and together they will find true love and peace.

November 25th

Lord! Dearest Jesus! What next?! Peggy Woodson, two months to live! How can this be!? I have wept, fasted and prayed and sought guidance from Your Spirit. I wrote what I believed was Your heart, a good word, instructive and promising! After talking with Greg, I was disturbed, trying to understand where they were coming from. It sounded like they were giving in to this hellish thing, they did not want any prayers except preparing for her death! They were accepting that You had allowed this and if it killed her, she still won — true — but? Saying they did not want but a few people to know and not to tell his mother because they did not agree with the way she might pray? WHAT! I had to ask carefully, "How do you want me to pray?" He talked about the peace that filled them both. They were praying for a miracle for it is inoperable and untreatable. They can only maintain and treat the symptoms. Oh God! I am only a friend, a spiritual sister, and if I feel this much shock and grief, what do Greg and Peggy feel? Unbelievable! Lord, all the plans, surely You are still Lord, even over our unbelief, shock and grief! Lord over sickness, disease, and all of these works of darkness! Thank You for Your mercy, Lord. Help us all, we are still such a needy people in need of Your grace.

In the midst of all of this, Your Presence sustains us. Each time we come together, the River seems to flow unobstructed. So many difficult situations surround us, and yet You have me seemingly on a 'timetable' concerning Your church agenda! I am almost overwhelmed with it all, and yet I am 'caught up' in this commission and cannot go any direction but forward. And I am amazed at the prophecy that flows under such an anointing, encouraging and imparting into the womb of our spirit for the future! And then You send us here and send us there to receive from other 'Gifts' of the body to keep us balanced and to further equip us. Lord, You are so good!

The Blessed Holy Spirit, as always, shines a light upon our present path of struggle to help us to 'see,' to understand His ways in the trials and tribulations we are experiencing. He began to direct me to 2 Corinthians 11:23-30; Paul's exhortation to the Corinthians concerning his many tribulations and struggles. In the light of his, and Christ's, ours seem rather small, but not to Jesus! Verse 30 is the answer: "If I must boast, I will boast of the things that show my infirmity of the things by which I am made weak and contemptible in the eyes of my opponents." What Paul describes here, the things he went through, that he would boast in these things that showed his weakness and made him contemptible in the eyes of those who opposed the gospel. This seems to be a contradiction. We have been taught in the past that it dishonored God to suffer, to be in want, that it might show the world His indifference or inability to care for His own and would show His word not to be true. Or demonstrate our lack of faith. In other words, it would put God in a bad light!

So why would Paul boast of those things happening in his life that seemed contrary to a Father's love and provision as if it bore testimony to the Truth of the word and proof of His love?!

The Key is in 2 Corinthians 12:6-10. The Message Bible: "If I had a mind to brag a little, I could probably do it without looking ridiculous, and I'd still be speaking plain truth all the way. But I'll spare you. I don't want anyone imagining me as anything other than the fool you'd encounter if you saw me on the street or heard me talk. Because of the extravagance of those revelations, and so I wouldn't get a big head, I was given the gift of a handicap to keep me in constant touch with my limitations. Satan's angel did his best to get me down, what he in fact did was push me to my knees! No danger then of walking around high and mighty! At first I didn't think of it as a gift, and begged God to remove it. Three times I did that, and then He told me: 'My grace is enough; it's really all you need. My strength comes into its own in your weakness.'" The true power is shown in how Paul responded in the situation, his patient endurance that God would be with Him in it and would empower him to walk through it! The purpose and ministry to which he was called would not be stopped unless Paul quit or gave up because of the tests and challenges. That Paul conducted himself not as an 'ordinary' man in adverse situations, but as a new creation man, empowered by the wonderful Spirit of Grace to weather any storm or attack from satan, was a true testimony of Gods faithfulness, power and Presence!

Thank You, Lord. The entrance of Your word brings 'light' in our darkness and we are comforted and strengthened!

PROPHETIC WORDS RELEASED OVER THE CHURCH IN '94

I was endeavoring to hear the Spirit concerning what He would have me include in the book out of the files of prophecies and journals. I was reasoning in my mind: "These were God's words to this part of His body in a particular season. Is there continual relevance for others?"

I heard in my spirit:

"My word is timeless, always a light in the darkness and relevant in all seasons and quickens the spirit of those who are in the season."

Word of the Lord to the Church, January 16th, 1994

"Listen, My children, My family! Listen to what I have to say!

"Do not close your eyes or turn your head away, for I will be speaking to you each day, each moment, so be listening. Pay attention to your dreams now and expect visions, for I have things to say to you that will protect you and prepare you for every evil day!

"Sometimes you forget that I am Omnipresent, One with you. I am the Source, your Source, the Author and Finisher of your faith!

"Now, there is a plan unfolding and many do not see nor can they understand. Only by My spirit can these times be discerned. There are many out there who have followed a strange light and so they do not know which way to turn. But this is not so with you and you must believe this is so!

Now things and times will not continue the way some think they will, and it may be hard for you to endure what lies ahead and live. But I have prepared the way before you. I have gone before you. Sometimes you have thought, 'Oh! I've lost my way,' or 'Oh! I'm off track,' and you've turned this way and that! But I say to you today that you have been within the boundary of My plans for you and you're on schedule, My schedule!

"*Do not be slothful and do not be lax, but fully depend upon Me.*

"*I'm looking for a people who are brave-hearted, people who have My heart and are not afraid, but bold indeed!*

"*These are My called out from the called out, chosen to see what I'm about! To do mighty exploits for the glory of My Name!*

"*I have clothed you and endued you with power from on high. I have given you authority in the earth! I am reminding you of your power in ME! I need you to walk in all that I have provided for you, for I have left you neither helpless nor hopeless. You are mighty in the Spirit and your weapons are mighty indeed! Be on the alert, be cautious and watch for the enemy. His warfare is intensifying upon the earth against My family!*

"*You are to stand in the full armor that I have provided you, relying upon the One who is faithful and true and He will guide you and see you through!*

"*Now there are many out there who are suffering, and some because of the consequences of rebelling against Me and going their own way and doing their own thing. My Father heart is grieved and I weep over them as I see them living in pain, poverty and misery! And all because they have not heard and they don't know the depth of love I have for them, they do not know Me!*

"*Who will go and share My love with humanity? Who will stand in My glory and show My love? Who will do it for Me? Who will speak for Me? Who will be a full expression in the earth of Me? Stewards of My grace, hosting My Presence? And see the captives go free?*

"*Do not say I am too young, too old, too rich or too poor! Give to Me that which you have and don't have! I call the old, the young, the rich and the poor to do what I have asked of you. Come bring your gifts to the table, let the generations merge and experience a surge of power that will bring you to your knees in worship and humility, and you will receive grace to meet the coming hour!*

"I will indeed bring unity and community, not conformity. There is only unity in and by the One Spirit and conformity to the image of the One Son who gave full expression and revelation of the Father and Creator of All! I will fold you together as sheep of My pasture into One fold."

January 23rd.

"For have I not called you forth? Have I not separated you unto Me? Have I not called you out to be a peculiar people? And yes, this peculiarity has sometimes caused you persecution, and it's caused you to fear and dread. But I say to you now, no more! You are to speak forth in the boldness of the new anointing that I have placed upon you and you will go as a holy people out of the refiner's fire! You are being brought forth even as gold. Beauty from out of the ashes! Shining forth in the light of My righteousness and holiness! God inside mindedness, righteousness consciousness. The day of compromise, of lukewarmness and intimidation is over for a called out people! I am fanning the flame of passion and zeal, and the smallest burning wick I will cause to flame up and flare up! My Spirit is stirring up My people, for the day demands it!

"For even as the enemy has mocked and laughed as you have labored and toiled, I say you will have the last laugh as you stand and see the fouler foiled, the spoiler spoiled!"

March 3rd.

"I have prepared a table before you in the presence of your enemies. Even as you have walked in desert places and wandered in the wilderness, I have watched over you, My eye has been upon you and My hand has held you when you stumbled and when you fell and I have lifted you up and given you hinds' feet to scale the mountains of trouble so that you made great progress! I have taken you through the valley of Achor, of troubling, but My bride indeed will come out of the wilderness staying very close to Me, holding to My

arm and leaning heavily upon Me! Your faith has become strong and will become even stronger. Independence and self-centeredness has almost disappeared and will soon no longer be evident. Increase is everywhere, and not without purpose! I'm going to move in unprecedented power in order to accomplish My purpose in this hour! So lift your voices and cry aloud as they did back then: "Behold their threatenings, Lord, and grant unto Your servants boldness to speak Your word and stretch out Your hand to heal and to perform signs and wonders by the Name of Your Holy Child Jesus. Grant it, Lord!"

"And then pray for rain in this time of the latter rains so that you can stop the river of pain. Pray to the Lord of the harvest to send forth laborers and don't hesitate, for these drastic times are going to require drastic measures! Now you need to forego some of life's pleasures, but you will not go unrewarded. So do not hesitate, for I want you to know that you can say to Me, Lord, here I am, I will go!

"You must not dread or be controlled by fears, for the things that I ask of you will not result in tears! Tears of joy, yes! Tears of gratitude, yes! Tears of surprise, oh yes! Tears of compassion, yes! Those kinds of tears will flow from your eyes!

"So put your hand in My hand, sons and daughters of the Most High, as a trusting little child. And then draw close to me so that you can look up into My face and see your Father smile! Hallelujah!"

April 8th.

"For those who have set their face like flint, for those who have answered when I called, those who have leaned into Me and leaned upon My bosom. For there are those that I have who are a close company of beloveds who lean in close to Me and run from the ways of the flesh and the ways they have walked in the past, knowing that it is a new day, changes in the earth have come, changes in the heart have occurred. A new time has come and you are in the season of fall and so I am calling for you to stand up tall. You can only do that as you bow down low, knowing that you can do nothing without Me, knowing that it is abiding in Me and the keys I give to you that will open the doors that have been placed in front of you! And as you walk through, oh, what will be waiting there for you! New adven-

tures await you beyond, and yes, new challenges, but worth every moment of revelation and glory! As you make this ascent, things will began to move more rapidly and you must walk in integrity and watch where you step, for there will be snares along the way! Pay attention, stay alert, be on your guard, watching as with the eye of the eagle!"

May 2nd.

"I need you to trust ME in the fire! At each temptation that comes your way, each hardship, every problem, every accusation. Stand. In faith, in joy that I have overcome and the accuser of the brethren has been cast down! I have made A Way of escape! And I AM the lifter of your head. I will lift you up into a new dimension and into a new realm of the spirit with Me. Right now I AM pulling on the reins and tightening the bits so that My people are not pulling this way and that way but walking in the furrow I have marked, on the line down the row I purpose! Now rest in Me, and apply the truth you know in every situation and wait! I will bring you through in victory! But you must pay attention and listen carefully to hear My Voice because there is a roar of a lion who is roaming about, seeking whom he may devour, roaring loudly to intimidate you. But the anointing and power within will enable you to triumph gloriously!"

May 5th.

"In my spirit I was seeing the Lord as He walked along the shores of Galilee and I heard Him crying out: Leave this and follow Me, leave that one, and follow Me, leave that and follow Me, Come and follow Me! The time is now, it's decision time. Many, many in the valley of decision! For My Spirit is sweeping across the face of the earth, hovering over the whole earth! I Am calling out a people, companies of people, placing them in troops! I Am indeed preparing troops, troops, troops! I am networking across the earth troop by troop, company by company! Selected according to their diversity of talents, anointings and gifts imparted and given by ME according to purpose. I have come and I AM taking over with My mighty army!

And they will put their foot on the neck of the enemy, and in the light of My glory all his evil works will be exposed, and destroyed, his camps plundered and his goods taken!

"There is a turning taking place, from one degree to another. A time has come to a 'turning place,' a turning point! And yes, there is about to be what some would call a great crisis. But My people will not see it from that viewpoint! Those who have chosen to follow Me will not have a world view, they will see through the eyes of the Spirit and understand the times and have a heavenly perspective! They will have an understanding, full of wisdom and revelation, and they will be lifted up above the earth, certainly not in the way you may have thought in the past, but you will be lifted up in HIM, in the anointed ONE, and you will began to demonstrate the kingdom, manifest the kingdom and ruling over all other kingdoms and the SON of MAN, SON of GOD will be lifted up and He will draw all men unto HIMSELF!

"MY troops will not break rank, they will hold together. If one falls, he will not fall all the way down, for the others will hold him up until he regains his strength. I will spread out the troops, I will take one here and one there and interweave and intertwine depending upon the time and what is needed to keep the flow and momentum going according to plan!

"My intercessors, My prophetic people who have humbled themselves and prayed and sought My face, have begun to come forth roaring, declaring and proclaiming, ripping and tearing, making a way, a highway for the God of Glory, the mighty Captain of the Host! He is on a mighty campaign leading His troops into battle, under the banner of Jehovah Nissi!"

July 3rd.

"Oh, I know! You have been turned this way and that. But I have never moved! I have not changed nor changed My mind! There is no shadow of turning in Me! Everything plays into My hands! No ground has been lost, only gained! For those I have called out are a people who have been in the process of being restored, being made whole, coming to know ME! And many, because of adversity and the

pressures of life, have finally come to the end of self! For often times the very strongest, who have struggled to survive and built such natural strength, they don't realize how truly weak they have become without ME. And now they are being brought to that place, to the end of self-sufficiency, and are now crying out to Me, "Father, I see. I see. I need You, help me!" Many, many are calling, crying out, desperate indeed! My heart is stirred and the Wind of My Spirit is blowing upon them and lifting them up into My Presence and blind eyes are being opened, deaf ears are being unstopped, prison doors are opening and I am bringing many out to be a part of the mighty army of the Lord! Some whom you never thought about, and some you would never consider, and some the church will look at and say, "Oh! What is this all about? This cannot be!" But I say, it certainly can be! For it is that no man boast unless they boast in ME! For I have brought it to pass! I never relaxed My hold upon them, I never took My eye off them! I never let them go, for they are a part of this end-time move, destined in their generation to be a revelation and carriers of My glory! It will confound the world and mystify even some who are called by My Name!"

July 11th.

"Lay aside every weight and every hindrance for this great encounter. Know that I, the Lord, make your burdens light and even lighter as you set out to follow ME. And you will go forth with a song in your heart and a dance in your step and praise on your lips and joy shall be your strength! I will continue to teach you My Ways and show you My paths. I will draw you to me, and cause you to experience God, who is Love. Only through this love will you truly be constrained to follow Me wherever I lead. I will place a hunger and a thirst within you that nothing else can fill or satisfy, but fellowship and intimacy with Me. I am available twenty-four hours a day. I pray you will come frequently! And when you open your mouth, I will fill it. When you lay hands on the sick, the Healer will be there. When you take authority over demons, the Deliverer will be there. For in obedience and surrender lies the power!"

PROPHETIC WORDS
RELEASED IN '95

January 4th.

"*As I was Israel's Husband, so I Am the Husband of the Church! I AM perfect in all My Ways. There is no flaw, fault or imperfection in ME. I please the Father perfectly. The church as My wife, I fulfill all My responsibilities and obligations toward her according to the law of Love! I love her with perfect Love and great affection and desire! And I will never be unfaithful to her!*

"*And because I fulfill My appointed role perfectly, her love for Me and trust in Me will grow stronger each day and our relationship will grow sweeter and she will blossom and be as the Rose of Sharon, and together, we shall bear much fruit and please the Father splendidly! And her life will become totally hid in Me and she will lack no good thing and her joy will be evident for all to see!*

"*Unless she turns away from My advances and rejects My Love and spurns My gifts or becomes rebellious and refuses to let Me lead and guide her and wash her with My Word! Or, if she becomes vain and puffed up and strikes out on her own and becomes unfaithful! Although I will never divorce her, those things will cause a separation! And by her choices, the consequences will be a lonely, barren life, without My company!*

"*Unless she repents and turns and comes back to Me again! Then I will forgive her and restore her to her place at My side! And we shall began again!*"

February 26th.

"Rejoice! I am releasing a floodtide of revelation upon the earth! Opening the gates of Glory! That you might more fully come to know the immeasurable power that is within you, so that you might walk in victory and share My truth, the truth that sets you free, that you might set others free! A day has come, a time has come for increase in the land. I am increasing your capacities, extending your boundaries, for this is the work of My hand! Lift up your heads, don't hang your heads in shame or despair, for it is time to rejoice and call upon My Name! I have heard your cries, "Do not pass Me by, Lord! Do not forget me!" Oh, I have not, My son, My daughter! I have your name engraved in the palm of My hand, I know you by name, I know the sound of your voice when you call My Name! I know the heart of all who believe in Me and all of you are about to see those greater things that I have told you about and spoken to you repeatedly! So walk uprightly with your heads held high. Remember you are the sons of the One Most High! Don't be cast down, say to yourself, "Why are you cast down, O my soul? You have nothing to be cast down about!" For though the storms rage around you and the pressures are intense that press against you, the Lord God says, "I will use them every one to shape and mold the vessels, the design of which has been in My mind since the beginning of time!" Take heart, dear children, trust fully in Me, for surely I will continue to thunder and cause it to rain down in every season upon you and you will be empowered to walk in My glory to the fullest degree!"

August 5th. Spoken during a service.

I was praying and kept hearing the words, 'consider and consideration.' What are you saying, Lord?

I began to prophesy:

"You have too much consideration for yourself. You are considering your feelings, your own needs, your own situation more than you consider what I have instructed you to consider!

"Yes! I have said, "Consider from were you have come, consider your ways so you can see more clearly how to continue on more

effectively and accurately!" But there are so many other things I have told you to consider that must have your consideration if you are going to continue to come up higher and dwell in the higher realms of love and glory in greater areas of victory and conquest!

"In every battle you face with the world, the flesh, and the devil, there is something for you to consider that will keep you in My Grace. That will strengthen you and set the course for a display of My Glory and power and your great joy!

"When persecutions come, when the emissaries of darkness speak evil against you and the unjust judge you, then consider, stop, pay attention to, and consider Him that endured the cross and such contradictions of sinners against Himself! So you will not be wearied and faint in your minds!

"When the times of discouragement come and hope is weak, know it this day and consider it in your heart; that the Lord, He is God in Heaven above and upon the earth beneath! Only fear the Lord and serve Him in truth with all your heart and consider and think on all the things He has done.

"When things press in around you, to frustrate and agitate, to steal your peace, hearken! Give attention to this! Be still and consider the wondrous works of your God!

"When the accuser comes to condemn and steal your joy, consider not the things of old nor consider the former things, for behold! I do a new thing in you and for you! Just consider this, My holy brethren, partakers of the heavenly calling! Consider the Apostle and High Priest of your profession, Christ Jesus, who was faithful to Him who appointed Him!

"And in the wilderness and the desert times, I will be with you, for I, even I will make a way in the wilderness and rivers in the desert to give drink to My people, My chosen, You whom I have formed for Myself, and you shall show forth My praises! Consider this and discover this as the means of success!

"Now, do not be anxious about yourself! But learn carefully of this; take note of this! Consider the lilies of the field, they neither toil nor spin, yet Solomon in his glory was not arrayed as splendidly as these! So learn thoroughly how they grow!

"And now My dear ones, My family, last of all but not the least! Consider fully, scrutinize and examine how to consider one another to stimulate and stir up to love and good works!

"And from your exalted position in Me, you will gaze upon the 'one' you have considered more than you should! And you will consider, saying, "Is this the one who made the earth to tremble and shook kingdoms?" I did not consider that from my exalted place on high that all things are under my feet and I am the one in authority!

"OH! That all men might fully consider My testimonies!"

'95, A PROPHETIC REVELATION FROM PSALM 23

In a time of prayer and meditation, I had read through the 23rd Psalm and certain words became enlarged in my spirit. For me it was further revelation of that passage.

I began to write:

Oh! The Green Pastures! For the sheep to find nourishment, strength, comfort, rest, refreshing as well as protection!

No longer the dead pasture of the Law that only brought death and could never bring transformation. But the life-giving SEED, THE SEED of redemption, that makes all things new, that brings transformation, raising the dead to life! That SEED would produce many seed to be planted into the very being of the womb of mankind! And all who would receive would produce within themselves the character, the genes that are inherent in the Seed! Even as Mary received the Seed of the Holy Spirit and gave birth to the infant, Jesus, who grew into the boy, then the young man, then the Son, to full stature. Even so, the Seed of the Father, His Holy Sperm of Life at the moment of conception by faith, in that Seed is ALL that Jesus THE SEED is! Many sons coming into full stature, many sons coming into glory!

Oh! The Green Pastures! The new Will and Testament! The Better Way! The Living Word! The Word of His Grace! Gathered unto Him, brought into Him to ever feed upon and take our sustenance, and strength from Him! Whatever we partake of or eat of becomes a part of us. We are in the Green Pasture, the Green Pasture is in us! In Him we are complete, there is no want! The Great I AM, the Green Pasture! He is to us all we need! He is our High Tower, our place of refuge and our defense!

JESUS, the Green Pasture, is also the Great Shepard of the sheep to lead the flock of God the Father! JESUS, the gentle Shepherd, who laid down His life for the sheep that they might be kept safe and sound. Who became the Door to the fold that all must come in through Him. The Door that opens and no man can close, and then it closes to protect the sheep inside, that no man or beast can open and come in and steal!

OH! The Gentle Shepherd who has led us by His Spirit into the Green Pasture, into Himself! Who ever lives! The Living Word! The Living Way! The Living Water, fresh and alive forevermore! Ever living, ever making alive!

The SEED that was dead was then planted into the earth, and in the darkness that SEED began to conquer sin, death and the grave! He burst forth from the grave, victorious! Death had put on immortality! The first of countless others! The Messiah, the Breaker had broken through and gone ahead and made a way for all who would receive Him and follow Him! He had been appointed and anointed the Great Shepherd of the Father's flock!

OH! The Green Pasture! Therein lies the still Water from which we drink and by which we lie down and rest! The Gentle Shepherd does not make us drink anymore from the turbulent waters of the past, but He leads us to the peaceful waters. Ceasing from our own strivings and labors and entering into His finished work. We lie down by the still waters in the fullness of His grace and provision!

"Come to the wells of MY Wisdom! Come to the wells of My Salvation and drink! Put your head under the water and let it run down your whole body and be refreshed, renewed and restored!

"I AM the Giver of Life! I AM the Giver of good gifts to My sheep and because I AM a Giver, I have made you a giver also so that what I freely give to you, you can freely give to others!

"Oh! Come to the waters and drink, there is no charge, only the self-surrender that it requires to drink! You cannot receive unless you come to Me, you cannot give until you have received from Me.

For you have nothing of lasting value to give except what you receive from ME!"

Selah

LOVE EMPOWERS

W hen you think of where we have come from, to where we are now, and to where we are going from here! Wow! Galatians 3:28; "There is now no distinction, neither Jew nor Greek, slave or free, there is no longer male or female, for you are all ONE in Christ Jesus. And if you belong to Christ who is Abraham's seed, then you are Abraham's spiritual heirs according to the promise!"

Father God is in the midst of us. His Spirit hovers over to see that His kingdom comes in its glory upon us and within us. His body is taking form, we are being formed into His image! The earth is about to receive the fruit of its travail! The revealing of sons, mature sons of God, who know how to host His presence, walk in an unconditional, all-merciful God kind of Love as described in 1 Corinthians 13, and walk [order their lives] according to Holy Spirit's instruction and leading.

We are experiencing the 'merging of the generations' that is a part of a move of God in the earth that will continue to bring the increase of His Kingdom as He turns the hearts of the Fathers to the sons, and the sons to the fathers in reconciliation. This will bring sons to maturity quickly. Revelation 5:9-10; "With Your Blood You have purchased men unto God from every tribe, nation and people. And You have made them a kingdom, a royal race and priests unto our God and they shall reign as kings over the earth!" What a future!

As I meditated upon all that has gone on these few years, it has been wild and glorious! Awesome and full of glory!

As I began to consider this new season and what the Lord has in store, I knew it would be a time of 'empowerment.' My mind went immediately to Ephesians 3:17; "May you be rooted deep in Love, founded securely on Love — so you will have the POWER"! John 17:21; "That they all may be one, just as You, Father, are in Me and I in You, that they also may be one in Us, so that the world may believe and be convinced that You have sent Me."

Suggested reading for a fresh reminder: 1 Corinthians 12,18,25,27. And 13:1-3.

The Kingdom of God is advanced and built upon God's kind of love, as demonstrated by the life and sacrifice of Jesus the Christ and our King. Ephesians 4:16. The church can only come to maturity building itself up in love. The love God requires does not originate from emotion or feeling. It can, but 'Agape,' kingdom love is much more powerful, it originates from the will! We choose to love with God's love as an act of our will! The challenges are indescribable. The demonic forces are surrounding us and putting intense pressure upon our 'flesh.' As Lot living in Sodom; David hounded by Saul; as Daniel in the lions den; Joseph in the pit and dungeon! Decision, the valley of decision, what will we choose? Will we react in anger, take offence, find ways, however subtle, to make 'them' pay, becoming judge and jury? Wallow in self-pity, submitting to the bondage of fear, be taken captive by the spirit of this world? OR, we have been crucified with Christ, empowered through His sacrifice and clothed with power from on high through the Holy Spirit who is God, who is Love. We choose to respond in love, resisting the devil and he flees from us! TO WALK IN LOVE! WE MUST NEEDS WALK BY FAITH! There will be all kinds of opposition from demons and our lower nature, our 'flesh.' All kinds of pressure will be applied upon our emotions to prevent our walking in love! But God will continue to present us with 'opportunities' to 'walk in love' — for love must be perfected in us for it is the 'EMPOWERMENT' to rule and reign with Christ! First upon the throne of our own hearts, and then over the territory that has been allotted to us to rule over, driving out the Hittites, Jebusites, Haggites, and Philistines! We shall overcome, and our Lord Christ shall indeed be Lord over all the kingdoms of our heart, and we shall be a body wholly filled and flooded with

God Himself, and this earth shall be under heaven's rule! His multi-faceted, multi-gifted, anointed body, giving full expression of Him in earth's realm, destroying the works of darkness and manifesting the works of His Kingdom! Yes!

I had felt insincere and hypocritical at times because I did not 'feel' the emotion of love. Phileo love is used in reference to family. It is a pure emotion accompanied by 'feelings' at many levels. Agape love, God's all-merciful love, is not based on 'feelings' and is much more powerful, for it comes from the 'will' in obedience to the Father! Although I was being merciful and extending grace and serving people, I was 'feeling' guilty because I was not 'feeling' the emotion of love. As I began to cry out to the Lord concerning this, the Holy Spirit straightened out the matter! As we will to do His will, He is able to download and infuse us with His love that is supernatural, for our human love can never rise to the level needed to fulfill His command! The accuser had been exposed and truth had set me free to love! Amen!

THE SHIFT

S hifting into another 'gear' to move forward, not without a few 'jerks' and 'jolts' and a little shaking! [I obviously spiritualized my difficulty in learning to drive a 'standard shift' versus an 'automatic shift'!]

The visit with Max and Norma was humbling and awesome and exciting! God the Holy Spirit had indeed made very clear His plans for them and they were constrained to step into His vision for them and Living Water Fellowship. Every motive of our hearts continued to be tested. Max knew that he would be sharing with me the Lord's instruction, no salary, just expenses as pertaining to the ministry, until He told us differently. Norma was with the Postal Service and Max worked for 3M. The Lord Most High was not only the owner of this vessel, but the Captain, and we had been 'recruited, shanghaied' [ha!] and given the awesome privilege of going on this adventure! The discoveries of hidden treasures, the tasks and resistance that developed our faith muscles, and the friction of the rubbing together of the 'living' stones as we worked together, began to smooth, shape and polish us to fit into our prepared place in the wall of His House! We seemed to stay on a 'learning curve,' which felt precarious oftentimes. But the Lord was SO faithful to always send one of His gifts our way or send us where they were that had just the revelation or word from Him for that particular season or ' place,' or confirmation of what we were hearing and seeing. And that kept us from 'tipping' too far to one side or the other, helping us stay on course. [Can you see this vehicle on this narrow road curving around the mountain, going higher and higher, and how you felt in the 'pit of your stomach'? You've been there, haven't you?!] The thing is, we ARE on this ascent, it IS a narrow way, a harrowing way, treacherous at times, with bandits waiting in hiding to attack and rob us, but it is the Glory Way of experiencing His Presence, His deliverance, His power and being changed into His likeness and image! He is always inviting us to come up higher. "Come up here and I will show you things which are to come." And it seems never to be about the 'things,' but a greater revelation of Himself and His glory and "and as we, with unveiled faces continue to behold as in a mirror the glory of the Lord, are constantly being transfigured into His very own image, from one degree of glory to another and this comes from the Lord who is the Spirit!" Oh! Yes!

Our times of coming together whether for prayer, fellowship or services were powerful in His Presence and anointing. Max and I did our best to follow the leading of the Spirit concerning team ministry. Giving each other opportunity without an agenda of our own. Being prepared but deferring to one another. And often ministering together. And giving opportunity for others of the church to share or testify. The Holy Spirit also dealt with 'traditional order of service.' We had certainly never been 'this' way before, nor had any of the congregants. We had awesome, unexpected experiences under the anointing and during worship, and the Spirit of prophecy was always flowing. For a better word, it was continuous revival for several years. Father God was continually giving us 'downloads' concerning connecting and relational oversight, His governmental order and alignment. And the importance of the body having opportunity to receive from all fivefold ministry giftings rather from just the pastoral and evangelistic.

I need to make you aware that the way the Holy Spirit was moving upon me, this ministry and the way the Holy Spirit was moving and manifesting His Presence upon us and in our midst was very new for Max and Norma. I knew it had to be jerking them around! But the moment they stepped up to the plate, they never backed down. They honored me in every way, were submitted and humble and kept their shoulder to the plow. It was amazing to me, and I continued to say that no one could doubt this was God's doing and His anointing. We all were blessed beyond words, and challenged more than we liked to say!

In '93, recognizing LWM's need for accountability and apostolic relational oversight, I felt the Lord was leading me to approach Billy and Angie Nunez, who pastored River City Fellowship in San Antonio, to connect with us in that capacity. I had an understanding that God was restoring order and His government to the church and through apostolic and prophetic connection He would bring unity, strength and increase to the corporate son in the earth. So I was praying into that vision and word, as well as 'looking' for the one to stand alongside me. Prophetic words had been released over me for years, as well as over LWM, a 'forerunner, pioneering spirit.' Billy was really clueless about this, but agreed. This was so new and different for them as well. They began to come and impart to us through his strong teaching gift, as well as through their music and worship and Angie's prophetic gifting. And we continued to pour into them and encourage them in their call and anointing. We were all breaking through the barriers of religion and tradition into the reality of the fullness of the Gospel of the Kingdom of Christ and His anointing. We recognized the operation of 'religious spirits.' And we understood that the old wineskin, the old structure could not hold the 'new wine' that God the Holy Spirit was pouring out. [The Holy Spirit referred to this 'event' as a 'prophetic seed' the size of a mustard seed, that would grow into a tree that would spread its branches over many and nurture many from its fruit!] Much of this took place at the house around our large round oak dining table. There were certainly 'knights' who sat around that table throughout the years, as the King gave revelation, correction and vision! I believe everyone could agree, those were blessed times!

We continued to pursue God in the attempt to apprehend all we believed we had been apprehended for! T.W, myself, Frankie, and her husband made a trip to the Brownsville Revival and stayed three days. We were in line for hours and God the Holy Spirit rewarded us beyond measure! Max and I went wherever we felt the Lord was leading. Rather, Max loved to say, Deep ruts are all over the country from my boot heels where Colleen dragged me!" The need was great for us to connect, to experience those who had revelation and were some of the mothers and fathers positioned to help the body of Christ through this new gate, as well as those who were in the same boat! We attended several of Sister Gwen Shaw's conferences, which introduced us to awesome, fantastic worship and testimonies from the nations. Then He would send us to the Copeland meetings for awesome prophetic teaching. And then there were the Rodney Howard Browne meetings, which were definitely 'way out of the box,' which brought some relief that we were not so 'strange' after all, this was really God the Holy Spirit! I was beginning to have revelation of those 'tables' God prepares for us in the presence of our enemies! He is definitely the Master Chef, and He knows how to prepare gourmet meals! Everyone is 'invited' and Holy Spirit goes out into the highways and hedges to compel us to come and 'dine,' that our 'body' become healthy and strong!

One of those was the FMCI yearly conference in the Dallas area. Founders were Jim and Jeane Hodges. I had felt especially drawn because it seemed everything that was in our hearts, for the church and kingdom vision, continued to be confirmed and affirmed through Brother Jim's teaching, revelation and the vision God had put in his heart. Also, Barbara Wintrouble, Dutch Sheets and several others were on the board, whom we greatly respected.

Max had been a part of the ministry for a year, and the Sunday before we were to leave for the FMCI conference, the Holy Spirit moved on me and said, "Tell him, he is My prophet!" I knelt by his chair and began to prophesy the word of the Lord. He was very moved and a very sweet presence of Jesus enveloped us. At the conference, which was awesome, the atmosphere heavy with the Lord's Presence. there was an invitation to come to the front for ministry. Several hundred were streaming up there! One of those ministers was Sam Brassfield, a prophet. We had not met him or should I say, experienced him! He looked like an Elijah and definitely sounded like him! [Still does! only with more authority!] Max and I were up there together and Sam went straight for Max. I was so intent on what he was saying to Max, confirming his prophetic anointing with impartation, and about that time someone came up to me and began to prophesy. At the same time, we fell out in the Spirit and later found we had ended up turned opposite directions with our heads touching!

We made an appointment with Brother Jim to be accepted into the fellowship of ministers and churches, for accountability and apostolic oversight. Through them, our hearts became connected with many others who imparted so much into our lives and ministry. Apostle Jim and Jeane have walked humbly with God, stayed the course and poured their lives into the body of Christ in every nation and helped bring many 'sons' to maturity for these end-times. Out of FMCI, the Father sent just those ones to bring the word and impartation that continued to fan the flame of revival, bring revelation and encouraging us on our journey. And I believe we made deposits into their lives and perhaps 'challenged' them just a little bit! Precious friends to the family of Living Water. Jim and Jeane faithfully came every year. Thank the Lord, messages were recorded. It was impossible to stay up with Brother Jim. We would have to listen to the tapes [yes, tapes! we didn't have CDs then!] for days to 'get it'! And we had to 'get it'! Bob Long with Rally Call Ministries, Gayle and their team of intercessors, Dr. Don and Cherrie Crum, Vance Underwood, and many others added along the way, depending upon the 'season' we were in. As I said in the dedication, without their sacrificial lives, integrity and perseverance, we could not have made our contribution to the increase of the Kingdom of Our Lord! Within and without! And had SO much fun!

One of our trips was to Colorado Springs. Peter and Doris Wagner were hosting, with Rick Joyner, Kimberly Daniels, Myles Monroe and several others. I don't remember all who were there, but we felt strongly we were to go. Tina was dating a young man, Rodney Bradley, who had barely ventured to the edge of the river. And because of his love for Tina, he came on this trip. As Jesus often does, the best way to learn to swim is to be thrown in the river! And Rodney needed to experience a deep rushing current of the river to move him into his place, and give him a 'jump' start on his journey of enlightenment! He not only survived, he and Tina soon married! The faithfulness of the Lord to illuminate our darkened understanding to know Him who is Love, and the immeasurable power of His Spirit within. What an adventure that trip was. We always traveled in my blue Suburban, always at least seven of us. The Holy Spirit was always taking every opportunity to teach, exhort, align, correct and bind our hearts together with one another, and surprising us with His ' suddenlies' and shaking us up! Max was always the driver and did an amazing job of holding us all together and keeping us safe, through the snow, ice and detours as well as through the unexpected 'eruptions' of the Holy Spirit! I'm certain He alerted an angel to come to Max's aid to assist him in keeping the car on the road and in the right lane! Also, I might mention, you needed to have a strong 'bladder' to travel long distances with Max! It seemed to me he might have become more understanding through the years!

It wasn't long before Tina and Glenda, Max and Norma's daughters, became a part of the fellowship. What a blessing they were, and increasingly so, with strong prophetic giftings. Tina is a deep river and Glenda's prophetic worship took us to another level. Others joined the worship team. We had such a heart to worship to the extreme of expression! We began to construct beautiful ornate banners, and worship flags, praying as we worked as a team. Franke, Linda, Charlotte, Joy, me, and others. What glorious times in His Presence! And what beautiful prophetic banners to display His many virtues, love and beauty! We just couldn't get enough of HIM!

In '96, a call came from Donny. He and Lori were getting married, just a simple wedding on the beach! Donny had brought her to meet us earlier, and she was all he had described! We loved her immediately! She was loving and gracious and loved the Lord. Very talented, had been with the San Francisco Ballet, and had a young son, Andreas. It was obvious they would marry soon. So I was ecstatic! I knew she would be very good for Lacey and a blessing to our family. Mother was delighted as well. The children spent the summers with Donny, but the family situation seemed to be the hardest for Lacey. [Just keeping you up dated on the family!] Randy had opened an insurance office and he and Betty were doing well. Jordan was in a private Christian school and he and Randy were 'two peas in a pod,' loved the water, fishing, surfing and boating. Both Donny and Randy loved Corpus and being close to the water.

They had always been avid surfers. So they were all at 'home' in Corpus Christi. And now a new beginning was coming together for Donny! Father's blessing and restoration!

We were able to acquire the property next to the church, which gave us the whole block. It had a large building that provided us a youth center as well as an apartment for guests. Glenda was a great organizer of events and great with the young people. Two years in a row, we hosted a three-day youth conference, "The Giant Slayers," with radical young worshippers, and groups that came from as far away as California! We put up a very large tent for the 'tabernacle of David' services. Rally Call participated, and others. The heavens over the region were impacted, the sound of the Shofar announcing the rising up of a new radical-for-God generation, and the increase of His kingdom! Many prophecies and declarations were released into the heavens, deposits made into young warriors' hearts. Many were never the same and have continued on to be world-changers and kingdom-builders!

Max was growing in the prophetic, Norma was a 'strong tower' for both Max and me, and we were all experiencing God at new levels. Services were never on a time schedule. We never wanted to leave His Presence. We came to meet with Him and He never disappointed us! Now I will say, the congregation had many opportunities to 'grow' in grace when I was preaching! I just didn't know how to make an exciting, good long story short! Still don't! And again, God the Holy Spirit used a lot of situations to lay the ax to the root of old mindsets of 'having church' to break us out of the mold of coming to 'a' church for an hour to get a fix for the week or to salve the conscience, or out of religious 'habit' or ritual. He was continually dealing with religious mindsets and motive, instilling in us that we were the church, coming together in a building to meet with Him, to receive from Him through the giftings in one another. To be strengthened, encouraged, healed and set free by His Spirit to affect the culture around us and bring His kingdom in our homes, workplace, or wherever He would lead us.

Lee and Becky Thompson joined our fellowship. She was an accomplished pianist, which added so much to the worship team. Lee was the school principal and added a bit of 'class' as well as a good challenge! They were with us a few years until they retired and moved to Virginia. How we missed them! So many wonderful people were a part of the fellowship through the years. Some were sent, some passing through, some stayed and some moved on. Seasons and cycles!

Several of us attended a conference in Abilene. A minister who did bronze sculpting, from another city, was experiencing gold dust falling heavily upon him and the sculptures. Everywhere he would go to minister, the gold dust would fall. At each service, pure gold dust would fall very heavily around the stage, upon the ministers at the front, and then lighter towards the back! Physical manifestations of His glory are so awesome. I still have the scotch tape stuck to my Bible that Rodney used to gather some of the dust!

I think I must have thought, because we just never backed down or backed off, and the fire just burned hotter, the devil would just give up and let us alone, that we were a lost cause! I learned he lies in wait until 'a more opportune time.' The Holy Spirit reminded me of Jesus' temptation in the wilderness. When satan did not succeed with Him, the word says he went away until a more 'opportune' time!

The Holy Spirit continued to bring enlightenment and vision. He has amazing ways to bring us into alignment with the 'picture' in His mind.

Prophecy released over the church, Sunday morning, 5/8/97:

"You are the Lord's spring, a fountain planted in a dry land. Planted and placed as surely as the springs and fountains of the earth were placed strategically for divine purpose. Springs are powerful, they provide life-giving water, food, cleansing and refreshing and have their source in the eternal supply! You are wells of Living Water. I have some wells that have been dug only as deep as the water-table, and so the water is not always pure or healthy to drink. Then I have some wells that have been dug to the next level, just to the surface of the hard rock. Then I have those wells that have been dug to the third level, through the hard rock and below. These need no pumping but spring forth from the force that is behind it! And

water from these wells refreshes and restores all who drink from it. And it shall be in My people a well springing up into everlasting life! The mighty power of the Holy Spirit! The deeper the well, the purer the water and stronger the force! How deep will you allow My Spirit to dig out the impurities and the soil and silt out of your life? Will you allow ME to dig through the hard rock of the self-life and take out the stony heart and put within you a heart like Jesus the pattern Son?

"I send the springs into the valleys to run among the hills. Most of My springs and fountains are small and hidden away, but remember, they are the source of the mighty rivers! And I, the Lord, say, 'You shall be like a watered garden and like a spring of water whose waters fail not. And when the poor and needy seek water and their tongue fails them for thirst, I, yes I, will open rivers in high places and fountains in the midst of the valleys and I will make the wilderness a well and the dry land springs of water!'"

Yes, Father, we come into agreement with Your vision for us as a people, one part of Your church in the earth You have gathered to Yourself to fulfill Your plans and purposes in the earth in this time. We yield to Your Spirit and will not resist His work within our hearts as He digs the 'wells' deeper, that Your water of life might flow with great force! And Your church be restored and the works of darkness be destroyed!

Thank You, Father!

We were introduced to Tim Shepperd and his family through Billy and Angie. He had such a powerful anointing of worship and the prophetic, and the heart and character to carry it, which always brought the manifest Presence of Jesus upon us in unexpected and powerful ways. There was a 'season' of a few years that the Lord sent him to minister. Billy and Angie would participate as well, as they both were anointed prophetic worshippers. Those times opened huge portals in the heavens and shook the gates of hell! We were extremely blessed personally, but being kingdom-minded, we knew it wasn't just about 'us,' but God was moving all over the earth, revealing Himself, the power of His spirit within His people, and shaking all that could be shaken, so that all that would be left standing would be His Kingdom! There were things going on in earth's realm that was strategically designed by God Himself to affect the powers of darkness in the heavenlies.

One of those times was particularly powerful. Tim was under such an anointing, water was pouring from him, not just natural 'sweat' but his shoes would fill up and run over! Oil was literally dripping off Angie's hands, not just a drop or two, but a stream from her hands. As she laid on hands, many were touched, and some received healing. Those two days were glorious, increase upon all of our lives. Anyone who came to minister was always ministered to and was never the same!

During this meeting, Tim prophesied that we were a 'Tekoah,' the place or school of the prophets. From this place, prophets would be trained and sent forth.

Just to remind you of the 'seed' of the word planted into the womb of the spirit, contained within the seed are predetermined purposes and destinies! First the blade, then the stalk, then the head and then the fruit. This was in '98. Ten years later, a school of the prophetic was birthed on Rosh Hoshanna in '08, led by Sam and Nancy Brassfield! Their testimony: Ten years before, Cindy Jacobs had prophesied to them they would be teaching a school of the prophets. They had been collecting material all these years, wondering and waiting upon God, and during a conference we were having in November of '07, the Holy Spirit spoke to Max: 'It is time for a school of the prophets!' He shared this with me, then called Sam. We set up a meeting with them in Bertram and they shared their testimony and bore witness that 'it was time'! We agreed, it would be birthed at LWM!

Our precious Mother went home February 21st, 1998, fourteen days after her 92nd birthday. Her heart began to fail in January, and even though her doctor did not recommend it, she insisted they do surgery. She came through the surgery, but her heart was just worn out. Pat would come on weekends and the grandchildren when they could. She had always been so strong, we just held on and believed she could make it through this and we would have a few more years with her. Pat was with her when she passed. I was at home, resting. I just didn't think it would be so soon. So when I got the call, I was devastated that he was there by himself and I was not there. He said they had been talking and she just closed her eyes and went to sleep, and he didn't realize it until the nurse came in. No matter how old you are, it is very difficult to lose your mother, even though we have the blessed assurance it will only be temporary. We still miss her. Cottonwood Baptist planted a tree in front of the church in her honor, with a memorial stone inscribed with her name. She had been a member since childhood.

The cycles and seasons of life. These times always causes us to come face-to-face with the brevity of our life here on earth, eternity, that there is life after death, and the choice we've been given as to where we spend life hereafter. "For God so greatly loved and dearly prized the world [cosmos, God's created order] that He even gave up His only begotten Son, so that whoever believes in, trusts in, clings to, relies on, Him shall not perish [come to destruction, be lost] but have eternal life. [He came to restore Divine order] For God did not send the Son into the world in order to judge [to reject, condemn, to pass sentence on] the world but that the world might find salvation, [wholeness and healing] and be made safe and sound through Him." Just a reminder of this SO great a salvation we have been given, and the peace He brings in all the cycles and seasons of life. We find not our peace and comfort through a religion but through our relationship with our Lord and Savior Jesus the Christ, and His indwelling Spirit! Thank You, Father!

Randy's son, Shawn, came to live with us in '98. The Lord's instructions. Many challenges, but rewarding. He had inherited his mother's mental illness, and after several years of great stress for the family, he had received treatment, was on medication, and was being released from a rehab center. The Lord said go get him for further restoration. After a year of ministry and deliverance, he received the Lord and was baptized. He moved into his own place and went to work. Max and others of the church provided an environment that helped him deal with his challenges and assisted me in the ongoing ministry it required.

In '99, I received a call from a woman in a nearby city who was involved in helping and ministering to those who had been ritually abused through satanic worship, some of whom were in hiding. She ask me if we would take a young woman and her young daughter into our home, whom she had picked up in a shelter in the Dallas area. They had assumed another identity and name change, and were very much in need of ministry. I felt very moved upon by the Holy Spirit to do this. I had no point of reference or experience for dealing with this depth of demonic activity, but knew from experience there are many things you cannot learn except through experience! We took them in as a part of the family. T. W. was gracious and fatherly to the young girl. He involved her in taking care of the goats and animals on the place, and she began to feel safe and heal. The mother had been in a family of satanists, and the documents and information she shared was eye-opening, and horrifying. She had attempted to escape several times, but they would find her. Her mind had split into several personalities through the years as she was subjected to the rituals and abuse. She had received some treatment and counseling from someone in Dallas. All of this greatly affected the daughter, but it was amazing how well she was learning the different personalities and coping with it. She was protective of her mother, a very precious young girl. Others in the congregation were loving and helpful. It was definitely challenging, to say the least. But also so amazing to be used by God the Holy Spirit as His gifts brought revelation, insights, discerning, and deliverance. Little by little she was functioning with much less fear, coming into her true identity and personhood. She required, and the situation demanded, much fasting, prayer and time.

Very few understood the ongoing demonic influence upon her personality. Even though she had received a lot of healing and deliverance and was an awesome young woman with an amazing knowledge of the scriptures and relationship with the Lord, there were demons who were able to manifest at times, and we had to be on guard. After about a year, we had a rental house that we moved them into. The daughter was being home schooled. I was not able to spend as much time with her as I had the first year. She seemed to be progressing great. One Sunday there was a manifestation, a threatening one, and it wasn't coming under my authority. It chose to manifest around others of the congregation, purposefully in order to gain sympathy and bring division, which it accomplished. The demon spirit manipulated so effectively because of the lack of discernment in others. That gift is SO important for all of us, and becomes even more so. We were certainly being taught and trained up by Holy Spirit not to be ignorant of satan's devices and his evil influences upon the mind and actions of human beings. This other family befriended her, and helped them for a while and then they moved on. The young girl came to see me at one point, asking to live with us. I prayed with her and we wept together. I did not hear from her for years. Lois called me from Arkansas, saying she ran into her in a restaurant, she was a waitress. She did not mention her mother, but seemed to be doing all right and asked about us and said how much she loved us. So that was very encouraging.

T.W. received a call from his son, Richard, and Karen. Their daughter, Tiffany, three years old, had a large cancerous tumor in her abdomen! They would do surgery and chemo. This was indescribable pain and heartbreak for us all, but for those parents, no one can know, only God. Of course we went, grateful they had a large church family for support, as well as family. So many prayers and struggles and challenges over the next few years, and little Tiffany was so brave and loving, such an angelic grace upon her, her parents and siblings, so brave, never losing their trust in their heavenly Father. After two years, God took her. God did give another child who looked so much like her it was uncanny. Life goes on, but not without scars.

Lois continued to live life to its fullest. Her zest for life and love for Christ and her fellow travelers on the journey was incredible. She kept fighting the battle of life for the beauty of life. Robert was such an awesome young man and loved her dearly and admired her greatly. They both had such a close relationship with the Lord, and through Lois's battle and their suffering, God was glorified! Each year she would plan a two-week vacation for her and us, and she would drive! T.W.'s health continued to deteriorate, with diabetes, then knee replacement. But he loved traveling and we really enjoyed those trips. Lois held her own with him and there were a few 'harrowing' moments, but we all lived to tell about it! And laugh!

In the situation for Lacey, the dysfunction in the home was worsening. Heath was at Texas Tech, Heather at McMurry, and Lacey was left in the 'heat' alone. Donny and Lori were doing their best. I was on the phone with her often and she would say, "Granny, come up here and rent an apartment and get me out of this house!" My heart was breaking for the precious child of my heart. I was bombarding the throne of God! Eventually Donny and Lori packed up and moved to Big Springs, rented a house, and stayed until she graduated and enrolled in Texas Tech. Her degree would be in family counseling and psychology. She received her master's, interned at MHMR, and has an anointing for working with the mentally challenged, the hurting and troubled. God's redeeming grace. Out of great trials and struggles, He brings help and healing for others.

UNDER ATTACK

We began to feel uncomfortable with the exclusiveness of FMCI. It felt like the networks were becoming another denomination. By revelation, I knew the networks were destined to be linked and intertwined, that this was one of God's kingdom methods meant to create a great resource for the body of Christ to serve one another in unity of purpose and bring accountability, purity and help define vision. Max had come over to the house with us to pray and intercede concerning this. As we were in prayer, the Lord gave him a vision and a revelation concerning the networks. And He pointed out that Billy and Angie were apostolically in our foundation and we were to be connected to River City as well as to FMCI. I began to prophesy. The Lord was sowing us as a seed of merging networks! The next Sunday, the intercessors of Bob Long with FMCI were in the services. Max, under the anointing, shared the vision [don't remember the details] and what the Lord had revealed to him, and I fully agreed, that we would be as a church connected Apostolically to both RC and FMCI, that all networks had to flow in and out of each other! Gayle [I love her dearly] and the intercessors were obviously concerned. She got up and more or less tried to 'correct' what had been said and what we 'thought' we had heard from the Lord! BUT a seed of merging networks and networks within networks was released and planted. Let me say here, that where all of us were in this time of another crossing over our 'Jordan' to reach the land we each at been given to possess, there was usually a 'jungle' to get through!

We had a meeting with Bob and brother Jim. They were gracious, but a noticeable division had taken place, a wall had been raised. But Max and I were under an anointing of grace and were convinced we had heard from God and we couldn't back down. But a seed had been planted and it would and did bear fruit and begin to multiply! Within a year, networks were beginning to form within the FMCI network, and some networks came together and walls began to crumble! The next year, Brother Jim called me and the relationship was restored! They were and have always been such a blessing! We're still on the same 'page'!

Prior to the reconciliation with FMCI, Jezebel was already on the scene, working very rebelliously, pridefully and strategically! We were of course dealing with this in much prayer and grace, [I'm not saying we had the fullest enlightenment of how to walk this out] but staying accountable to our apostolic oversight and believing God for restoration and His glory! And then Belial arrived on the scene, and quickly made connection with Jezebel for the dismantling and destruction of LWM and the death of me! No one can be fully prepared for the intensity of warfare against kingdom people and be 'ignorant of satan's devices.' The control, influence, deception, manipulation and wicked plots of the Jezebel and Belial spirits cannot be 'taught' effectively. It takes 'experiential knowledge, pure hearts, motives and abiding in Christ to successfully defeat these principalities and dismantle their structures. The Lord's works are marvelous.

We were caught up somewhat in the Y2K concerns. And because most of us had enough revelation to know there would come a time of crisis and greater stress than we had experienced in our lifetime, we felt it was better to be as prepared as we could be if this was the beginning of that time.

Lois was back on chemo and radiation. I was making trips to Arkansas to help her. T.W was having more health problems: in 2001 he had colon cancer surgery and part of his colon removed! Gene was helping, but I was under extreme duress! [remember the 'more opportune time'?] Max, Glenda and the team were in full swing. Jamie Lipe had come on board, another precious gift from Father. The Lord had sent her from Fredricksburg to be a part of the ministry and worship team. The team, now including part of a family that had joined the ministry after our big youth conference, were being invited to many of the conferences, writing prophetic songs and very powerful worship. The kingdom of darkness was under assault big time! So satan sent out some big guns, already knowing those they could access for the job! The Holy Spirit alerted some of the intercessors and they warned us, but some couldn't see it. And through very sly manipulation, the worship team and Max were being swayed to come into agreement with satan's schemes. I was aware and praying, but couldn't seem to hold back the tide. I had absolute trust in the hearts of those who had been set in leadership and I had confidence in God's faithfulness as my defender and the Guardian of His House. There are many times our position in a battle like this one is to 'rest,' stand still and see the salvation of the Lord! With all that was going on around me personally, I had no choice but to trust Him to bring an increase of faith and grace and strength with which to stand.

I had just returned from one of my trips to Arkansas, and Max came by. He was obviously in great stress. He started talking, with tears pouring down his face. [Jezebel and Belial always set others up to do the 'dirty' work; it would not work any other way.] I was heartbroken for Max, knowing his integrity and love for me, and the ministry, and recognizing once again, even the very elect can be deceived. I understood that 'Jezebel' hates the prophet, and this 'scheme' was surely designed for Max's downfall as well! There was an incredible anointing of love and grace upon me, powerful weapons against those spirits! Ephesians 6:12, "Our battle is not against flesh and blood but against principalities, rulers of darkness and demons," etc.!

Max began hesitantly, stumbling but believing he was doing the best thing for all concerned. "We have decided it is time for you to step down, and others agree." And then he began to state some of the reasons. The breath of God was gently blowing upon my face. I thought I was going to die, literally, with all I had endured and was still going through in my life and for this work. Within my spirit I was saying, "Let me die, Lord, this is too much! This cannot be You, I know You and You know me, all You would have to do is tell me and You know it would have been just fine. I cannot 'blow' this, or give any legal right for satan, so I am trusting You for the wisdom to bring satan down, and bring Max to his right mind." It was almost as if I was 'out' of myself.' I cannot describe the peace, the gentle flow of tears, the love that poured out to Max. There was no reaction. I just said, "All of this is the Lord's, to give to whomever He chooses. I don't own anything, He owns everything and everyone, so whatever He wants, I come into agreement with. I know this is very hard for you." He hugged me and left. Then Franke came with almost the same thing. I still wasn't sure I wasn't going to die. I just went to bed and tried to rest. I couldn't even pray. But I was 'at rest.' Dead!

Bob Long was scheduled to minister on Saturday night. Max had called the day before and said he felt led to go to a conference and would try to get back for Bob's meeting I went on early to the church as usual, still in some kind of a 'cocoon,' absolutely free of any negative feelings. I couldn't believe it myself! This was certainly 'supernatural'! My flesh was DEAD!

Worship was almost over. Bob was running late. He came through the door and a few minutes later he got up to minister. He was moving along and suddenly he stopped and very loudly said, "Leviathan is in this place! Jezebel is in this place!" I couldn't believe it. My spirit began to leap inside of me, as Bob began to expose and dismantle apostolically those principalities! He did not have a clue to any of the circumstances or what had just previously taken place. A little later, Max came in the door. The Holy Spirit had sent him to that conference to RIP the veil of deception and expose the works of darkness and he came out of agreement with that thing. With an anointing of wisdom and grace, he let it be known and prophetically acted out some things that began to expose, dismantle and cut ungodly cords and strengthen godly cords! From that moment, every attempt was made to bring restoration to the parties involved, and supernaturally, every hidden thing continued to be revealed!

His ways are beyond knowing, but to watch the evidence of His bringing those spirits down and showing Himself mighty on our behalf was something none of us will ever forget! We took no pleasure in the consequences some experienced because there was no repentance, brokenness or turning for them. Those spirits had several prime targets. We hate the devil and his evil ways, but we dearly love the people and hurt for them, and believe and continue to pray for their restoration. For His glory.

Our source of power is the Holy Spirit and the Word of God. We build ourselves up in faith when we confess the Word of God. We experience greater confidence when we understand the Word and walk in revelation. Prayer plugs us into the power source, connects us to Father God, and allows His power to flow to us in any situation. Psalm 65:3 says that calling upon the Lord will bring salvation and deliverance from your enemies. This has always been a key to deliverance. We can pray ourselves out of any adverse situation. God has provided 'a' way of escape for His people. Believers must know and operate in authority. Jesus gave His disciples power and authority over all devils, to tread on serpents and scorpions, and He promised that nothing would hurt us. We are positionally seated with Christ in heavenly places far above all principalities and powers! We use this authority through prayer and confession, allowing the Holy Spirit to use all of our faculties and gifts at any given time with weepings, travail, tongues, prophecy, and prophetic acts, as He leads us into victory! He gave gifts to men and led away a train of vanquished foes!

We are not to be ignorant of the devil's tactics! We can overcome all the schemes of the devil. He is a 'schemer' with a plan, design, or program of action. The Bible talks about the 'wiles' of the devil. A 'wile' is a trick or trap. A trap is a snare. Traps and snares are hidden. People fall into traps unknowingly. We are delivered from the snare of the fowler. A fowler is a hunter. Satan is a hunter of souls. Multitudes of people are deceived by the enemy. There are hosts of lying and deceiving spirits that work under the authority of satan. These spirits include delusion, deception, lying, seducing, blinding, error and guile.

All of the struggles and battles of God's people in the Old Testament were natural enemies. Behind these natural enemies were spiritual ones that were opposed to the Davidic Kingdom. Jesus was to come from this line and sit on the throne. David was fighting something beyond the natural. Through the Holy Spirit, he was contending with the powers of darkness that were set against the arrival of the kingdom of God. The kingdom of God has come! Through Jesus' sacrificial death and the shedding of His divine Blood, the devil has been brought to an open shame, Christ has risen, and God the Holy Spirit has come down to earth to reside, dwell within and empower all who receive Him by faith, to enforce the victory at Calvary! That age-old serpent, that old dragon the devil and all his 'cohorts' are still opposing the rule of God, His kingdom and principles and law of love. Where did Jesus say His kingdom would be? "The kingdom of God is WITHIN YOU!" The story of God's people under the old covenant, the battles they faced of seduction, idolatry, the 'kings' they had to battle and overcome, the consequences and hardships they endured, are all 'pictures' in the natural of the spiritual forces of darkness that we battle today. Behind the idols of the 'gods' and' goddesses' the nations worship are demons, evil spirits that manifest in the natural through these idols. Jezebel is an example of a female principality. The Bible uses strong words that pertain to spiritual warfare. Abolish, beat down, break down, cast down, cast out, chase, confound, consume, contend, destroy, smite, wrestle. Jesus warned the church in Thyatira in Revelation 2:20, "I have this against you: that you tolerate the woman Jezebel who is leading astray My servants and beguiling them." The spirit or children of Belial are mentioned many times in scripture. Demon spirits operating under the rulership of Beliah seduce people, to lead away, to persuade to disobedience or disloyalty, to lure away. The instigators of 'wicked plots' are the ancient serpent, Leviathan, and his fallen angels.

Truth is powerful! The truth will set you free! We are responsible for the 'renewing of our mind.' We must take spiritual responsibility for our life, not depending on anyone else for our spiritual well-being. We must confess the word over our lives, praying strong prayers that rout the enemy, not allowing self-pity to hold us back, but stirring ourselves up to prayer and fellowship with God the Holy Spirit. It all starts with a decision, taking the initiative, disallowing passivity to rob us of our inheritance in Christ Jesus! Our deliverance is as close as our mouth!

Out of a time of fasting and seeking the Lord during this time, I began to prophesy the word of the Lord:

"There is something greater that you cannot yet see. Fearlessly look and SEE and walk softly with ME. I will stir and shake and see that you stay awake! So much is at stake! How important now for purity in thought and motive, how important now to keep laying it all down upon My altar of sacrifice, keeping all released, giving in, giving up, dying, crucifying, resting, trusting, loving and devoting yourself to ME! Oh, it does My heart good to hear your words and songs of love that I give to you that you give back to ME! But more than that, your trust and faith and devotion to ME cuts right through the enemy's territory and demons flee! What power I desire to release! How heady and intoxicating is the new Wine ready to be poured out upon those who are fully submitted to ME!

"Hang on to My words from the mouths of My prophets, and then pay close attention to the inner witness and do not let men's words override that witness! Judge all things by My Spirit and be alert and on your guard, all of you! I AM with you! Be courageous, the days ahead require it! Be at peace, seek that place of inner peace. Look for righteousness, peace and joy manifested in those around you. By their fruit they shall be known! Know no more by the flesh, but know them by the spirit! Not by words or failures or successes, but in contriteness and humility of the heart, you can trust! How watchful and close is the enemy, ready to pounce! But how much closer am I, and through the authority I have given, you must not give him an ounce! I AM your defender and I will preserve you and keep you for Myself alone! I will protect you. Believe that I will, for I AM committed to you to bring you through! You are not working for me, you are alongside of Me, partnering with Me. Lean heavily upon ME and learn of Me continually and let love do its perfect work in you! Do not think that I AM displeased or disappointed. You do not yet know 'perfect love'! One day I will see you BE! One day you will just BE! Oh, the joy and satisfaction in My heart for you, your total fulfillment in ME!"

Thank You, Lord

I highly recommend Steve Samson's book, ***Discerning and Confronting Jezebel,*** as well as John Eckhardt's books, ***Prayers That Rout Demons and Break Curses,*** and ***Prayers That Bring***

Healing. Let's get free, church! Let's get healed! The harvest is plentiful, but the laborers are few!

Prayer:

Father, forgive us for being tolerant of the Jezebel spirit. Open our eyes to all its influence and tactics. We bind the stronghold it has on our minds and the minds of those in our lives, churches, communities and nation. And we release the Spirit of God to expose all its works. We pull down every stronghold and fortress this spirit has built up, in which we live. We choose to humble ourselves and walk before You with purity of heart and mind and a submissive spirit. In Jesus' name. Amen!

While we must have compassion for those who are bound with the spirit of Jezebel, we must also have compassion for those who have experienced great damage by the operation of that spirit. Therefore, we must not come into agreement with their ways and controlling tactics, and we must be willing to confront them. Repentance is the key. Those who have opened themselves up to that spirit must not only feel sorry, but also genuinely seek repentance. Apologies can become manipulative without true brokenness and repentance. Because of the deep pattern of control, those who recognize this must be willing to confront boldly and specifically point out his actions. The weapon we have is truth spoken in love, and it is the truth that sets people free! If the people 'see the light' and seek repentance, they can be delivered. This will become a process. They will need to humble themselves, not only before God, but to others, renouncing the behavioral patterns of control in their life, which may go back to childhood. Jezebels have personality traits that are deeply entrenched that have been shaped by continual demonic thoughts. Flesh cannot be cast out, it has to be crucified and subjected to the Holy Spirit daily. A person may not necessarily have a Jezebel spirit, but may have thought structures that help a Jezebel find a home.

All Christians must face up to the fact that their real battle is with their flesh. The power of the flesh, which is capable of opposing the Holy Spirit in all He wants to do, far exceeds the power of the enemy!

A Jezebel personality is almost always motivated by insecurity and is a product of the flesh. Paul called the works of the flesh 'witchcraft.' It is a behavior that operates through a person to control by the use of manipulation, domineering, and intimidating tactics. What is most deceiving is that they are 'religious' and often very spiritual and talented and do religious things. They are normally always available, involved whenever possible to gain the greater amount of influence, ingratiating to gain favor. Religion, legalism, and works are the most used anesthetic to numb the conscience and hold people in the kingdom of darkness.

They are independent and avoid true intimacy. Some of the greatest effectiveness of this spirit is intimidation. Elijah responded to fear instead of to God. He surrendered to self-pity, which is a conscious resignation and surrender to a victim mentality. When you see yourself as a victim, you literally enter into sin with Jezebel, because you are not resisting her! She must be resisted by commitment to truth, to the 'law' of love. There must be a willingness to confront lies without compromise, absolutely taking no offence, relenting, zero tolerance, no sympathy and much prayer!

The most cunning yet most common way the spirit of control works is through manipulation! This manifests in countless ways such as flattery in public, and criticism in private. The old saying, 'Eat you up in your face and tear you down at your back!' But all done very smoothly and manipulatively.

In marriages it takes on another form, usually as silent treatment, sulking. The wife may withhold sex or use seductive charms to get what she wants. The husband may control finances or find countless ways to get his way. There is nothing more repulsive than a man or woman who puts his wife or her husband down or belittles them in front of people. They are also good at continuing to point out flaws and mistakes to make themselves feel superior, but also build an idolatrous structure that swallows up the true person's identity. Manipulation is also used to put guilt on people, being condemning and judgmental. This is an evil in that illegitimately controls people into the response the person desires. The voice of the 'accuser' to bring guilt and condemnation, a sense of failure, which acts as a 'curse,' bringing people into captivity, stealing their destinies!

Jezebel uses intimidation, seeking to move people through threats, to move a person into fear. And fear is used to paralyze the person and capture a specific response!

The most drastic method of control is simply dominating the will of another person, It leaves the controlled person no option. Husbands use this method over battered wives. Men experience this method of domination as well. Victims feel controlled by the threat of disapproval or violence and they fear to speak up. It is difficult for women to protect themselves because of men's strength, and difficult for men to protect themselves from this manifestation, other than in a defensive position, without being physical.

Jezebel exhibits varying degrees of stubbornness, mean-spiritedness, arrogance and jealousies, but can then turn on the 'charm' and be almost sickeningly sweet! This is always self-serving. And the stronghold of pride is closely tied with insecurity. Her theology is that the end justifies the means!

Jezebel gets others to do her dirty work! She commonly stirs innocent people up through defiling them with her self-pitying, victim mentality and garnering sympathy until their emotions are out of control and they do the 'dirty work,' while Jezebel is the 'good guy' with a convincing performance! Jezebels can seduce another person [often wife or husband] to the point of becoming a puppet in their hands. The Jezebel is clever in its agenda. The saddest part is the way that spirit destroys the fruitfulness of others, bringing confusion and bondage. The mistake many make when dealing with a person under the influence and control of Jezebel is that of being too easy on it. And we certainly must not be easy on its traits or influence in our lives personally! Just as Jehu commanded her to be thrown down, we must be aggressive and not tolerate it, be it husband or wife, or whomever! Those who serve Jezebel, die first! Ahab was spineless and so intimidated and in order to please her, abdicated his own throne and convictions. How pleased God would have been if Ahab had stood up to the manipulating, controlling spirit. Instead, he entered into her sins and took her part! Those who have been victims of that spirit and have come under the control and influence of that spirit must rise up in the power of God and be ruthless against it, compassionate to the person, but give no quarter, never surrendering to fear! That spirit makes you feel suffocated and powerless to disagree! Victims feel controlled by the threat of disapproval or violent reactions or scathing rebuke!

God is raising up those in this hour who will be militant against that spirit, not only by becoming unyielding and aggressive against it, but living in a spirit of repentance and walking in humility and loving truth and pursuing God more than popularity or reputation! Remember God's words to Thyatira! I believe almost all of us have been, at one time or another, on both sides of the Jezebel experience, exhibiting her traits as well as becoming a victim or being victimized! I believe there is no other way of bringing understanding and revelation of the agenda of this spirit and the effect it has upon the body of Christ without going through the experience. Once you are out from under that deception and influence and dealing with 'flesh' and 'light has dawned,' you definitely hate it with a purple passion and are very discerning when it is operating at any level! Thank God, the Holy Spirit is bringing revelation, understanding and correction and we are indeed becoming the ones who are militant against it and with great love and compassion will be bolder to confront it!

Jezebel destroys churches, families, businesses and relationships. God hates it and will bring judgment upon it. It seems that people who yield to it get away with it for a long time. First of all, Father is merciful and gives His children time to repent. He always reaches out in many different ways to bring that person to repentance before judgment comes. "What peace as long as Jezebel and her witchcraft are so many?" 2 Kings 9:22

Jezebel hates the prophet because prophetic words come with a creative power that renders the enemy helpless! The prophetic voice demands repentance and surrendering of self-will. Jezebel cannot accomplish its agenda with the prophet around! It is strong and deceptive and waits for opportunities.

God is exposing and dealing with Jezebel in the church and in leadership. Many leaders with mighty anointing have been seduced by this spirit and fallen into adultery, homosexuality and a compromised lifestyle. The eunuchs around Jezebel were robbed of their masculinity. Those who have been tolerant and sympathetic to Jezebel's nature are no longer powerful, authority-filled believers!

To defeat Jezebel, there must be intolerance for all types of her influences in ourselves and in and through others. There must be consistency in our private lives as believers. When we tolerate her influence, such as immoral entertainment, unholy desires, self-centeredness [it's all about 'me'], treating our wives or husbands treacherously, manipulatively, gratifying the flesh, we give inroads to the sanctuary of our lives and we greatly hinder the flow of God's power in our lives, and our effectiveness for Him. What cripples the power of darkness more than anything else is when believers surrender totally to the person and nature of Christ and 'self' is dethroned! Manipulative love says, "I will do something for you if you will do something for me." Sadly, many are unaware when they are being manipulated. The manipulation is nothing more than action performed to get you to agree and conform to someone's plans, agenda or desires. Divine love gives and expects nothing in return, no strings attached. It leaves you totality free to make your own decisions. Jesus Christ is the expression of divine love and God desires that Christians mature into this kind of love, abandoning selfish gain, motives or ambition!

When you come against the spirit of control, you can expect retaliation of some sort! Or when you began to free yourself from the constraints of that spirit, they do not like to be wrong, they fight, often venomously, and they have a way of collecting or gathering information and using it against you, should you ever challenge or contradict their decision or plans or fail to support them or threaten their influence!

It is very important for leaders to remain teachable and have a servant heart, to be connected and accountable. So much has been shared and taught for several years concerning the orphan spirit, and certainly we have a fatherless generation that gives opportunity for Jezebel. The sons and daughters must return to the Father and forsake their rebellious ways, and go to their spiritual fathers/ mothers in humility and submission, transparent and honest for correction and wisdom. This affords protection that is unquestionable. One of the most dangerous things the Jezebel will tempt you with is isolation and separation from fellowship. Independence is one of its traits. It is easily threatened by anyone who could potentially question its position or authority or methods. There can be no true fathering without humble, submitted sons. The principle of submission preached through legalistic thinking produces death because it has no foundation in love and trust, but the teaching of Christ is humbly submitting to one another in love. Confessing our faults one to another will bring healing!

As long as the victim mentality is present and someone else is to blame, Jezebel will have her way.

Other traits to consider;

They can turn on the charm and make you believe blue is red. They lie very convincingly. They can look you in the eye and weave a 'story' you can't help but believe! They have endless nervous energy, largely looks to be busy, although may work hard but have little to show for it. Their motives are seldom pure. They may drive others, exert pressure and are users.

Jezebel is clairvoyant. A familiar spirit helps in 'knowing' and sensing information in a 'supernatural way.' It is very deceptive as it masquerades as the Holy Spirit.

It uses the element of surprise to catch you off guard and have the upper hand. It has a 'spiritual' vocabulary that is very convincing.

When Jezebels are confronted or questioned, they commonly spiritualizes the situation. This protects them from owning up to responsibility required. "You're the one with the problem, not me."

If people are near to being confronted, they are very adept at twisting the situation or conversation to make the other person look like the one attempting to control and in the wrong. They will always try to look like the ones in the right. This makes it very difficult to 'corner' them and bring satisfying results. Only the Anointed One, Christ within, can be effective against it.

You will know them by their 'fruits'!

It goes without saying, it is not fair to pick one or two traits and determine that someone is dealing with a Jezebel spirit. All people have character flaws and blind spots. Paul in Galatians 6:5 says,

"For every person will have to bear [be equal to understanding and calmly receive] his own [little] load [of oppressive faults."] However, when a number of these traits coincide, it is easy to conclude that the person is dealing with the personality of a Jezebel spirit!

The cross is still the place to take your guilt and sin. Mercy still flows, forgiveness is ours, healing and deliverance are ours! It is the Father's good pleasure to give to us the kingdom, righteousness, love, peace and joy in the Holy Ghost! His agenda: to transform and form us into the image of Jesus Christ!

The scriptures plainly say that the Lord corrects the sons He loves and 'if we receive' correction, then promotion follows! He is the God of increase and change. It is easy to be spiritual when one is under the anointing or when in the presence of those moving with the anointing. However, God's concern is not what we are when we minister under the anointing, but that we become transformed permanently into 'another man,' into the image and character of Christ, "speaking the truth in love, and may grow in all things into Him who is the Head!" It is not what you've done, it is what you have become. It is not how you start, it is how you finish! God is always taking us to the 'other side,' to our destiny and to fulfillment. "We went through the fire and through the water, but You brought us out to rich fulfillment!"

May the God of all grace who called us to His eternal Glory by Christ Jesus, perfect, strengthen, establish and settle you!

Prayer:

Father, I acknowledge that I have yielded myself to the spirit of Jezebel. I come to You, humbling myself before You. I desire Your standard of righteousness and holiness. I ask You to forgive me for my tolerance of the Jezebel spirit and for any way I have opened myself to its influence and of being sympathetic to its ways. I renounce all participation and agreement that I entered into knowingly or unknowingly, willingly or unwillingly, with idolatry and with Jezebel! I renounce and pull down this demon Jezebel! I submit to You, Father, and will submit to the elder fathers and mothers for accountability and confess my faults, that I might be healed. I pull down every stronghold in my life, I declare it is dismantled, pulled up by the roots, and every stone of the structure destroyed, never to rise again! I declare Jesus Christ is Lord and King over every area of my life and every kingdom of my heart! Now Holy Spirit, completely fill that place with Your all-merciful love, joy and peace! I present myself, body, soul and spirit, to You, Holy Father. Renew a right spirit within me. Through the power of the Holy Spirit, I will live by Your standard of righteousness and conduct and help to bring healing to any family member or any others in the body of Christ who have been wounded and defiled by my words or actions from a Jezebel spirit. In the Name of Jesus.

Thank You, Father!

It looked like the 'seed' had died! But resurrection power, the 'Life' is in the 'seed'! Contained within the seed are predetermined purposes and destines! It has to come forth out of the grave, it cannot help itself, the fullness of a time will come! On the fourth day, it will burst forth! Four being the number of completion, or however long it takes to complete the cycle of the throes of change, the jolting shifts of reconstruction, transformation. A resurrection happens! God's new order for the new day! And the garments worn in the last season will no longer be appropriate in the new place of advancement, the new level of glory! The outward appearance will begin to reflect the new inward transformation!

Released over the church 6/15/02

To:
The Family of Living Water Ministries
From:
The One Who Walks Among The Candlesticks

"You are on a growth curve and in a cycle of blessing and moving into a broader sphere of influence; in spite of the opposition and the assignment against you from satan. Surely you are spiking upward and you will continue to break through!

"Satan apposes those who are becoming the greatest threat to his kingdom. Be very watchful and pray for discernment. Do not ignore or allow even a small indulgence of pride or self-confidence. It can mean disaster! It puts you at risk and puts you in agreement with demons because it expresses a lack of trust in Me. Sin can break the cycle of blessing and interferes with My power flow. Rush into My Presence in grief over disobedience and rebellion, no matter how insignificant you think it might be, and make things right that the miracle begun in your lives does not stop.

"Faith in Me and walking uprightly will bring a release of signs and wonders, and you yourselves will be signs and wonders! I will not withhold any good thing from those who believe and walk uprightly! I desire faith, unwavering faith in Me and My love and My word, and then all things are possible! I do display My glory so some will believe, but My Heart bursts with joy when My children trust Me and believe Me and cling to Me, even when they do not understand and cannot see My dealings with them! When things seem to be going contrary to My promises and still they believe and trust in My love for them and My justice, then all things truly become possible and My love and glory will never disappoint and you will never be ashamed!

"So do not grow weary in doing good, do not faint in the work that I have assigned to you. I see you in your toils and in your distresses. I see you in your crying and despair. I see you in your celebrations! There is nothing that escapes Me! I Am He who goes before you, scattering your enemies seven ways before you! I am He who stands before your Father and My Father, interceding in your behalf. I Am your vindicator and I will execute justice on your behalf!

"I walk amongst My church, examining and inspecting it. And I see the wounds, the scars and the blemishes, says the One who is faithful and true. I come to heal, to purify, wash and cleanse my church. I will pour out the oil and wine of My Spirit for the healing of your wounds and that your heart might be merry. I am sending the fire of My Spirit to purify and bring you forth as pure, translucent gold, more pure than the gold of Ophir! I am polishing you and you shall shine as a priceless pearl. I have gone before you in all *things. The way is made, only an open door in front of you, nothing to stop you, so run, MY child! Run the race set before you, I Am with you! Come ride with Me through the earth and the heavenlies! Come ride with Me as the victorious bride now! Awake and arise, Warrior bride, the Bridegroom calls! Mount your steed and draw your sword. The One who calls is your warrior Lord!"*

THE REVERENTIAL FEAR
OF THE LORD

It is very important for us in this time to understand what the 'Fear of the Lord' IS and what it ISN'T.

We will try to define this fear of the Lord that the Holy Spirit has brought to our attention recently, continues to remind us of, and which the scriptures so often and repeatedly admonish and exhort us to do. From Genesis to Revelation, I believe this phrase is more often repeated than any other. Until I began this search, I don't think I was aware of this.

Luke 12:4-5, "I tell you, My friends, do not dread and be afraid of those who kill the body and after that have nothing more they can do, but I will warn you whom you should fear, fear Him who after killing, has the power to hurl into hell, yes, I say to you, fear ye HIM!"

We are not to be afraid of the Lord, for we were created for His pleasure and intimate friendship. But when we have the worshipful fear of the Lord, we will fear no man, no beast, no devil, no circumstance or situation! We will have the peace of God and the assurance that will indeed pass our human ability to understand!

Always the fear of God is coupled with worship. It includes reverence and awe and will always motivate us to obey Him!

Proverbs 8:13, "The reverent fear and worshipful awe of the Lord [includes] the hatred of evil, pride, arrogance, the evil way and perverted and twisted speech I hate!"

Job 28:28, "But to man He said, 'Behold! The reverential and wor-shipful fear of the Lord — that is wisdom! And to depart from evil is understanding!'"

Malachi 3 tells us that the fear of the Lord is to stand in awe of His Name, to give glory to His Name.

The scriptures tell us that those living in the last generation call evil good and good evil [the spirit of compromise, humanistic, man-pleasing spirit]. But we must have God's attitude toward sin at all times and His attitude toward the sinner or the one who falls, caught in the devil's snare. The revelation of the fear of the Lord should produce in us the same attitude toward sin as God has [abstain from all appearance of evil]. Every idle word will be judged, making no excuses or justifying our sins and failures, but judging ourselves that we are not judged and receiving our forgiveness through the river that flows from the mercy throne! Ever reaching toward the mark of the 'High Calling,' not accepting less than God requires, not resting on our ' laurels' of salvation but ever seeking the Kingdom, ever moving upward and onward in our pursuit to 'know' Him who loves us so! Fear of God should produce in us a deep respect for the purity and holiness of God and the power of God and the total sufficiency of God! And to instill in us the desire to obey Him at any cost, loving not our lives unto death! Because of Who He is, His love compels and constrains us!

The fear of God is directly related to obedience.

When Abraham was about to slay Isaac in obedience to the Voice of the Lord, the angel said to him, "Now I know that you FEAR GOD! seeing you have not withheld your only son from Me."

When Jonah was on the ship going to Tarshish, running from God, he told them, "I'm a Hebrew and I FEAR the Lord! The God of Heaven who made the sea and the dry land!" But — but — but — obviously he did not have the true fear of God or he would not have been in disobedience! I wonder how many of us, how many of God's people would say, "Oh, I fear the Lord, but yet go another 'way,' take a path of unforgiveness, of lust, rebellion, pride, anger, etc.

But now the ship's crew had a genuine FEAR of the Lord! Even though they didn't know Him! They were afraid of what they were experiencing at His Hand when Jonah told them the terrible storm was an act of God on his account! And before throwing him over-board, at his suggestion, they cried out to the Lord not to let them perish or lay Jonah's blood on them, for the Lord had done what pleased HIM! Jonah learned through some pretty horrifying experiences that the consequences of the disobedience of not fearing God are far harder than the act of obedience! God's grace will always enable us to obey! After Jonah's repentance in the middle of the fish's belly, God delivered him, and then Jonah exhibited genuine fear of the Lord and delivered the message to Ninevah.

In the old covenant, the punishment was pretty severe when the Israelites did not heed His word to 'fear and revere the Lord.' In 2 Kings 17:26, He sent lions among them, killing some of them! [I am 'quaking,' not with condemnation, but recognizing how often we take the grace that has been extended to us and flows through and over our lives for granted, and 'use' it conveniently!] Oh! Father! Continue opening our hearts to the revelation of our need to reverently and worshipfully fear YOU! Thank You, Lord, for Your faithfulness!

Like all who repent of sin, we experience the truth of Psalm 130:3; "If You, Lord, should keep account and treat us according to our sins, O Lord, who could stand! But there is forgiveness with You [just what man needs], that You may be reverently feared and worshiped!"

Romans 11:22; "Then note and appreciate the gracious kindness and the severity of God"!

Hebrews 1:26; "For the Lord corrects and disciplines everyone whom He loves, and He punishes, even scourges, every son whom He accepts and welcomes to His heart and cherishes. You must submit to and endure correction for discipline. God is dealing with you as with sons. For what son is there whom his father does not thus train and discipline?"

I believe He is bringing us to the place where 'what' He tells us to do is not nearly as important as 'Who He IS,' Who gives the order! Many times, God tests us by telling us to do things without knowing why. We don't need to understand the why but to understand 'Who He IS' that is speaking!

Abraham could have written a book on why he should not be sacrificing Isaac, according to his reasoning and desires. But he hated the sin of disobedience to God, he feared God! So, he exercised great faith by believing God to raise Isaac from the dead so God's promise would be fulfilled!

The fear of God is the only way to be released from the fear of man!

The fear of man s, being more impressed and influenced by man's 'reaction' to our action than with God's reaction!

We have to get free from the concern of what people may think or do, or we can be guilty of not fearing and reverencing God!

When we have the reverential fear of God on us, we will be concerned only with how God feels about a thing. 1 Peter 1:13-16, the fear of God will bring us into God's holiness. His holiness is the most important part of God's character! True worship comes when we truly fear the Lord and stand in awe of His Name! His holiness is above all His attributes! His holiness is the basis for our respect, honor and fear of God and our being able to submit and commit ourselves to Him!

Malachi 2, where God was making reference to Levi the priest, "My covenant with him was a covenant of life and peace and I gave them to him that he might fear, and he feared Me, he stood in awe of My Name." What is His Name? Exodus 3:14; "I AM." He is everything excellent, complete, pure, perfect, just, sufficient, who has always been, is now and always will be!

Psalm 33:8-9 gives another dimension of the 'fear' of the Lord; "let all the earth fear the Lord! Let all the inhabitants of the world stand in awe of Him for He spoke and it came to be, He commanded and it stood forth!" This means we are to be arrested with awe and wonder and consider the limitless power and supreme authority of the spoken word alone that brought the universe into being!

Hebrews 1:13 tells us, by the same word of power, the universe is being upheld by that same power! Also 2 Peter 3:7 tells us this same heaven and earth that now exists have been stored up for fire, being kept until the day of judgment and the destruction of ungodly men! So! By God's word He creates, folds together, destroys and recreates! That's power! I believe Father God is strongly reminding us of all of this because of our need to rise to another level of understanding the importance of His word of instruction; to fear Him and stand in awe of His Name! For the now more obvious reasons! David tells how his understanding of the fear of the Lord heightened his praise and worship of the Lord. Psalm 22.

Thank You, Holy Lord, that You by Your Holy Spirit continue to deal with us concerning YOUR ISSUES, because You love us and desire we apprehend to the full, all that we have been apprehended for! For Your honor, glory, and praise and our being raised up into new heights in the Realm of Your Spirit. That we might come to know the fullest measure of the unlimited power of Your Spirit within us and what is the breadth and length, and the height and depth of Your Love for us. We ask You for wisdom and thank You and praise You for continuing revelation and enlightenment, meeting all our needs and the grace that is always available and sufficient for all things. In the Wonderful NAME of JESUS!

Let THE TRUTH come forth uncovered, unadulterated, not watered down, diluted, twisted or hidden! Let THE GOSPEL of THE KINGDOM come forth in the fullness of its power and glory that the body of Christ be filled with reverent fear and awe of THE LORD, that His Kingdom might be fully manifest through His Mighty Works and the earth be filled with glory and justice reign! AMEN!

PROPHETIC WORD: JUNE OF 2000

Prophecy:

"*Many of My people are like children on the playground on a thirty-minute recess from classes. Running to the swings. Whee! Running to the see-saw, up and down, bumpity-bump. Whee!! Running to the slide, up and down. Whee!! Running to the monkey bar, competing, testing their strength and agility, falling to the ground, plunk! Whoops! There goes the bell! No more fun!*"

I believe He's speaking to us about discipleship. Too few are interested in being discipled. Let's think about this.

Disciple is a military word: Webster's. Training to act in accordance with rules; instruction designed to train in proper conduct and action; the training effect of experience, adversity, etc. To bring to a state of order. A disciple is a follower as a pupil to be taught and trained.

Matthew 28:18. Jesus approached and said to them, "All authority in heaven and on earth has been given to Me, go then and make disciples of all the nations, baptizing them into the name of the Father and of the Son and of the Holy Spirit. Teaching them to observe everything that I have commanded you, and behold, I Am with you all the days [perpetually, uniformly, and on every occasion] to the very close and consummation of the age!" It obviously wasn't His plan to get people born again and put them on the battle-field without training.

So the Lord is saying many want the blessing of ministry, the benefit and thrill of the anointing, the joy of celebration, only the thrills and chills!

BUT! Discipline's of the Faith! — I don't know about that! I like the freedom on the playground, under no authority, no discipline or accountability, no responsibility!

Let's talk about the true followers of Jesus Christ! Oh! The miracles were awesome and exciting! The water turned into wine, feeding the five thousand with a boy's lunch!! Calling Lazarus forth out of that tomb, four days dead!! Casting out a legion of demons and seeing all those pigs drown!!

BUT — BUT —! There was all of that rejection and persecution and betrayal and the cross!! Those all-night prayer meetings, all the love, mercy and forgiveness, turning the other cheek! Always sub-mitted to His Father, always submitted to authority, a sacrificial life given for others! A true disciple.

We must be an eager and joyful 'pupil.' A learner, teachable under authority. The Holy Spirit is our 'School Master.' He designs the courses and prepares the 'tests,' purposed to train and prepare us for the spiritual 'vocation' Father God has called us to!

The Classroom: Life! Relationships! Tests! Correction! Discipline! — OH! That hurts! Whittles away at pride! The flesh screams!!

Let's play hooky! I don't want to go through all of this, I don't need fellowship, I already know enough, I don't have time for this! Let's just go have fun on the playground!

6-2-2000 DREAM

Lord, I believe last night was a time of 'ME,' the spiritual man fully present while the natural man slept! I felt so 'unobstructed' as spiritual concepts and visions and revelations flowed unhindered through my 'mind'? 'spirit'? ' being'?

My spirit man was fully alive unto the Holy Spirit! No fleshly interferences. I was acutely aware of the freedom and ability to articulate out of the spirit, and in the dream there was a longing, a desire for this to become a reality in ministry. I was also acutely aware of the difficulty of this 'river' flowing through the flesh man. I was seeing the effect and restrictions of the flow of life because of resentments, offence, pretensions, fears, need for recognition, approval. Even a small blemish or bruise from others not resolved is a hindrance. I began to pray and yield myself up to the Father, knowing this would require much further work for 'The Minister of the interior' on the dismantling of strongholds and ungodly structures and further revealing of the mysteries of the kingdom, as well as the unveiling of Christ to my heart. I began to experience divine love engulfing me, and fear and apprehension leaving. Ecstasy

It really did feel like a 'river' flowing through my being. Your words are life-giving water that must flow from Your throne through our spirit into the earth. I see more clearly "Jesus is The Word [Water], in the beginning was the Word [water] and the Word became flesh and dwelt among us," so we could see it, touch it, feel it, experience it, so we could know what it was when He left, so we would recognize Him, the Word, the Water in His invisible form, the Holy

Spirit! That flowing out of us isn't just a river of love, grace, mercy, healing, tongues, prophecy, authority, peace, life — It is HIM! The Water Of Life! He who drinks of this Water will never thirst again!

Revelation 22: "Come and drink freely of this water of life, at no charge, just the surrender, the humbling of yourself it takes to drink and when you do, you become a part of the supply!"

Lord, I felt something was released in the earth last night that is very significant.

I know You must tear down before You can build up. This is taking place simultaneously. It must be pure water, not filtered through pride, lust, rebellion, stubbornness, unforgiveness, self-pity, immorality or impure thoughts or impure motives. These are all in the outer man, the flesh man and he overpowers or overrules the spiritual man at times. Whatever is released out of the spirit is pure, but if the outer man is not broken into humility, then the soul-self-flesh is mingled with the pure. Grace is in place for this, grace is greater than all our sins. The cross has removed our sins from us as far as the east is from the west, and the power of grace through the Blood will empower us to overcome the flesh and the devil! An absolute need of the revelation 'we have been crucified with Christ.' An 'I die daily,' 'considering myself dead in Christ,' lifestyle! This fountain is in our spirit, everything that is God is in His Spirit within us! We're on a journey of enlightenment, taking us on to greater glory, a body wholly filled and flooded with God Himself! Ephesians 3:19-21! So be it, Lord! There will be a generation that You will bring to this level of glory. In Your great grace, you give us previews of that which is to come, and not only did you give me the dream experience, I am reminded of a few other very special, awesome times when I had similar experiences. I was fully awake when suddenly I was in a place of Your having taken me over and I was in another 'realm,' fully functional. But signs and wonders followed me for three days, and love melted me! I know those were prophetic seeds planted in the earth that will produce a generation that will operate under an anointing that we cannot imagine!

Thank You, Father!

During this 'night vision dream' happening, through my mind began to flow revelation concerning the gates of pearl and the parable of the Pearl of Great Price, hidden in a field. The kingdom of God is as a pearl ... 'and the man sold all he had to obtain it.' It seemed very significant, the Spirit was drawing my attention to gates of pearl and that the entrance to the City of God was through gates of pearl. I began to see a huge oyster, open with a glistening white, perfect huge pearl in the center — and I began to see a form that I knew was Jesus in His earth journey: the world as the oyster, the friction, the pain and disappointments, the rejection and His obedience to His Father unto death that formed and shaped the pearl and how we, the believers, are being formed and shaped in the same way in the oyster of the earth. As we go against the ways of the world and take our position in Christ to obey God, a pearl is being formed — the bride without spot or blemish. I could see why heaven's gates were enormous pearls, symbolic of Christ's sacrifice of obedience, and ours as well. Our earth journey is forming a pearl. "I have been crucified with Christ, it is no longer the 'big I who live,' but Christ lives in me and the life I now live in the body I live by faith — by adherence to the word and complete reliance on the Son of God who loved me and gave Himself for me." Selah

He has crowned us with grace and made us His dwelling place by His Spirit!

I have a river of life inside of me.

Break through, break through and flow out from me to release the power and authority of the Kingdom of God in the earth!

PROPHETIC JOURNAL
AND TEACHINGS

1999, 2000, 2001
Released over the church, 9/16/99

" *J*ust as a new season in the natural is upon you and beginning, so a new season in the spiritual realm is upon you and
beginning. As I have drawn you and called you up to the mountain
of My Presence, and I gave you the seed of My Word and increased
understanding, the word of My instruction, correction, hope and
vision; now in this short season of Autumn you must carefully prepare the ground and quickly plant and attend to it devotedly, to see
and enjoy the harvest before the cold of the winter season sets in!
You will, in the winter season, find newfound joy in relationships
and times of rest. And the fire of the hour will warm you and I will
comfort you and fill you with My peace. My Spirit will bind you
together even in stronger family relationships. The family of God
must be all for one and one for all, giving and receiving and gracing
and gracing! The spirit of strife and contention will attempt to bring
disagreement and division, but through your obedience and the
humbling of yourselves before Me, it will do the opposite! For I will
work all things for the good. And at any time the devil is at work,
you can know he has come to defy Me and attempt through deception to stop and interfere with My plans and purposes and blessings
for you! So, be on guard! Do not allow your emotions to be manipulated! Do not accept excuses for rebellion at any level, fight with

My word, the Word of My grace, and the promises! And pray for discernment! Ask of Me for that which you need and I will supply it!

"Remember, by their fruit you will recognize the true and the false disciples. The true disciples will be known by their love for one another! And by the same measure you will judge your own state of heart and be quick to repent and turn, that you not be judged. Strive for true peace, beware of false peace when your soul has its way and it seems there is harmony in the natural. Look for and seek to know My peace, which is the peace that comes when My Word, My Love and the Voice of the Spirit all agree and your soul surrenders to these! Peace will always be the result of full surrender! Remember, you are My garden, My field being cultivated, conditioned and sown! I AM the Husbandman and the Harvester and the Owner of the harvest! And yet, I have made you to be cultivators and sowers and harvesters! We are co-laborers together and you are inheritors together with Me of the blessing!"

Selah!

10/99

"This visitation, My Presence in your midst in this unique and special way in this time, is not about acquiring more knowledge about Me, or even experiencing the supernatural manifestations of My Spirit. It is about opening your hearts, your spirit, to the powerful touch of My Love!

Sometime it is easier for my precious daughters to receive love, for it is inherent in them to respond to love. But My precious brothers desperately need a touch from Me, to feel and know Love, to let go of pride and the need to be in control, and surrender to Love!

"My people, both men and women, must surrender their feelings to Me! The powerful love relationship between Jesus Christ and His bride, this is very pure and holy indeed! Remember the Apostle John saying, "the disciple whom Jesus loved"? This revival at this time is about overcoming every obstacle in your lives, dear man, dear woman, dear child, to receiving more of My Love SO you will follow Me, respond to Me! I am wooing My Beloved company of Beloveds,

to unashamedly draw ever close to My breast to listen and hear My heartbeat and My slightest whisper. Oh, the comfort! Oh, the peace! Oh, the glory!"

5/3/01 Dream:

I was in this large open room alone. The room was bare. I was talking to the Lord [I don't remember what it was about] and I began to sense His Presence very strongly, and there was a quickening in my spirit and my body. It seemed His presence was filling my body more and more and I was almost crying, the sensation was so glorious. Then it was as if the Holy Spirit filled me so full, earth's gravity could no longer hold me. I began to float or levitate up and around the room or inside the open area. It was so real! This went on for a good while. It was heavenly! Then I found myself in my recliner, but my body kept rising up and then T.W. was there and someone was with him, I do not know who, and T.W. would wrap his arms around my legs and pull me back down into the chair, and I kept saying No! No! Let me go, don't make me stay down! But he wouldn't stop. I was very upset and weeping. I awakened soon afterward, wrote the dream down, and meditated on it. Okay, Lord, I know that in the natural I do feel like that is happening, but what are You saying to me?

He let me know this was not about T.W. This was about me. He only represented 'the cares of this life' and the frustration I was allowing to influence me negatively and interfere with my not pressing on to enter into His Rest and where He wanted to take me in the spirit!

5/25/01 Vivid Dream

I walked upon my porch, and through the door sensed someone there and knew he had a gun. It seemed I knew the possibility of being harmed and made no attempt to run or protect myself. I felt no fear. Suddenly he shot me! I felt the impact of the bullet. It knocked me down and out, and yet I heard the man say as he stood over me, "I'll make sure you are dead," and he shot me again! I felt the impact of the bullet, but felt no pain, and he walked away. I felt detached from my body. Someone else, who I knew lived with me, but I was not aware of who they were, assumed I was dead. He just stood there. After awhile I was able to speak and said, "Help me!" It was like he couldn't hear me, or was ignoring me. I repeated, "Help me!" He didn't respond, and walked away and left me. I managed to crawl to the front yard of a house close by, where a woman lived who I knew was a friend, who I knew could help if I could get to her. I began to cry out, "Get me help, I am dying!" Then I thought, it's a miracle I am not dead, I have been shot at point blank range twice, and I am not dead! God is not going to let me die! He is protecting me! He was my shield!

The woman managed to get me back to my house, and this man who had not helped me earlier was there, as if he lived there. He still ignored me and the situation, very uncaring. With the help of this woman, I insisted he leave, and he did!

Then in the next scene, we were in a hospital ward and this man was on the floor on a pallet or bed on the floor, lying on his back, looking a little fearful. I had a water hose in my hand and I began squirting water in his face and he was helpless! He would sputter, twist and turn, but I would determinedly and gleefully squirt water in his mouth and eyes! This woman and I had him pinned down, standing over him!

Then I awakened suddenly. It was so detailed and shocking, I immediately recorded it and prayed concerning it.

I wish I could say I recalled the dream when the 'attack' came! But afterward, I did remember and read what I had recorded. And I marveled at God's omniscience and omnipresence. I have no words to express the awesome reality of those words that swept over me as I wrote them!

2002 DREAM REVELATION

As a child, I was sitting in the lap of my father in a rather large truck and I was 'driving'! My hands were on the steering wheel, His left hand was on the wheel at the bottom, sort of hidden under my arm. I was aware of how big the steering wheel was and how important it seemed and how good I felt that 'Daddy' and I were going to drive this! His right hand was on the gear shift. I was stretching my toe to the gas pedal, but His foot was on the pedal. The gear shift was like the ones on a big truck; it had twelve gears. As we began to move forward, I felt confident and unafraid, but then as we began to pick up speed and 'Daddy' began to shift gears, I became fearful, knowing I was unable to drive this truck! Then I saw His hand on the wheel and His foot under mine on the pedal and His big hand on the shift and the ride began to be very exhilarating and I was laughing with joy! The windows were down and the wind was blowing my hair back.

My attention was drawn to the numbers of gears. The numbers He emphasized were 5-10-12. And the words: ' trans-mission' and 'transition.'

I began to have an understanding that God was moving the church forward with each shift with predetermined timing and destination. I also heard, "sovereign pronounced change." I awakened and immediately reached for my Bible and pad. Following is what I believe to be the message:

Transmission: Trans — Latin word meaning: across, beyond, through, transference of power or force, a shift,
Process of being sent forward, release of power. Process of transmitting.

'Mission' — a specific task to be accomplished.

Five is where I begin.
5 speed: Number of grace and number of equipping ministries.
I believe the church has been in a time of the equipping ministries setting Christ, the anointed One, and His anointing in place as governmental Head of His Church. Through the giftings and offices of the Holy Spirit operating in the believer, He leads us. And the operation of these fivefold ministry gifts is the power of divine Grace. It is by His Grace we are chosen, given gifts, changed, set in place, prepared and equipped, and as we behold His Face, His Glory, the spirit of Grace works mightily within us! And His Kingdom is built within and around us!

We have shifted and are picking up speed::
10: Number of perfection and divine order. Ten is a corporate and double portion number.
He has been drawing our attention as we have been 'shifting,' to the corporate son. Discerning the 'Lord's body.' This is a relational number, not organizational. No longer me and mine, existing as a local body, operating behind church doors, but merging, linking up. The Body of Christ! Christ the Supreme Head of His body universal! He came to set things in order! To bring Love to perfection is us!

In the dream, I felt He was saying things were accelerating through many shifts, but the big shift coming is setting His apostolic government in place.

12 is a governmental apostolic number. The foundation of His spiritual house, the Apostle and Prophet..
12: Product of 3 and 4 — the divine and earthly and the number of the nations. ["Ask of Me and I will give you the nations"]

As the gears were being 'shifted' into the next position, the motion had to follow a certain pre-determined path. If not followed precisely — there's a lot of 'grinding and noise'! It just won't shift to the next power level unless we follow a predetermined path, unless we are fully responsive to His touch, to His Hand. We can't force it into place, there is a 'flow' we follow! Thank God! His Hand is on the 'shift,' guiding this shifting! So we don't STRIP the GEARS and break down and stop the 'Trans-Mission'! This 'shift' sends us forward with a transference of power for the new season!

The Big Wheel. The eternal realm! Father God, the Alpha and Omega, ever existing and we are In Him. We have been given a sphere of authority to establish the rule of God through the power of His indwelling Spirit! We are the connection, conduit between heaven and earth. Nothing can stop or interfere with God establishing His Kingdom and restoring all things back to Himself. He rules and reigns NOW and will always be Supreme over ALL!! Amen

Joshua 3:1-5, 4:1-7
The church is coming out of the old order into the new governmental order and into the vastness of the Kingdom of God! This transitioning and shifting and change is setting the stage for the restoration of the church back to God's original design and pattern. And restoring back to the church the power and glory it once had! And to do this, He must set in place His divine governmental order! I believe we have been in that 'three day' time period of preparation, and we are the third day church and we are arising!

Hosea 6:1
"Come and let us return to the Lord for He has torn so that He may heal us; He has stricken so that He may bind us up; After two days He will revive us [quicken us give us life] on the third day He will raise us up that we may live before Him!"

The year 2000 did thrust us into a new millennium in the natural realm, but it is even more significant in the spiritual realm. I believe we can all agree the church, as we have known it, will not be the same. We have been in birth-pangs and we're coming through quickened and made alive by the Spirit into a new place, new levels of revelation, faith and love. Moving forward: reformation, transformation, transfiguration!

Before every great move of God, He always exhorted the people to be of good courage, do not fear, be strong. Now obviously if this was going to be an easy campaign, there would be no reason to stress this issue. Be not afraid! We must rid ourselves of fear at every level. Fear is the opposite of trust and a spirit of fear is of the adversary!

We are beginning to understand that God sends forerunners ahead, and until we catch up and our eyes are open and we can began to 'see,' we can't understand!

There are some things in these scriptures that are so relevant today. Just as the church is coming out of an old order and crossing over into a new order, so was the nation of Israel. This is a picture of the progression of true believers and the corporate church.

Joshua 1: God came to Joshua and told him Moses was dead. He of course knew this, but what God was saying to him, the old order is dead, it's gone, now you rise up, lead these people over into the land I promised them. This was not the same as the Red Sea crossing. That was under the old order. Our Joshua. When we are delivered out of bondage, washed in the blood, baptized in water and immersed in the Holy Spirit, our Yeshua Jesus brings us out to bring us into our destiny and inheritance! Where we're going and where we are headed is what the Father is concerned about! We not only have a purpose, but a destiny in the Lord!

One thing we notice that was different between the old Moses order and the Joshua order was a very important thing. In the old Moses order, our enemies and God's enemies were chasing us! But in the new Joshua order, we are pursuing our enemies! Our enemies are not at our backs chasing us — we're pursuing them! "The righteous are bold as a Lion and the wicked flee!" He is on the run! If we draw close to God and resist the devil, he has to flee! So a Joshua order of people are not intimidated by giants, by the enemies of God, we are a people following the Holy Spirit and His purpose in this hour, and we have him on the run and that's why he's counter-attacking! That's a perspective in God we have to get hold of! It's about mandate, dominion, subduing the inhabitants and taking our land of destiny!

Joshua was a man of destiny, with a history. He had crossed the Red Sea and had been through the desert wilderness experience and kept his faith and trust in God and His Word, and he was not going to be denied the Promised Land! He had been faithful and now he was the leader, and now he would take many over the Jordan. Those who went over the Jordan had been born in the desert except Joshua and Caleb. I believe God is saying we have to know our history and from where we have come. We don't live back there, but we build on that so we know where we're headed as God's people. As we continue to move forward in this progression, we must avoid the 'ideal' of 'the newer — the truer' and the 'latest is the greatest'! and conserve what is true and right and good! The surest way forward is always first to go back, seeking to always be faithful to the good news of Jesus Christ and to the scriptures. He is our standard measurement for righteousness, and His word is our standard for His ever-proceeding Word! We confess that we have betrayed our beliefs by our behavior all too often. We have trumpeted the gospel of Jesus, but we have replaced biblical truths with therapeutic techniques, worship with entertainment, discipleship with growth in human potential, church growth with business entrepreneurship, and trying to meet real needs with pandering to 'felt' needs, and marketing concepts. In the process, we have become known for a commercial, diluted and 'feel good' gospel of wealth, human potential and religious happy talk, which is indistinguishable from the surrounding world. That said, let's go on!

At one time, the old order was the new order. When Moses led them 'out' from Egypt, that was new compared to living 'in' Egypt. In the desert, that old order was dying off because of unbelief and disobedience. But all the while, the new order was coming up! Now when we think about these things, we like for God to do something quickly. Patience has not had its perfect work. We are a 'drive through' generation! But God phases out the old and brings up the new. The new IS coming up!. We need to be encouraged, we are 'moving' on !

A new order Joshua church comes up out of the river and takes cities! Thank You, Lord, for the refreshing of the river, for the thunderstorms and downpour and even the 'dew.' We need Your touch! A fresh anointing. A deeper revelation of Your kind of Love!

The new order Joshua church is commanded by the Lord to take communities, cities and nations! Once again, it's not all in the 'sweet bye and bye,' because the earth is the Lord's and the fullness thereof, and He has declared it will be filled with His glory as the waters cover the sea!

The Lord's inheritance is to be 'received' by the meek so Jesus has His full inheritance in the earth!!

New order Joshua church, the apostolic government, came out of the river! Remember, they pulled twelve stones up out of the river? There are many apostles, but there were twelve apostles of the Lamb! After He went to heaven, there were many apostles. Ephesians 4 tell us He ascended and He gave gifts to the church, Apostles, Prophets, Pastor/Teachers, and Evangelists for the perfecting and maturing of the body of the Lord Jesus Christ, for the works of the ministry until we all come to the fullness of faith!

I believe the church in this hour is coming into apostolic government out of the strength of the river! This apostolic government is not being established by religion, but this one is being established out of the anointing of the river! And you know before they passed over, they sent twelve Levites carrying the ark and twelve more men picking up a stone on each man's shoulder. Shoulder means government. Upon the Messiah's shoulder is God's government [Isaiah 9]. Stone speaks of Jesus, the Cornerstone of God's House, He being the Head of the church being built with living, lively stones. We are His shoulders! The church is being built now upon the foundation of the Apostles and Prophets. Hallelujah! [Coming out of the river, and yet having to stay in the deep of the river, continually 'over our' heads, suspended in the Spirit to be 'carriers' of the glory!] The church will be the church!

When we see this apostolic government in the church, we are going to see more glorious things in the church and outside the church walls! We will see the works of Jesus like we have never seen! Just like the crossing of the Jordan was more glorious than coming out of Egypt, because coming out of Egypt involved Moses with a staff in his hand, up in the air, believing God! But Psalm 106 says the people at the Red Sea were in rebellion! The only reason they wanted to get out was because Pharaoh was breathing down their necks! They were not full of faith! Only Moses basically believed when he lifted his rod up and the sea split. It didn't take faith to go through, it was the only way of escape!

But at the Jordan River, Joshua didn't raise up a rod. The old way would not have worked. The Lord said to take the Levites and get that ark and get them out there. The Jordan was at flood tide. Jeremiah says at flood tide it was a maze of jungle full of lions! Now faith is not walking through the water after it parted — faith is stepping in before the water splits! Once they stepped in, that water parted and they put that Ark in the middle of the Jordan and 2 million people crossed over! Twelve men carrying that ark, not one man, corporate anointing! This was a whole nation believing God! Twelve Levites and twelve men carrying stones. Twenty-four represents nations and governmental anointing. A whole nation got baptized that day!

He's putting us together as stones as a glorious House of Zion! Coming out of the river under apostolic government, fulfilling God's purpose to take the earth out of the hands of the enemy and give it back to God, because the Bible says the nations are going to make up Jesus' inheritance!

The church is moving into the latter glory. It is harvest time!

Be encouraged! Stay in the "truck," enjoy the ride as Daddy presses on the accelerator and shifts the gears! It will get a little "scary" and challenging and death-defying! Just keep remembering "WHO" is driving and don't get focused on the "destination," or you'll miss all the MARVELS along the WAY!!

MOVING ON

The church purchased a house, to be used as a safe house for anyone needing ministry. Franke would move in as housemother.

It seemed our home continued to be filled with those coming and going for ministry. There was a family working for the airlines, living in Fort Worth, who were driving back and forth on weekends to attend church and receive ministry. Three children were living at home and very needy. They wanted to get the children in a better situation and enroll them in school in Cross Plains. This is one of those 'long' stories I'll try to shorten! They ended up moving in upstairs and driving back and forth to work! And I definitely was in 'full-time' ministry!

Pat had decided to sell our mother's farm. Max and Norma were living in town and they wanted a place, so Pat worked with them and they bought our home place! This gave us all great comfort! They rented their house to the Duran's. They moved back to Fort Worth after a few years, but heart connections remain. Many deposits were made into their lives, and we have seen a blessed harvest. Some of the children come 'home' to Max and Norma's frequently, staying accountable to Father Max!

There was never a 'dull' moment in the Father's House! Many signs and wonders continued to manifest around us and the people God had connected us to. After experiencing the gold dust, then came gold fillings and other miracles in the mouth! This was happening frequently in several meetings we attended. Then the Lord graced us with the manifestation in our midst of teeth filled with gold, continuing to awaken us to the reality of His Presence, His Glory and Power. We made the yearly FMCI conferences, which were always such a blessing in so many ways, as well as staying in contact with regional ministries. We hosted a conference each year as well, and there was always awesome fellowship and communion with God the Holy Spirit and with one another.

Gene had moved in with us to help take care of T.W. It was a very challenging situation, very sad. I was beginning to show signs of 'wear and tear,' and our family doctor began to talk with me about a nursing home for T.W. Randy and Donny were making trips as often as they could, and of course we had an awesome support group around us, but it was just tough. In 2002, he went into a nursing home in Abilene. Donny, Beverly and Richard had come to visit and help me with the situation. Robert called: Lois was back in the hospital, her sister could only stay a week, and could I come? So Donny stayed with T.W. and got him settled in the nursing home and I took off for Arkansas for two weeks. It was very difficult for all of us. There was much grace and always wonderful times with the Lord. Without Him, we just could not make it through. T. W. was in the nursing home a year and made many friends with the residents, praying for people, counseling and helping everyone he could. He was a blessing. He passed February 23, 2003. Donny had to leave the day before to go back to Corpus to get Lori. All the family drove back the following day in the worst ice and snowstorm we had seen in several years! He and Randy drove through barricades and no telling what else to make it through! Lacey was already there with me when T.W. went home. He had suffered much. It was over and he was free.

Lois had been writing a book of her journey, ***Running as Fast as I Can.*** It was a beautiful testimony of the Lord's grace and faithfulness and her love for Him and her faith. She had been a runner, which helped her to get through those years. It was published and their church had a book signing event for her and she wanted me to be there. Also, it was impossible for her to get up and down the stairs anymore, so she wanted me to help her find a house. We got all of that done, their home sold quickly, they moved into their new home, and then things took a turn for the worst. Donny and I drove up to stay a few days so they could talk and say their goodbyes. They had been truly brother and sister through the years, always there for each other. They laughed and cried and relived old times. Donny told her it made sense that God would take her home before the rest of us, so she could get everything ready the way she wanted it before we got there! She was a 'take charge, get it done right' leader! Her battle ended eight years after it began. She passed May of 2002.

I didn't realize how close I was to a breakdown, emotionally and physically. For several months, I don't think I knew who I was. It was a very difficult time. Much grieving. I was so grateful for my children and family, my beautiful home and the peacefulness of my surroundings. And for the family of Living Water.

River City fellowship was transitioning to become RCHP. The pastors, Billy and Angie, had been interning at Mike Bickle's House of Prayer in Kansas City for a few years, and felt this ultimately was their call to San Antonio. Glenda and Jamie, the worship leaders of LWM, had been participating in their conferences leading praise and worship. They began to feel called to that ministry for a season. This was difficult for us, especially Max and Norma, but we knew the girls had heard from the Lord, and of course Billy and Angie were in agreement. So we released them to go and with our blessings. The apostolic prophetic anointing that is upon them is quite amazing, and Holy Spirit uses them for breakthrough and opening portals. There were others God had prepared to step up for our worship team for the next few years, and God kept moving us on and blessing us mightily.

AUTHORITY SHIFT

May of 2003 was a season of joy! There was something in the 'air' and our spirits were 'lifted.' I was experiencing an inappropriate 'giddiness' at times. Within I was just joyful, regardless of the circumstances! As we progressed through the months, there were times during services when an anointing of His love for the body would just overwhelm me, I would be weeping and hugging on every one, even grabbing some of the ladies as they walked by and setting them in my lap, like a mother would a child, and weep and hold them! It was weird! But Jesus just had to caress and hold His dearly loved ones. And they realized it was Him. It was certainly strengthening and healing for me, supernaturally. The anointing, Christ the Anointed One, Who is Love Personified, breaks the yoke of trauma, grief and pain and enables us to move forward!

In September of 2003, I was in prayer and intercession [always with my notebook in my lap!], and the Holy Spirit said:

This Ship, [LWM] one in the fleet of our Commander-in-Chief, is continuing to sail into uncharted waters with each wave of the Holy Spirit lifting her and moving her forward, the Wind of the Spirit catching her sails and moving her steadily on her determined course. She has been fitted out by the Lord Christ for the journey she must take, and He has set the sails to stay the course! She will not fail to fulfill her purpose and destiny. No storm is powerful enough to capsize her, no beast of the sea is fierce enough to prevent her from delivering her cargo and fulfilling her assignment!

Others may see her as tossed, torn and battered for a season, but she will come through with His brightness shining and in glorious triumph!

Then He said, "It is time for an authority shift!" Max and I were to exchange positions! "You have taken LWM as far as you can. I AM placing a new mantle of apostolic and prophetic authority upon Max to lead the church into deeper uncharted waters of kingdom purpose! This is not demotion for you but promotion as well. I am extending your boundaries! As always, this has far-reaching implications and is for more than I can show you at this time."

He let me know that Billy and Angie would come and apostolically establish this before the church.

I was worshiping and praising the Lord and began to sing a little joyful song of the Spirit!

"Third day church arising! No more compromising! No more one-man show, teamwork, don't you know! Kings and priests we are, gone through the fire! And we are not for hire! We are sons of Jehovah Jirah!"

I had known this day would come and had watched it unfold by the hand of the Lord. So often I had felt like a mother making a way for her child to move forward. He gave me instructions to ordain three ministry coordinators, and to set Franke in as head of the intercessors and prayer coordinator. And Max and I were to start receiving a set amount of income each month.

I was weeping, tongues flowing like a river. I called Max, he was still sleeping [he worked shifts at 3M], and he started to interrupt me as I was pouring out all of this. I 'very strongly ' told him to be quiet and listen to every word I was saying while I was under the anointing! Father was speaking! He shared with me later how the Presence of the Lord engulfed him and also that He had been dealing with him concerning retiring early from 3M and give the ministry his full time!

I called Billy after I spoke to Max, and he was in awe of all the Lord had done with me and us through the years, and as always there was so much more to this than we could know. HE was continuing to work HIS plan!

Once again, I stood with arms uplifted, my mouth full of praise and my heart in awe! Of course my mind shifted to the few years back when satan attempted a 'takeover' and to wreck havoc with the purpose and destiny of many! And how God fought for us and did not allow what He had purposed to be destroyed! And now, according to HIS plan and HIS timing, an authority shift would take place. It would be given, not stolen! And Max would be set in place and I would stand by his side as second-in-command! And Norma, as always, the pillar in the middle!

The message I shared with the church the following Sunday morning:

Vision I had received 1/3/03:

Numberless people, young and old, pressing in, demanding the enthroning of a King! It looked like an insurrection, a revolution. It was all very passionate as they were crying out with upraised arms! God the Holy Spirit said, "There is a change in government taking place in the earth! It's being changed from a democracy to a theocracy! There is a King, only One, the God King Jesus. He is being enthroned in the hearts of His people and His Kingdom is increasing and spreading rapidly!"

As I meditated on the vision I was led to Micah 4:1

"But in the latter days it shall come to pass the mountain [government, kingdom] of the house of the Lord shall be established as the highest of the mountains; and it shall be exalted above the hills, and peoples shall flow to it." I believe He will be revealed in His Bride the Church before He comes at the end of the age in the clouds of glory, and every eye shall see Him.

Looking back at the part that prophecy, visions and dreams has played in the founding and raising up of LWM and in my own life and all of yours as well, it is PROFOUND! They cast vision, revealed and strengthened our purpose, established our identity, and gave us guidance and assurance beyond measure! All of the ways the Lord communicates with His people is to strengthen our relationship with Him, our trust and confidence in His love for us, and through us the culture will be changed and His kingdom will spread, and certainly through all the giftings and anointings of Holy Spirit! It is all through His empowerment.

Psalm 127:1. If God doesn't build the house, they labor in vain who build it.

We are still under construction! There is no place where we take over! No, there is less and less of us and more of Him! He came to rule and reign in the hearts of His people and His government will be established.

I want to remind us of the vision Father God set before us as a called out people of His kingdom, what He has named us or called us. We need to be reminded of the work He has called us to, the assignments we have been given, the glimpses He has given us of ' things to come' as HE continues to flood our understanding with 'Light' to enable us to be 'a part' of His body, functioning smoothly with other parts of the body.

Colossians 2:19; "Holding fast to the Head from Whom the entire body, supplied and knit together by means of its joints and ligaments, grows with a growth that is from God." Paul says: "Now you collectively are Christ's body and individually you are members of it, each part severally and distinct, each with its own place and function." We must begin to 'see' with more clarity the corporate son, and understand the Lord is not into conformity but community. It is the multi-faceted body of Christ, expressing the multi-faceted nature of God, each body part and organ with gifts, anointings, and callings, purposed of God. Living stones being shaped, chiseled and formed to fit into the walls of His spiritual house, His Tabernacle in the earth. God the Holy Spirit draws and divinely connects people together who will 'fit' together, unity through the Spirit, for divine purpose. He creates the 'joint,' the 'organ,' the part of the body to connect to another part of the body to form a whole, healthy body and supernaturally His kingdom is spreading, His House is being constructed as a place for all people called by His Name! His power and marvelous works are manifesting all over the place and His glory is experienced and seen all over the earth! And we begin to

SEE JESUS in HIS GLORY, in His Church! Can you see it?! Okay, let's move on!

He has given us personal names and corporate names. Names to live up to through our relationship with Him and obedience out of our love for Him. He said, "I will give you a new name, a name no man knows, only God." He also said we would be called by His name! I don't really care what man calls me, I care what He calls me and I want to hear Him when He calls me! Let's hear some of the names He called us when we were born again of His Spirit, when we gave our lives to Christ. Righteous! Sons of God! Holy! Free! Delivered! Priest and kings! Saints! The Called! Witnesses! Then He named some Apostles, Prophets, Teachers, Evangelists, Healers, Workers of miracles, Administrators, Helpers! And the wonderful news is, what He has called us, He by His Spirit will work in us and will provide an abundant supply of His grace and Spirit to anoint us and prepare us as vessels He can work through, and the 'river' will be loosed to flow from us! I'm telling you! This 'flood' that is covering the earth is the River of God, flowing from under the door of the threshold of His Temple! Who is the temple? Where is the river? Where is the kingdom? Put your hand on your belly and declare, "Out of my innermost being shall flow rivers of living water, this He spoke of the Spirit!" Come on, Church!

The Holy Spirit was specific in naming us. He said clearly we were to be called Living Water Ministries Fellowship, not just "ministry," but "ministries" that would pour out living water! This brought some identification and cast vision before us and set us on course. Before the visitation of the Lord, He had planted in my heart a revelation of the process of restoration according to God's plan and purpose, as set forth in scriptures. I began to understand 'reformation' and 'restoration' on the path to 'transfiguration'! The partial understanding of the third day church rising in the earth, and a partial understanding of the corporate son emerging. When the Holy Spirit called me up and out of the church 'box,' 'denominational box,' out of my darkened understanding into His marvelous Light, it was and is and will forever be AMAZING! And AWESOME! I can say now, I didn't know the terms then. I was given Kingdom vision in my generation. I was being moved along by the Holy Spirit in the current of the river called, "It's Time" and I've been 'moving' ever since! Halle! I believed in the restoration and the glory that was coming back to the church and the absolute need for God's government and order set in place through the five-fold ministry offices and giftings and the restoring of the apostle and prophet to the church. Paul said, "You've not had many fathers." This was certainly true at my beginnings.

Building had begun in earnest! In the early years of this revelation, I didn't fit in too well in the organized church! I was rather isolated until He began to connect me to a few of the multiplied thousands in the earth whom God was raising up and gathering together and bringing to the forefront. What a mighty work the Holy Spirit has done in seemingly such a short time. And in this hour, the Patriarchs and Matriarchs are coming forth for the discipling and training up of the sons of God. HE is truly in the House and in the earth, ruling and reigning! I have no doubt He will finish what He has begun in His Church and in the earth, and the knowledge of His Glory shall fill the whole earth, and His kingdom will be on the earth as it is in Heaven!

The day King Jesus was born on this earth, the Kingdom of God on earth began! He came to bring the gift of redemption to all those who would come to believe in Who He was, the prophesied Messiah, Savior of the world! He came to become the sacrifice required, that through His Holy Blood, fellowship would be restored with our Creator as sons of God, inheritors with Christ Jesus the Lord, the First Born Pattern Son!

Besides the prophecy released from within the fellowship, God continued to send His ministers to us, bringing His word for the hour and season. And with each new revelation and prophecy, we would go through a season of shaking and change and growing, preparing us to walk in what He had called us and shown us of His will and plan for us. Some of those new names released over us were: An intensive care unit, and gave us Luke 10:30-37; special services core; little Bethlehem, where Jesus would be revealed and worshipped and gifts of sacrifice, worship and joy would be brought to Him; a young David, giant slayer, a battle-axe in His Hand, pioneering, breakthrough anointing, incubator for nurturing gifs and callings. Apostolic and prophetic, sending others out to the nations. A Tekoah, school of the prophets; an Antioch church with great grace upon us, God's favor upon us for His manifest Presence and great grace operating in us and through us to one another as we go through the process of being changed from glory to glory! Wow! Talk about being living proof of "but God chooses the insignificant, the weak, the small to show Himself Mighty, that we can only boast in Him and bow before Him!

LWM is twelve years old this year! It is the number of government, and has to do with rule. The product of three, which is a divine number, and four, that which is earthly or material. Twelve is three multiplied by four — hence it denotes that which can scarcely be explained in words but which the spiritual can appreciate. It denotes fruitfulness, multiplication and increase!

I remind you of the visitation and vision in '92, the year of the beginning of LWM, with an emphasis on Ezekiel 37, Nehemiah 2 and 4.

And the night vision in '02 concerning the 'big truck ride with Father'! One of the things He said: "There is coming a pronounced 'shift,'" and the church was coming into order governmentally. In the vision I was only aware of up to the number twelve. That doesn't mean that's the year of the end of this age! Even though things are accelerating and this glory train is movin' on, we have a long way to go yet!

We have been in our building ten years! Ten being the number of completeness of order, completed cycle, marking the entire round of a thing. Also a corporate number.

Max is in his eighth year. The number of a new era or order, and of resurrection!

A few days ago, as I was on the porch praying and seeking the lord, I was enveloped in His spirit with much intercession and weeping, and He said, "It is time for an authority shift." Max and I were to exchange positions! "You have taken the fellowship as far as you can take it. I am placing a new mantle of apostolic and prophetic authority upon Max to lead the church into deeper uncharted waters of kingdom purpose! This is not demotion for you but promotion as well, as I am extending your boundaries. As always, this has far reaching implications that I cannot show you at this time." So it is a completion of a cycle for me, and a new beginning for Max and the church. As we transition together in the days ahead, a familiar verse of scripture kept coming to mind, Matthew 6:33, "Seek [aim at and strive after] first of all His kingdom and His righteousness [His way of doing and being right], and then all these things taken together will be given you besides!"

We are to seek God's rule and righteousness, His government in our lives. The kingdom is not some 'thing' that we seek, we're seeking a Person and a right relationship with Him. I know you are aware of this. The Holy Spirit is reminding us and encouraging us to persevere.

Psalm 27:4-8, "One thing I have desired of the Lord, that I will seek after, that I may dwell in the house of the Lord all the days of my life, to behold the beauty of the Lord and to inquire in His temple. When You, Lord, said, seek My Face, my heart said to You, Your face, Lord, I will seek."

We are seeking a face-to-face relationship with God. Out of that relationship, God will continue to add all things we need to our lives. We are to live our lives unto the Lord and our needs are met out of the overflow of His life! When we are in this kind of relationship, we don't have to ask, they are graciously added to our lives by the Father, because our hearts are set upon knowing Him!

Seeking is a process. Asking is an act. Seeking takes time. If I ask you for a gift of money, you might give it to me, but if I go to the mountain to search for gold, it will require something much more of me. If I seek and find a treasure, it's not a gift, it's a reward for my diligent searching.

Hebrews 11:6, "Without faith it is impossible to please Him. He is a rewarder of them that diligently seek Him"

There is a type of faith preached for years that asks and receives from God, but there is a deeper realm, another type of faith that is seeking and finding. Something that is not given until it is found.

Proverbs 25:2, "It is the glory of God to conceal a thing, but the honor of Kings is to search out a matter."

Jeremiah 29:13, "You shall seek Me and find Me when you shall search for Me with all your heart."

1 Corinthians 2:9, "What eye has not seen and ear has not heard and has not entered into the heart of man all that God has prepared, made and keeps ready, for those who love Him."

We are not only to seek Him, but we are to seek to excel in spiritual gifts [1 Corinthians 12]. We are to seek to prophesy to build up the corporate son, and the gift of tongues is to be sought after and practiced for personal edification, revelation and the prophetic. There is more than desiring the gifts of the Spirit, and that is to LIVE by the Spirit, and walk in LOVE. You and I both know this shift will take us way beyond where we have been and what revelation we have received up to this point, and obviously the Holy Spirit is directing us to a season of 'seeking' and experiencing God at another level, coming into another level of maturity in our giftings, but more than that, that faith and love might abound more and more as we move forward together.

I commend you for your walk of love, the grace and mercy that has been extended to me and the leadership through these years and all the prayers and encouragement. In all of my failings and choices that were not always the best, I believe I can say before our Lord and King, I was transparent and accountable before Him and you. I was so honored to be called to serve His people, and my heart was always to care for you and love you as He would. I have been honored to be on this journey with all of you, and plan to continue until the Lord says otherwise. I believe you will support Max and Norma and come into agreement with the Lord's plans and be in prayer for Max and me as we shift into another 'gear,' that we are able to follow the 'flow of the Spirit' as we transition, and there be no 'grinding or stripping' of the gears and the 'transmission' is smooth! We are in awe at the Lord's faithfulness to us and are excited for the coming days. We lean heavily upon your prayers and intercession for us and the body.

I want to leave you with this: John 1:14, "And The Word [Christ] became flesh [human, incarnate] and tabernacled [fixed His tent] among us; and we actually saw His glory [His honor, His majesty], such glory as an only begotten son receives from his father, full of GRACE and TRUTH." His glory was seen in His compassion, mercy, forgiveness, sacrifice, holiness and purity, as well as the miracles and His conversation. He was full of grace and truth. His Glory is His Goodness and Grace in demonstration!

He is a fountain overflowing. We receive Him, we receive from Him. The best and greatest saint cannot live without Him! The meanest and weakest may live by Him. This excludes all boasting. Jesus was full of grace, so he was qualified to intercede, to take our place. He was full of truth, which qualified Him to instruct, lead and guide us and be our example.

As the branches receive sap from the root, as the air draws light from the sun, as the pool receives water from the fountain, so we receive grace from the One Who overflows with grace. So great a gift, so rich, so valuable! We have received no less than GRACE! Paul said, "Oh the unsearchable riches of His Grace! It is blessing poured out that there shall not be room to receive it!" It is FREE for the TAKING! For the RECEIVING! But have you received it in salvation and in the baptism of Holy Spirit, and like the Galatians are now in bondage and are trying to earn God's approval? Earn the blessings? Operate in the kingdom through self-effort, controlled by the old nature?

As that grace does its work upon your soul, the grace we receive from Christ changes us into that same image and we overflow with that grace upon those around us so His Glory can be experienced! Grace is the performance or reality of all Old Testament promises! It is the substance of all Old Testament types and shadows. Jesus, the true Passover lamb, the true manna from heaven. They had grace in pictures, we have Grace in TRUTH!

Passing the staff

In February of '04, Pastors Billy and Angie came to officially oversee setting Max in as Senior Pastor before the church. It was an awesome service. The Presence of the Lord was so heavy upon us all as I passed the staff of leadership to Max, and prophecy was flowing.

Angie's word over me: Father, the cross that she took, the death that she took, Father, death is a weapon! Show us, Lord, how death is a weapon against the enemy, just as you were hanging on the cross, Lord Jesus, and the devil had thought he'd won and he was kicked in the face forever. You disarmed the principalities through your death on the cross, and just as this death of this cross has taken place in Colleen, there has been in the spirit realm a disarming of the religious principalities in this city and this region, and what is done in Heaven will be manifest on this earth! Her eyes will see it, we will no longer say, 'Oh, when she is gone it will happen.' No, it is going to happen now, her eyes will see it happen and Father, You're turning the cross into a staff, a shepherd's staff in her hand. The cross of Cross Plains has now become a shepherd's staff in her hand and mighty signs and wonders will come from this staff, just like Moses when he threw down his rod and it became a serpent and he picked it up and it became a rod again. This is going to release miracles in this region, mighty signs and wonders from the death of a cross to the staff of a shepherd, signs and wonders shall come forth in Jesus' Name.

Billy's prayer and word: I declare that every slanderous word spoken against her through these years, through these years of perseverance, of hanging in there, stick-to-it-ness, I declare in the Name of Jesus the blessings of God tenfold over you because of the humility you have shown. There is a new anointing, a new grace coming to her, a new level, a promotion. This wasn't demotion, this was a promotion. Colleen, in the Name of Jesus, you have been pro-moted in the Kingdom. God says, "It's not just this flock, you have inherited a golden heritage of His flock wherever you go. God gives grace to the humble and humility is created unto unity."

Billy prayed over Max: "Father, we thank You for Max. We thank You for the wisdom that is on this man, even by the evidence of the color of his hair. Lord, I declare in the Name of Jesus that Max would not try to fill her shoes, her shoes won't fit Max, and you don't look good in high heels, Max, so don't try to put on Colleen's shoes. We declare that Max is to be who Max is in Christ Jesus. I declare the anointing of God is rising up in the five-fold giftings of God and in the apostolic gift that he has. He's the thumb that can touch all the other fingers, and I declare in the Name of Jesus he will function, oh God, at new levels of the prophetic and oh God, even now You are adjusting the apostolic mantle upon him for greater authority. The gifts and calling of God upon your life are without repentance, Max, and as I wrap my arms around you in the name of Jesus, I want to prophetically picture the Father's arms wrapped around His boy, the Father is so proud of you, He is so in love with you, He just loves you, Max, and He wants you to know that His burden is easy and His yoke is light and the government does rest upon His Shoulders. Father, we thank You for the way he has proven himself under Colleen. He has walked the walk and he has talked the talk, and he has been trustworthy. Thank You, Father, that this was not something he took from her, Lord, even as Absalom would want to take something, even as others would try to take something, this man has not taken anything. It was given to him. As there were three anointings upon David, I believe, Max, there was a time when you heard the Lord say, "One day you will pastor this church," and then there was a time a few months back when Colleen made it known to you and the church you would be taking this position. I declare that this is the third anointing, Max, and now it is not just that you are going to rule in Hebron, you're going to rule in Jerusalem, the place of God's Presence. I declare a deposit of God's Presence into this place, even more so than it has ever been, in the Name of Jesus! Now Father, I declare in the Name of Jesus that Max will take this congregation where You say to go, and because he does not trust in the arm of the flesh but leans upon the Lord with all of his heart, You will certainly make his paths straight and his future glorious! I now call Max into his position in a maximum sort of way, in Jesus'

Name! I call this church to its maximum now in the body of Christ in Cross Plains!"

Angie prayed over Max: "I have a word for you, Max, from the Lord that I want you to pray about. It's Jeremiah 16:15-17, but specifically 16:16, and I'm gonna call forth in you this morning something from this word.

"And the Lord said, 'I call forth for you this day, because from this day forward, Colleen prophesied in her house today, from this day forward every day will be a "marked day." And I call forth in Max the fisher and the hunter. The time of the man has come, the time of "father" has come, as Father's children have been driven out by their own iniquity into mountains and hills and cliffs of rocks, into hiding, into religious bondage serving other gods, behold! This day I AM anointing you, I AM sending you, Max, in your maximum gifting. I want the max from you, Max! You give Me the max and I'll take care of the "minimum." You, Max, are what I want for Me. I want the maximum out of you to Me, for I Am very jealous for you.' And now the Lord spoke this phrase to me that he gave Billy in his secret place. As you hunt for Heaven, Maximum, that's your new name in the spirit, Maximum. As you hunt for Heaven, you will hunt out the sons of God out of the mountains, out of the hills, out of the cliffs of the rocks, into their destinies in the Kingdom. You will fish them out as a fisher, you will fish them out of religious bondage, out of religion into Father relationships. So by faith I call forth the hunter and the fisher, the time of man has come, your whole life was molding you and shaping you for this moment, Maximum. For this moment you were molded and shaped. You learned about farming and horses and hunting. You are the hunter and fisher of our Savior's finest hour in this region! I call forth for you right now, fish them out of the mountains, hunt them out of the rocks and the hills. Hunt them out of their religious bondage, fish them out of hell into their destinies in the kingdom! And I say to you, Max, the Father is calling the maximum from you. You are able, you will have the anointing and the authority. If you will give Him the max, He will take care of all the minimums! We seal it up, Father, with Your signet ring.

For I have written a decree from the heart of Esther. I have written a decree in this place and it will be so in Jesus' Name. Amen!"

My exhortation:

The Holy Spirit said: "You are having a kingdom experience in order to experience Kingdom reality. I am dealing with you as sons, not as children."
I felt to read over us Matthew 11:12 and 16:19.

"And from the days of John the Baptist until the present time, the kingdom of heaven has endured violent assault, and violent men seize it by force [as a precious prize — a share in the heavenly kingdom is sought with most ardent zeal and intense exertion.]"

"I will give you the keys of the kingdom of heaven; and whatever you bind [declare to be improper and unlawful] on earth must be what is already bound in heaven; and whatever you loose [declare lawful] must be what is already loosed in heaven."

The kingdom is being entered by desperate people with intense interest and deep need. They press their way into the kingdom! The formula of Jesus' ministry was disregarded by His people and He said the people were acting like domineering children who blamed their companions for being spoilsports! He spoke in irony, chiding them when He said, "They were so wise in their criticism — Wisdom is justified by her children." Let's look at the scene here: children playing in the street, boys were saying, 'We wanted to play at wedding' [the round dance done by boys]. We wanted to play at funeral [mourning dirge done by women]. They said John was a mad man because he fasted when they wanted to make merry, and Jesus was a glutton and a wine-bibber because He ate and socialized with the sinners.
The point Jesus was making: "All the people wanted to do was play childish games while missing the Kingdom!" Children, unspiritual, versus mature sons. [1 Corinthians 3:2-3] They were in the kingdom and the kingdom was in them. They were experiencing

the liberty and blessing, but the kingdom was not advancing within them or around them because of the carnal nature, men of the flesh in whom the carnal nature predominates under the control of ordinary impulses! They were infants in their new life in Christ, unable to talk yet. It is one thing to have knowledge about something, but quite another thing to have understanding and revelation that brings transformation.

We are kingdom people. Kings and priests unto our God. Servants to His body, a holy sacrifice through His Blood, unto our God, given the keys of authority to lock up and unlock. To reign over the flesh, old nature, and the devil in the power of His Spirit, advancing His Kingdom!

It is not 'church as usual,' nor has it ever been for us! We are under new orders, new direction, ever on the move! Max has not walked this way before. The word of the Lord to Joshua as they were crossing over the Jordan at high tide: "You have not been this way before, Maximum! Be strong, vigorous and very courageous, be not afraid, neither be discouraged, for the Lord your God is with you wherever you go." The water parted as they followed the ark into the Jordan. As Max follows the 'ark,' the Holy Spirit is working in him, 'working him over,' positioning him comfortably beneath the mantle that has been placed upon Him by the Father. Man did not call him and 'set' him in place, we only confirm and prophetically act out what has already been established in heaven and purposed of God according to His plan! Max has for eight years followed the 'ark.' He has been a submitted son and conducted himself with honor. He has never followed man. If I had ever tried to be his 'god' at any level, had tried to 'steward' rather than 'host' the Holy Spirit, he would have 'high-tailed' it out of here long ago!

He has been set here, in this place, but it is also about the body of Christ and the advancing of His kingdom, not only here but to the nations. "God has set some in the church for His use."

It's never been easy, and it won't get any easier! It will become more glorious! Metamorphosis is taking place. Maturation. A steady ascent to the mountain of transfiguration! We have been selected, chosen of God to be positioned on the earth, in a specific nation, country, city, place, family in our generation. Acts1:7, "It is not for you to become acquainted with and know what 'time' brings [the things and events of time and their definite periods] or fixed years and seasons [their critical niche in time], which the Father has appointed [fixed and reserved], by His own choice and authority and personal power!"

This is the day of the Lord and many are fainting. A hundredfold calling and a thirty fold commitment! It is a day of decision. It is always a day of decision! What do we really want? How bad do we want it? What are we willing to pay, to give up, to die for? How fast and how far will we run? Kingdom people are to rule and reign with Jesus NOW! Not every Christian will rule and reign. Multiplied millions will be serving the Lord in the light they have. The Father does not love them any less.

Within Max is the voice of a king, urging us on, raising the banner, as well as the staff of the gentle shepherd, leading us to green pastures and still waters and urging us to drink. I encourage all of us to awake and arise to the challenge set before us. Those who do will become as David's mighty men and will die 'custom designed' deaths to the self-life.

It's closet time! Seeking, pressing, listening, worshipping, praying and fasting time! I close by praying this pray over us all. Philippians 1:9-11:

"And this I pray; that your love may abound yet more and more and extend to its fullest development in knowledge and all keen insight [that your love may display itself in greater depth of acquaintance and more comprehensive discernment], so that you may surely learn to sense what is vital, and approve and prize what is excellent and of real value [recognizing the highest and the best, and distinguishing the moral differences], and that you may be untainted and pure and unerring and blameless [so that with hearts sincere and certain and unsullied, you may approach] the day of Christ not stumbling nor causing others to stumble. May you abound in and be filled with the fruits of righteousness [of right standing with God and right doing] which comes through Jesus Christ the Anointed One, to the honor and praise of God, that His glory may be both manifested and recognized! Amen!"

BURNT STONES

8/30/03 Message:

Word of the Lord, February '02: *"I have taken the 'burnt stones,' the foolish and the weak, insignificant and despised and I have made them a mighty army of mighty men and it has been by My Mighty Right Arm! It is time for My Coronation in My House and before all heaven and earth! I AM ready for the marriage to My betrothed! How beautiful is My beloved in her adornments and holy garments! How sweet is the fragrance of her love and obedience! My warrior bride! She is the battle-ax in My Hand!"*

There have been, in my lifetime, three distinct moves or outpourings of the Spirit in revival that called out or 'thrust' out a people, 'burnt stones,' that began to be laid in the foundation of the third day church. The church is now beginning to take on a form, the image of Christ is emerging, signs of the kingdom are increasing. Because of the refiner's fire, the 'living stones' have been exposed to a kind of testing that causes them to be stronger and more valuable.

In Nehemiah 4:1-2, there were taunts and accusations from the enemy — "God isn't in this, all you've done up to this point has been in vain. All your sacrifices have been for nothing. You can't finish this work. It's impossible. The material for the walls, the building stones are scorched and burned and in a pile of rubbish, not fit for building material any more. You think you can revive them? Besides, what you build, if a fox climbs upon it, he'll break down the stone wall."

Ezekiel 13:1-5 describes the apostate church system or religious system. Ministers, preachers who preach out of their own
intellect or training and not from the Father's heart or anointing of
the Holy Spirit. Those who preach through a veil of men's tradition or denominationalism neutralize the power of the gospel of the
kingdom. A social gospel results in sectarianism and division in the
body of Christ, and when those who have preached a compromised
gospel and declared peace when there is no true peace, people have
died and gone to hell!

People have stayed in bondage to their sins and addictions
because ministers have preached grace without law and have been
men-pleasers, rather than preaching the true doctrines of Christ,
which are confrontational to sin and lawlessness and have the
power through grace to set men free! God says My people have been
seduced by these false prophets! Consequently, because they have
been like 'foxes' in the middle of the construction of God's House,
the gaps and breaches have not been healed. There is still disunity,
division and strife and the 'walls' have not been built up and made
strong that it might stand in the day of battle!

Isaiah 26:1, "In that day shall this song be sung, we have a strong
city. The Lord sets up salvation as walls and bulwarks! Open the
gates that the righteous nation which keeps her faith and her troth
with God might enter in."

Leaders who have not experienced Jesus as the baptizer in the
Holy Spirit and do not have a kingdom revelation and vision can end
up consuming people into their personal desires, or vision for success, or empire building, and rob them of their destiny and purpose.

There has operated a kind of church system even among
Pentecostals that centered upon its own success and promotion.
There has been a lot of politics in man's religion and traditions. A true
apostolic church or apostle understands that God reveals Himself
through His many-membered body, drawing their gifts, call, and
anointing out of them to see they are equipped and prepared to serve
God's purpose and receive fulfillment and true blessing! Apostolic
people see destiny in you. They won't let you stay in the same old

place. They see the best in you, they recognize the giftings, and this is their reward, their fulfillment to see you become all God has purposed you to be. God's desire is that His people come to know the fullest measure of His love for them, that through the revelation of His love we are compelled and constrained to lay down our lives for others.

Now, the devil is fully aware of the condition of the church, but he doesn't know everything! Not about Jesus or His bride! He managed to get Jesus crucified, which just played into the plan of the Father to reproduce Himself! The devil thinks he has neutralized the church through religion and deception, but Jesus ROSE and the Church is RISING! This is a new day! Third day church arising!

Ezekiel 13:21 declares that God will deliver His people out of the apostate church and its deception, no more to be hunted and ensnared!

"Because with lies you've made the righteous sad and disheartened, whom I have not made sad or disheartened and because you have encouraged and strengthened the hands of the wicked that he should not turn from his wicked ways and be saved, therefore I will deliver MY people out of your hand and then you will know that I AM the LORD!"

Here come the rest of the 'burnt stones,' a mighty revival, outpouring and visitation to revive them for the completion of the walls of the spiritual house. 2 Corinthians 1:4 says only the free can help others become free. Only those who have been comforted by God the Holy Spirit can bring comfort to others! 1 Corinthians 1:27-29, "For God deliberately chose what in the world is foolish to put the wise to shame and what the world calls weak to put the strong to shame. And God also deliberately chose what in the world is low-born and insignificant and branded and treated with contempt, even the things that are nothing, that He might depose and bring to nothing the things that are, so that no mortal man should have pretense for glorying and boast in the presence of God!"

Every one of us needs what the church is supposed to be, a safe place where 'burnt stones' can find restoration, healing, fruitfulness and the path of intimacy with the Holy Trinity. Only revived, restored burnt stones in the foundation can restore the burnt stones that are coming in the harvest to find their place, purpose and value. Only committed, devoted worshippers who have reached another level of 'loving the Lord your God with all your heart and soul and others as you love yourself' can help them discover their purpose and destiny in God and His Kingdom.

In Nehemiah 4:4, because of prayer intercession there was divine intervention. Because Nehemiah prayed with authority, God frustrated the enemy's purpose! We must persevere and fight for family members. There must be a continual increase of 'fathering and mothering' for further restoration and increase of anointing on the next generation, that the church continue to rise up in fullness of power and glory for His Name's sake! We have a responsibility not only to rebuild and restore, but to continue in the process of ever reaching for the 'high' calling of God in Christ. We not only labor in building up the body of Christ, but we engage the enemy in order to preserve it!

As 'burnt stones,' we must enter into a mature interdependence with other kingdom builders, being sensitive to God's leading.

For every bit of spiritual progress, there is both life and death. Paul says in 2 Corinthians 4:2, "So death works in us, but life in you." The church is an army, and most times we march into battle, there will be casualties. This is one of the hardest things for any leader or serious believer to come to grips with. Often God brings issues to light that are very complex and difficult to deal with. God wants to reclaim and restore the offended, hurt, stumbled, rejected and those in spiritual bondage. Faith works by love. Through faith and patience, we inherit the promises. We are by God's grace called to build and reveal His Kingdom on earth!

Our position must continue to be, "Forgetting what lies behind, I press on towards the goal for the prize to which God in Christ is calling us upward. So let those of us who are spiritually mature have this mindset and hold these convictions!"

2002, '03, '04 PROPHECIES AND JOURNAL

February '02
Prophecy released over LWM

"*I have commissioned you. You have received your orders. Your mission is assigned. The Captain has selected, trained and prepared the 'special services corps' and it seems to the natural mind you've been given a 'mission impossible' assignment! But all that you need to accomplish each mission will be given as you go forth, as you move forward, knowing that the One who leads you has already gone before you and will lead you to victory! Do not let your eyes focus on the works of darkness and evil, for there is more than you know concerning My works and purposes in the earth. I rule over all! My Presence and manifestations of My glory are spreading! Do not forget the I AM is in full control and that I will not fail to see the fulfillment of My Word and Will upon the earth! There is an exceeding great host advancing, My great army, a formidable force in the earth, and they will not be stopped!*

"*I have taken the 'burnt stones,' the foolish and the weak, insignificant and despised, and I have made them a mighty army of mighty men and it has been by My Mighty Right Arm! It is time for My Coronation in My House and before all heaven and earth! I Am ready for the marriage to My betrothed! How beautiful is My beloved in her adornments and holy garments! How sweet is the fragrance of her love and obedience! My warrior bride! She is the battle ax in My Hand!"*

5-20-02 Journal

"I have been courting My Beloved. I have been wooing her love and devotion. Many have spurned My Advances and have come to many woes, but many have responded and have received My gifts of love and have adorned themselves with humility and contriteness and their beauty stirs My Heart, and I say, 'Prepare the wedding feast! Get ready the bridal chamber!' For My heart beats wildly for My church! Her warfare is intensifying, but the victory is sure and it is almost time for all things to come into divine order! The whole earth is in travail for the revealing of the sons of God! Numberless are those looking ever the banister of heaven to view the glories of My kingdom as the Ancient of Days sits with His scepter of righteousness extended, releasing His authority over the earth!"

"My worship and response to His word: How beautiful is His Holiness! How dazzling is the brightness of His shining! Oh that He would take notice of 'me'! That He knows 'my name'! To think He knows 'my' thoughts! And the number of the hair upon 'my' head! That the King of the universe and Creator of all things is my redeemer, and He loves me!"

1-17-03 Journal

Holy One, pure and perfect in all Your ways! This is so comforting to me, so motivating to me. I so love your holiness and I am awed at the depth of Your love and commitment to Your own!

I think some of my reactions are because of my own imperfections and frustrations at the evidence that I am still, at this point in my life, imperfect! I seem to be too much aware or too focused lately on faults and imperfections. Help me, Dear Heart, to stay balanced, and please, Holy Spirit, continue Your work within me! I so want to be pleasing to Him! I don't want to be caught up in what I'm not yet or where I'm not yet, but who I am becoming and where He desires to take me!

I think I might have presumed that somewhere along my journey, I would somehow have reached a plateau of 'perfection' of saying the right things always, behaving always godly, and the flesh having finally been conquered for good! That is a 'set up' for disappointment! I think I more fully understand Paul's words: "The difficulty of having to bear the burden of your own imperfections and faults!" But one day, we will be as He is, in our immortality, in our new bodies! It's hard to imagine the freedom from the flesh and the devil! But I can and do believe it will come! In the interim, GRACE! The BLOOD! The New Covenant! Forgive me, Lord, for being more 'self-conscious' than 'righteousness-conscious'!

18th:

Even this extra sensitivity to the 'flesh' right now, which causes me to often focus on 'me,' which I know is spiritually unhealthy — You must be after 'something'! Okay, Holy Spirit, what? "The word of God is sharper than a two-edged sword, dividing the soul and spirit." My goodness, Lord! That's been going on for years! But still it must continue?! You must continue to expose the deceitfulness of the flesh man, its betrayal, that we continue to be even more dependant upon You! That we put no trust in the flesh, we must be continually reminded that 'in my flesh dwelleth no good thing,' I owe it nothing! But to the Spirit of Christ I owe all! In Him only am I righteous! He has covered my whole body, soul and spirit, my whole 'self' with His Robe of righteousness! He has come into His temple within me and His Presence has created a Holy of Holies in the center of my being! His Life, His Presence is consuming all that is not of Him! He is the Hand that fills the glove; that's me! Oh! Thank You, dearest Lord, dearest friend, for loving me, for choosing me to be Your own! Father! I love Your Son! I want to love Him more, I want to be able to bless Him and bring Him joy! He must have my whole heart, always first above all else! I ask that the latter glory of this house be greater than the former glory. That You bless me, Your hand be upon me, that I might not cause pain. Increase my territory for the establishing of Your kingdom! Jesus, manifest Yourself through me in power to others! Do mighty exploits through this vessel that I might honor You! "Not that I have attained this ideal or have been made perfect, but I press on to lay hold and make my own that for which Christ Jesus has laid hold of me and made me His own. I do not consider, brethren, that I have captured it or made it my own yet; but one thing I do, forgetting what lies behind me and straining forward to what lies ahead, I press on toward the goal to win the supreme prize to which Christ Jesus is calling us upward! So I will, in the meantime, hold true to what I have already attained and order my life by that!" Selah!

The Lord's response: *"You must fling away the limitations of past injustices, for I Am the God of justice and I Am your defender. You must choose to shake yourself free of the shackles of past failures, for they will sap your energy and obstruct your view of kingdom purpose, for there is no failure in Me and no defeat for those who trust Me fully!*

"You must also choose not to be satisfied with past revelation and spiritual experiences, but press on to lay hold of Me and the mysteries of the kingdom and the greater works. You are pregnant with the seed of greater revelation of My glory and power, and these will indeed come to full term, for there is no end to the unfolding revelation of My Glory for all of you!"

[He then shifted to the church] *"Do not fret, little flock, little army, for little is much where I Am the Shepherd and the Shepherd over you. I AM! And you have experienced My jealous love, for you are mine and I guard you jealously! Press on through the pressures, your destinies are in My Hand, just stay with My plan! Press on, mighty warriors, for you are mighty in My strength and you shall run fast and you shall walk in love and not fail or faint! I will bring further revelation of My love and My glory and you will be compelled and constrained onward and upward in ever-increasing faith and devotion to Me! Please accept My gifts, the jewels, ornaments and holy garments which are priceless and are given to you, My bride, as evidence of My seal and ownership! Trust Me implicitly! Now is the time to fully enter into My rest, fully confident in My love and faithfulness. Don't struggle, don't worry, don't fret! All of that is just a waste of good energy! I have brought all of you this far, each one with a special purpose. You are the paintbrush in My Hand for the portrait of My love! You are a thread being woven into the fabric of My coat of many colors! Again, do you doubt you are My planting? I Am building this house and I Am networking and connecting to other houses. So do not get impatient with the process, stay in the peace of God and follow the word of God and be quick to obey! Sometimes you will need to tread softly, sometimes you will need to put your foot down hard, but always hold up your shield of faith and always keep your sword drawn!"*

Father.
Thank You, Father.

3/15/04
Prophecy

This is a 'springtime' season for the church, and the Husbandman, who keeps and tends the garden of your lives, is determined to have a bountiful harvest! He has tilled the past winter's harvests back into the soil of your hearts and it has become as 'organic compost,' mulch incorporated back into the soil, and the tilling and cultivating has broken up hardness and loosened the soil and prepared it for the rain of My Spirit to be poured out and the 'compost' will release 'nutrients' for a healthy, vibrant, bountiful harvest, as well as a protective covering against the growth of 'weeds' that interfere with production! The seed will spring up quickly, and whereas in the past there was a long season before harvest, behold what has been spoken by the prophets of old and released as a now word to you in times past: "The days are coming and now are, says the Lord, that the plowman shall overtake the reapers and the treader of grapes of him who sows the seed and the barren and unfruitful shall overflow with spiritual blessing!" Yes! Amen!

March 30, 2004

These are six visions given to Linda Fortune, with each followed by the interpretations given by the Spirit to Colleen Anderson.

Two of the visions, the third and the sixth, represent the saints and the glorified church.

Intercessors had gathered to pray, listening to the CD, ***Breath of God,*** by Graham Ord.

Linda's Account:

The Holy Spirit began to catch me away in visions. They were like scenes and did not appear to be related. Each person or place seemed to be in Old Testament times. After each one, I thought it would be the last, but I continued to have visions until the end of the music.

Vision 1:

There was an old man with long white hair and beard, wearing an off-white colored tunic with a scarlet-colored cloak covering his head and shoulders, and he was carrying a staff. I sensed that he seemed harmless. His sandaled feet were moving to the rhythm of the music, which was tribal-like drumbeats.

He began moving in a semi-circle towards me, and when he got directly in front of me, I could see there was a white goat by his side. He was not leading it or pulling it in any way, but had his hand resting on the side of the goat and the goat was just walking with him, as if it knew the man well.

As the man walked away, still to the beat of the music, following behind him were other goats, one or two at a time. They weren't hurried or rushing, just following peacefully behind him. Some were tan, some were brown or black, but there were no other white ones. The man walked out of my range of vision into the darkness with his long line of goats following him, hundreds of them, as far as the eye could see.

Interpretation:

Long white hair = wisdom, philosophy, ancient, rebellion
Beard = uncleanness

Off-White = the mingling of truth and error for evil

Scarlet Cloak = Isaiah 1:18 talks about scarlet being a symbol of the nature of sin

When he circled in front of me = means the prophecy of future events has come and is now

Staff = Authority

Goat = sinner, unbelief, unyielding, strife, licentiousness, lecherous man, scapegoat, the sign of Capricorn in the zodiac, and is an important satanic emblem or sign.

Max said at an auction, sheep will not enter the auction ring, so the sale barn uses a 'Judas goat' [this is literally what it is called!]. The Judas goat slowly, peacefully walks into the ring and the sheep follow. The goat then slips out and goes back to lead another group of sheep into the ring! This Judas goat is trained to obey voice commands.

Judas Goat = Leading many into the auction arena of satan, into slavery. This is religious deception. The lost, as well as deceived believers, will follow this seemingly harmless religious deception. Goats and sheep will follow a 'Judas goat'!

2 Thessalonians 2:1-3 speaks of the latter days, or prior to the return of Jesus Christ, and the 'great falling away' or apostasy of those who profess to be Christians.

Walked off into the darkness = he returns into the darkness from which he came. He is called the mind-blinder and this darkness is ignorance, witchcraft, and that which is hidden.

The man in this vision represents THE SPIRIT OF LEVIATHAN, the ancient serpent, the ANTI-CHRIST SPIRIT.

Vision 2:

A woman was dancing in front of a crowd of men. She was wearing dark green bloomer-type pants like you would see in an Aladdin movie. There was a sheer yellow veil covering her head and lower face, with only her eyes showing.

She carried another yellow veil in her hand and she waved it back and forth as she danced almost seductively. Her eyes were mysterious-looking, like she had a secret or ulterior motive of some kind.

Interpretation:

Unknown woman = the spirit of seduction. Her dancing is a seducing spirit.

Green Bloomers = represents the life of flesh, carnal nature, envy, wickedness

Yellow Veil = represents gift or deceitful gift, counterfeit supernatural gifts, false prophets, fear, cowardliness

Eyes = reveal the window of the soul; seeing into the soul of man for the purpose of finding a weakness or sin in order to seduce

This woman represents THE SPIRIT OF JEZEBEL.

These two, the SPIRIT OF LEVIATHAN and THE SPIRIT OF JEZEBEL, are working together and people will be caught up in this deception, as satan knows his time is short. How important it is for the gift of discerning of spirits to be in operation in the Church in this hour! For it IS possible that the very elect CAN be deceived!

Vision 3:

A man, maybe a priest, wearing a white tunic and cloak with gold trim, was in a large room, perhaps a temple. He was on his knees on a white pillow, bowed down very low, with his arms outstretched in front of him. He appeared to be in prayer.

Interpretation:

THIS REPRESENTS THE THIRD DAY CHURCH, RULING AND REIGNING IN THE MIDST OF THE DARKNESS!

White Tunic = saints that are sanctified, righteous.
Trimmed in Gold = truth, glory, wisdom.

On his knees = saints submitted to God, intercession.
White pillow = represents the Holy Spirit, the Comforter.
Bowed low = humility, submission, worship.
Arms outstretched = dependency upon God, as well as reaching out
    to others.

This represents spirit-filled, end-time saints, walking in truth and wisdom, clothed in the glory of God, humble, dependant, leaning and resting on the comforter, in full dependence on God, standing in the midst of darkness in humility, operating in the power of the Holy Spirit, a light in the darkness, leading many out of darkness into His marvelous light!

Vision 4:

In this scene, I was above what appeared to be an African village. It was at night and it appears everyone in the village is sleeping, not realizing there is danger lurking near. As my eyes scan this village and beyond, I see a man off in the distance. He is walking away from the village.

He is wearing an off-white cloak, which covers his head, and he is carrying a staff. He has been walking for a while because I see his footprints in the sand as he has gone down one sand dune and up the side of another.

Interpretation:

Africa = a key nation, as well as represents the nations. It has been
    one of satan's targets.
Man = this is the same man as in the first vision.
Night = represents darkened understanding and ignorance, unknown
    course of action, under the cover of darkness as being hidden or
    covert.
Sand = improper or wrong foundation, flesh, weakness, weariness,
    hindrances, childish, unclean. Satan's house is on the sand. IT
    WILL NOT STAND. IT WILL TOPPLE! The kingdom of dark-
    ness is on shifting sands. He won't be able to leave his mark on

the "ROCK." JESUS IS THE ROCK, THE ROCK OF AGES! The Kingdom of God is the ROCK! The footprints of satan will wash away and disappear! There will be absolute victory over the powers of darkness!

Footprints in the sand = Leviathan has left his mark, his footprints on the continent of Africa and on the nations. But the wave of the powerful army of the Living God, empowered by His Holy Spirit, will hit the shores of every continent with such force, every footprint, every mark, every sign will be washed away by the tidal wave of His Presence and Power! Just as Jesus wrote in the sand concerning the woman caught in adultery, His words of love and forgiveness and restoration washed the words of the accuser away and she was free. AFRICA WILL BE FREE FROM SATAN'S DOMINION AND CONTROL. What is printed in the sand will be erased by the waves!

Vision 5:

Now I'm in a fairly large city with streets made of stone. There are crowds of people standing on both sides of the main street and I am standing among them.

I see a procession coming, and at the head is a man being carried on a lift, like a king or other dignitary. Behind him is an army marching down the street. As they pass by, I have this sense of foreboding, as if there is a trial or judgment of some kind about to take place.

Interpretation:

Five is the number of Grace

City = a whole segment of society, not just a place or an area.
Streets of stone = represents witness or testimony, as written in stone. The very stones are crying out, speaking of sins, works of darkness and deception.

Stones are bearing witness for judgment, for He is a God of justice and vindication! Judgment must come for the fulfillment of scripture and for the separation of the sheep and the goats. But judgment will not come in the way that we think. It will be a time of reckoning for those who have denied Him and have fought against His Kingdom. At the same time, a glorious, unspeakable revelation and revealing of Himself to those and in those who are called by His Name!

Vision 6:

I see an army on horseback, lined up on the side of a hill. They are prepared and waiting for battle. In the distant horizon, in front of them, the sun is rising. I feel peacefulness settle over me and I sense that I am safe. I see that I am sitting on one of those horses on the side of that hill. Below me, a group of men are dancing and rejoicing, cheering and raising their weapons in the air!

I realize that I am not a woman, but a man of about thirty years old, not a boy, but mature. The horse I am sitting on begins to move slowly, gently, and sits down, like a camel would, with me still on his back! As he does so, I step off and begin walking toward the sunrise. I feel drawn, compelled to do this, leaving everyone behind.

As I walk, I take off my helmet, but I still have my sword in my right hand. I see, on the ground in front of me, what at first appears to be briers or thorn bushes. But as I get closer, I see they are bodies of men and horses killed in battle. I look around at them as I pass through, with a sense of sadness and resignation.

Interpretation:

Six is the number of man and the corporate son and will be revealed in all of his glory.

Revelation 19:11-24
Revelation 20 and 21

This vision represents victorious King Jesus astride His horse with His army of saints. Jesus was thirty years of age when He came into His fullness and maturity. I believe this is a picture of the fulfillment of Ephesians 4:13. His end-time army, armed and ready for battle, riding with Him for the final defeat of satan.

There is no stopping the advancing army of the Lord in this present time. And there will be TOTAL victory at the consummation of all that has been spoken!

Briers = wicked persons.
Thorn bushes = people who are persecutors and bear false witness.
Was able to pass through = knowing this was their lot.

THE REFINER'S FIRE

Message I brought before the church the second Sunday in April of '04

The first week of April, I was meditating on Linda's visions, especially concerning the falling away and deception, and a vision Jamie received the following Sunday morning during worship. She saw a large golden ball, bright, shining like fire, coming down and hanging over us. I was searching out the matter, following the clues for revelation and just leaning into the Lord. He said, "Do you think I came to bring peace on the earth? No! But rather division! I came to cast fire upon the earth, that fire to refine and purify and kindle a flame in men's hearts! I came and cast fire upon the earth. A cleansing, purifying, devouring fire! For My Word, when believed and obeyed, brings division, even in families and households! Commitment to Me can result in division and rejection. There is separation taking place by My Hand, saith the Lord, separating the precious from the vile! The flesh from the Spirit! The lies from the Truth! The false from the True! The counterfeit from the Genuine! At the same time there is a joining, a coming together in covenantal relationships within My House! I AM Zealous for My House!"

These are the scriptures I was led to read:

1 Timothy 3:16, 4:1-2; "And great and important and weighty, we confess, is the hidden truth [the mystic secret] of godliness. God was made visible in human flesh, justified and vindicated in the Holy

Spirit, was seen by angels, preached among the nations, believed on in the world, and taken up in glory. But the Holy Spirit distinctly and expressly declares that in latter times some will turn away from the faith, giving attention to deluding and seducing spirits and doctrines that demons teach, through the hypocrisy and pretensions of liars whose consciences are seared."

Matthew 10:34-39; "Do you think that I have come to bring peace upon the earth; I have not come to bring peace, but a sword. For I have come to part asunder a man from his father, and a daughter from her mother, and a newly married from her mother-in-law. And a man's foes will be those of his own household. He who loves and takes more pleasure in father or mother more than in Me is not worthy of Me; and he who loves and takes more pleasure in son or daughter more than Me is not worthy of Me; and he who does not take up his cross and follow Me, cleave steadfastly to Me, conforming to My example in living and if need be, dying, is not worthy of me. Whoever finds his lower life will lose the higher life, and whoever loses his lower life on My account will find the higher life."

Malachi 3:2-3; "But who can endure the day of His coming? And who can stand when He appears? For He is like a refiner's fire and like fuller's soap; He will sit as a refiner and purifier of silver and He will purify the priests, the sons of Levi, and refine them like gold and silver, that they may offer to the Lord offerings in righteousness."

Zechariah 13:9; "And I will bring the third part through the fire, and refine them as silver is refined and will test them as gold is tested. They will call on My Name, and I will hear and answer them. I will say, It is My people; and they will say, The Lord is my God."

A few days prior, Franke received an e-mail entitled, 'The Refiner's Fire'!

Some women in a Bible study were wondering what this scrip-ture was saying about the character and nature of God. One of the women called a silversmith and made an appointment to watch him at work, not mentioning her reason.

As she watched the silversmith, he held a piece of silver over the fire and let it heat up. He explained that refining silver, one needed to hold the silver in the middle of the fire where the flames were hottest, to burn away all the impurities. She thought about God holding us in such a hot spot; then she thought again about the verse that says: 'He sits as a refiner and purifier of silver.' She asked the silversmith if it was true that he had to sit there in front of the fire the whole time?

The man answered yes, he not only had to sit there holding the silver, but he had to keep his eyes on the silver the entire time it was in the fire. If the silver was left a moment too long in the flames, it would be destroyed.

Then she asked, "How do you know when the silver is fully refined?"

He smiled at her and answered, "Oh, that's easy — when I see my image in it!"

Obviously God is after something in each of us and corporately! If the church does not know her true identity, value and purpose, and is not walking in revelation and obedience, many may be in the number of those who fall away in the days ahead.

Our hearts must be established, our feet planted securely upon the Rock of Truth as it is in Jesus Christ and Him crucified, risen, ruling, reigning Messiah and our position in Him! Our wineskins must be well oiled, and flexible enough, pliable enough to receive the flow and increase from His Spirit within and upon our lives, that we might walk in resurrection power and victory. An understanding of the incredible love and plans Father God has for His people would produce a deeper humility, worship and obedience, which increases our capacity to receive more of Him.

Father God has a high destiny for man. We are destined for the Grander, the more Glorious, and the Greater!

Hebrews 4:12; "For the word that God speaks is alive and full of power, making it active, operative, energizing and effective; it is sharper than any two-edged sword, penetrating to the dividing line of the breath of life, the soul, and the immortal spirit, and of joints and marrow, of the deepest parts of our nature, exposing and sifting and analyzing and judging the very thoughts and purposes of the heart."

The WORD is the Fire! The Refiner's Fire! As you believe it, receive it, conduct your life by it, and apply it in the situations, circumstances, trials and tribulations of life, the good times as well as the bad times. Supernaturally, the word will separate the precious from the vile, the lie from the truth. Freedom will come, healing will come, light will swallow up the darkness, and the Day Star shall rise in your heart! The Fire by Night, the Cloud by Day that led the children of Israel to the Promised Land! The Word and God the Holy Spirit. On the day of Pentecost, the Holy Spirit came like a mighty rushing wind and sat upon them as tongues of fire! The Spirit and the Word are inseparable! He is a consuming Fire!

Hearing Him, obeying Him, trusting that as His sheep we recognize His voice, and another's we do not follow! The 'elect can be deceived,' but those who are intimately acquainted with Him, in fellowship with Him and follow His leading will not be deceived! We will be doing those mighty 'exploits' in His Name in the glory! I believe this hour of refining will bring us into deeper revelation of the supremacy of Christ within us. His nature will be more evident in us, for He will have separated us from ungodly attachments, and ungodly soul ties and idolatry, dismantling and destroying strongholds and fortresses of demons!

"UPON THIS ROCK I will build My church and the gates of hell shall not prevail against it! You are My living stones that comprise My spiritual house. You are My Priesthood, a Holy Nation. My kingdom on earth now and in the new order to come, My ultimate Kingdom. You are destined to rule with Me over all things, even the angels!" We were created for this! Christ is bringing us toward God's goal, restoration unto God's purpose through Christ bringing us to the Mount of God as participants in a kingdom that cannot be shaken!

Hebrews 2:8 says all things have been put under man's feet, but we do not yet see all things subjected to him yet. But there is one thing we do see, WE SEE JESUS! LOOKING [to stare at attentively, to discern clearly, to experience, take heed] UNTO JESUS, the Author and Finisher of our faith, do not look down on yourself, look up! How can you look down on yourself when you are high and lifted up, seated together with him in heavenly places by virtue of your being in Christ? Jesus did more than bridge the chasm between God and man — He has broken the power of death that blocked God's high purpose for man and paved the way to "bring many sons into glory to fulfill the original intention for mankind! WE SEE JESUS! LOOKING UNTO JESUS! THE ROCK OF OUR SALVATION! GLORY!

Psalm 8 and Hebrews 2:5 says angels watched while the wonders of the work of the Godhead in creation were taking place, then asked, "What is man that you visit him, that he has a place in Your Mind?" [The angels may have had to 'call' on God but 'this man' God visits.] You have made him a little lower than 'angels' [Hebrew, 'Elohim,' a little lower than God]!" Eternity past had been this order: The Godhead — archangels — angels. Now there is a new order in creation, man ranked just under the Godhead! God the Father, God the Son, God the Holy Spirit and you and me, sons of grace! Then the Angels said, "You have crowned him with glory and honor!" God Himself crowned him! Who wears crowns? By this, God established the place of man in God's heart and plans. He crowned him not with gold, but with glory and honor! The glory of God is His manifested Presence! God's glory sat upon man as his crown and clothed him as his covering and fitted him for fellowship with his creator!

In verse 9, Jesus was crowned with Glory and Honor! Man fell from glory in the garden and the Father of Glory sent the Lord of Glory to lift up the man who had originally been crowned with Glory but had fallen from Glory, back into the Glory of His Presence AND gave him dominion!

If I lift off, whoever is here can take over! I am GETTING this even more than when I was preparing this message! Awesome!

Through the blood of the everlasting covenant, God is committed to work in us "what is well pleasing in His sight through Jesus Christ, to whom be all the glory forever and ever!"

Matthew 3:11-12; "I indeed baptize you in water because of repentance [that is, because of your changing your minds for the better, heartily amending your ways, with abhorrence of your past sin]. But He Who is coming after me is mightier than I, whose sandals I am not worthy or fit to take off or carry; He will baptize you with the Holy Spirit and fire! His winnowing fan [shovel, fork] is in His hand, and He will thoroughly clear out and clean His threshing floor and gather and store His wheat in His barn, but the chaff He will burn up with fire that cannot be put out!"

The fiery baptism of the Holy Spirit consumes all the chaff in our lives. The Spirit exposes sin and all things contrary to His nature, then begins the refining process, consuming it in the fire of His passion and Love, to bring us into the reality of, "we are the righteousness of God in Christ Jesus," bringing us forth into the true identity of our new nature. It is the Holy Spirit's assignment to fulfill WITHIN us God's commandment TO us: "Be Ye holy even as I Am holy!" Now is coming the 'unveiling' of the bride!

Chaff is a figurative type of sin that He convicts us of. John says in 16:5-11, "When He comes He will convict and convince the world and demonstrate to it about sin and about righteousness of heart and right standing with God and about judgment!"

What chaff does He need to burn away, separate from our hearts and lives? Let us name a few: Pride, anger, offense, lying, hypocrisy, lukewarmness, gossiping, rebellion, laziness, prejudices, and immorality. All works of the flesh, old nature. The Holy Spirit's fire within us will make the interior of our lives His sanctifying crucible! When we step out of 'darkness into His marvelous Light,' the Light is not only revelation, illumination, it is HIM! His Holiness, His Presence, the consuming Fire! His redeeming Blood has provided through Grace a covering that protects us from being burned to a cinder in the glory and excellence of His Holiness! The more He removes from us, separates us from, the more glory we receive and experience! Going from one level or experience of glory to another!

The fire of the Spirit is not only purging and cleansing us, we are also being set ablaze with the fire of His passion for Jesus Christ and His body! Repentance, confession, worship are the kindling for this fire! When we enter into His Presence, coming boldly before His mercy seat with sin in our lives, His fire convicts, purges and cleanses us so we may dwell in His Presence, secure in the benefits of His Grace! Isaiah 33:16 tells us of those benefits: "These are the ones who will dwell on high. The rocks of the mountains will be their fortress of safety, food will be supplied to them and they will have water in abundance!"

In 1 Corinthians 3:13-15, Paul tells us that fire from God's Spirit proves and tests each person's works done in His Name. If we submit our thought life, motives, words and actions to the Word and the Spirit, He will consume the chaff. And He will work in us and through us powerfully!

What should our course of action be when the Holy Spirit shines the Light of Christ upon something in our walk, conduct, and thought life?

1. Do we repent immediately, seeking the Father's forgiveness, His cleansing fire and new direction?

2. OR, do we rationalize, justify, make excuses, blaming others? Refusing to accept responsibility, not holding ourselves accountable to God and before the Fire, which will result in our withdrawing from intimacy with God the Holy Spirit and often isolate ourselves from others of the church? The Lord says: Embrace the Fire and follow the Cloud!

Because it is God, by His Spirit that makes us holy, sanctifies and purifies us, there are two questions we ask:

1. What does God require in holiness?
2. How does He make us holy?

Holiness means to be 'set apart' unto the Lord. That which is holy is for God's use only, belongs solely to Him! You are set apart as God's special, unique and prized possession to be tried and tested by fire!

Every believer has been made holy by the poured out Blood of Jesus. This is called 'positional sanctification.' Because of the CROSS, WE ARE NOW IN A POSITION TO RECEIVE THE HOLY SPIRIT'S ONGOING WORK IN WHICH HE IS MAKING US HOLY! BODY, SOUL, AND SPIRIT, FOR THE REST OF OUR LIVES ON THIS PLANET! We are the Tabernacle and Christ is our High Priest. The cloud of His Presence rest upon us and dwells within us. The baptism of fire from the Holy Spirit was accompanied by tongues, to purify the tongue and lips, so what we speak brings life and not death.

One of the ways He makes us holy is through trial. He uses trials to test and refine our faith the way fire refines and purifies silver and gold. Oftentimes, we misinterpret the trials and challenges of life and allow satan a foothold. Satan comes to tempt. He is the tempter, deceiver, seducer, accuser and destroyer!

1 Peter 1:6-7; "You should be exceedingly glad on this account, though now for a little while you may be distressed by trials and suffer temptations, so that the genuineness of your faith may be tested, your faith which is infinitely more precious than the perishable gold which is tested and purified by fire. This proving of your faith is intended to redound to your praise and glory and honor when Jesus Christ, the Anointed One is revealed." James 1:2-4; "Consider it wholly joyful, my brethren, whenever you are enveloped in or encounter trials of any sort or fall into various temptations. Be assured and understand that the trial of your faith brings out endurance and steadfastness and patience. But let endurance and steadfastness have full play and do a thorough work, so that you may be people perfectly and fully developed, lacking in nothing!"

Abraham's faith opened his life to a covenant with God that was sealed by blood and fire! Then came the time when Abraham's faith was tested in the hot fire of covenant. He was asked to put his son

Isaac upon the altar. Abraham first encountered Jehovah upon the mountain, manifesting Himself as the Consuming Fire in a burning bush.

God seeks to know by fire if there are other gods in our lives, if there is anything or anyone that comes between us and our covenant with God through Christ. God's covenant is given by grace and received by faith. We will be tested on the altar of fire to be melted in our love for Him and consumed with desire for His abiding Spirit! Matthew 5:14-15; "You are the Light [fire] of the world." When the Holy Spirit sets us ablaze for Christ, we bring His fire into a world blanketed in the darkness of rebellion and deception. Our fiery love of Christ cannot be hidden, it burns brightly in the 'darkness' to light the way for all to see! Jesus is the source of all light! The fire of God's Spirit does not burn within us for our glory or satisfaction, it shines through us so others can see the glory of God and give Him praise and honor!

We are responsible to fan the glowing coals of the Spirit's fire within us into flames. 2 Timothy 1:6-14; "Fan into flames the spiritual gifts God has given you." Seeking, knocking, asking! [Luke 11] Being faithful to the Holy Spirit and humble in His Presence. [James 4:5-10] Praying as directed by the Lord, fellowship with other believers in worship, ministering to those in need, and serving are just a few ways the 'fan' works! As the flame grows brighter, we must be yielded, ready and available. The fire is our friend! We emerge from its holy work a vessel unto honor!

One of the things that will keep us steadfast, stable and in peace in the days ahead is the understanding of God the Father's ultimate purpose and goal for His church and His kingdom. His WILL to be accomplished on earth as it is in heaven. We are a part of the answer! The Lord Jesus created this world for man and His purpose, and only those who are aligned with His purpose will have the authority that can stand the pressures of the times we are entering! And only the human authority, based upon kingdom principles of truth, righteousness and justice will stand!

The story in Matthew 8:43 is of the woman with an issue of blood, WHO PRESSED THROUGH A HUGE CROWD TO GET TO JESUS FOR HER HEALING and a new beginning. The church has some ISSUE'S that need dealing with! Jesus is still standing in the midst of the crowds, fully available. And there are a lot of groups and crowds of people who have gathered 'around' Jesus, but few are bending 'low' and paying the price, making the sacrifice, reaching for Him in order to touch Him, to know Him, be healed and changed by Him. But, there are people who have been bent over, bent down with some 'ISSUES,' who are now determined to PRESS through! They have their eyes upon Jesus! The Word! They want all HE has for them. They aren't running everywhere else, relying on others or things for their needs to be met. They cannot bear staying in the same 'rut' they have been in for years. It's becoming unbearable! In spite of the pressures, opinions of others, intimidation, weakness and pain, they are pressing through to the Master! However, they are not just after touching the hem of His robe, but wearing it, receiving His robe, new sandals for their feet and His ring for their finger! They are no longer just after their inheritance, they just want to be in His Presence, experiencing kingdom glory, walking in the glory, carriers of the glory, His word fulfilled in their lives! As kingdom people they are living in kingdom benefits through the power of His Spirit, the Water of life that He changes to Wine in these water pots! No longer bent over, looking down, with a limited perspective of God, themselves, others and the circumstances! Now overcomers! Victorious!

Job 4:17-29, Psalm 40:2, and Daniel 2:33-44 tell us 'clay' is in reference to the 'old nature.'

Genesis 2:10:11, Job 23:10, and Psalm 45:13 tells us the 'new nature' is referenced as 'the gold.'

He is 'stoking' the fire in the furnace of His Word in this hour. A revival of His word. The Wind of the Spirit of wisdom and revelation is blowing anew upon the Word in revival. That honed and sharpened two-edged, fiery sword, dividing the soul and the spirit even unto the deepest parts of our nature to reveal who we are — Clay or Gold!

As we drink anew of the Water of Life, light is dawning. Our eyes are opening, vision is opening up, our hearing is keen and sharp, hearts are surrendered, conscience is tender and clear, strength is returning, and we are a determined people. We are leaping upon the mountains of spices, going from faith to faith, strength to strength, and from glory to glory! Vessels of gold, vessels of honor, fit for the Master's use!

Fire hardens clay but melts gold so it will flow as the river of God, which is redemptive, restorative, healing and liberating! Everywhere the river goes, there is Life!

2005 THROUGH 2006 JOURNAL AND PROPHECIES

12/17/05
Word from the Lord out of intercession:

"*I will not put a bit in your mouth! You will come and you will follow Me wholeheartedly and with joy and expectancy, or you will not! You will not have to strain to know My Way, to strain to hear My Voice. I will make Myself heard and I will make My Way plain. Unless you deliberately turn the other way and say in your heart, "I will to do this my way, I will to do this without God, I do not will to hear or see, I am satisfied!" Only then will you be unable to hear and unable to see, then the consequences will be your responsibility!*

"Yes, the signs are all around and yet so many are fearful to 'look' and 'see' and accept what has been spoken from eternity. Yes, it is hard, I fully understand all the 'ins' and 'outs' in the nature of man. It would be profitable if those who are called by My Name would not be among the scoffers saying, "I've heard all of this since the beginning of old, but I don't think I believe all I've been told!" Now is the time as never before to know and understand for yourselves what I, the Lord, speaks and no more! Do not mistrust Me now, do not misjudge Me now, in this day! You must continue to hide My words in your heart and then listen carefully to ALL I say!

"Now is the time to lay in store. Be wise and prudent in all you do and all you say, and you need to begin to keep score of all that's

coming in and all that's going out, and let Me help you to spend where it will count! A spiritual winter season is approaching the earth. Even nature knows how to prepare. I do not raise dumb children! Now is not the time to sit and stare! To many I will give many resources to provide the needs of many more, so all will be provided for!

"Don't sit and wonder and mourn! How will that benefit you or those who scorn? Be an example in all your ways, and you will see it pays and pays! Don't waste your substance on prodigal living or on things that are not practical or needed, as if you think things will continue on the same course. Learn even more to be self-controlled and you tighten up the reins! Let not your appetites or desires of the flesh rule your lives to any degree! See that you get yourself fully into agreement with ME!

"And remember, the devil and his crew have no surprises for ME! So don't be unduly concerned about what he will do, but pray and intercede with purpose and authority! Your words and declarations propelled by faith must be sent! And many will be saved and many will repent! This is not the time to be cast down, for soon My Glory will erase every frown!

"So rejoice on your way, no matter what may be your lot, and let ME search your heart for any dark spot. Not to condemn or bring shame, but to heal and set free, for you are mine and I want to promote you to display My Grace and Glory and cause you to shine!

"Pull together now as never before, and as much as is in your power through Me, pull the family circle in closer and help them understand and 'see.' For I know what your children and families mean to you. For I am Father and Brother too! And I grieve just as you do! Please read the large print, small print and the words written in red. Abide in the covenant set forth and your faith will increase and you will see that charity. Love is the door and obedience is the key to the reality of all you have been told! Worship and praise and seek My face and I will continually remind you of the power of My love and grace!"

Father:

We are listening, Father God, with great desire to be obedient. Your faithfulness to us as Your family is unspeakably humbling, and at the same time strengthening and encouraging. It causes us to feel so secure in Your love, and watchful to heed and obey. We trust the Holy Spirit will lead us to give you worthy praise!

May 2006

Pastor Nunez had come to teach concerning the 'orphan' spirit that was affecting the body of Christ and so many of the "Baby Boomers."

As we were praying for the 'family' after having heard his message, the Holy Spirit began to move upon me in weeping and great travail in tongues and much warfare. The words from the heart of Jesus began to flow like a river of love and encouragement:

"Oh! My children, you are so loved! I lavish My love upon you because you are Mine! Sow seeds of love, forgiveness, grace, goodness, and humility! Be liberal to sow seeds of patience, perseverance, joy, trust, and peace! Sow these dear ones! Give and it shall be given back to you, pressed down and running over shall I, the Lord, give back to you! OH! I have made a way when there seemed to be no way for you! For I AM the way maker! Trust Me now and align yourselves up with your true hearts and the truth you know in your spirit. I have been your Father from the beginning! You are a Holy Seed in the earth and not without purpose! My heart aches for you, for your fellowship, for relationship. I have never left you! How could a father leave his children? Earthly fathers, yes, but I AM the I AM to be all you need, to fill every void and empty place. To be your strength, joy and peace, for I AM your righteousness! I am well aware of the challenges you face, the plans and the deceitfulness of the devil to steal from you. But I have given to you all things needed to rise above the circumstances. My word is yes to you, each one of you, and My grace is always over you to bring you out and to bring you through! There is nothing you have done or haven't done that I

didn't know from the foundations of the world. I know every word in your mouth not yet spoken! Every evil thing that has ever been done or will be done was and is known to Me. You are forgiven! You are the righteousness of God in Christ. Now receive your forgiveness and forgive yourself, so you can forgive others! Remember, "Love the Lord your God with all your heart and soul, and your neighbor, brother, as yourself." That can't happen until you receive what you have been given. It is a free gift, take it and open it and walk in the love and joy of it!

"Now, about all this shaking you're going through! Let it shake you free from all that is not Me! Let it shake you free from depending upon anything or anyone more than Me! This shaking can shake you into the right place and right position. Shakings have the potential to set you free and bring order and move you forward.

"Pray like this: 'My Father Who is in Heaven, Hallowed be Your Name! Your Kingdom has come, Thy will shall be done, on earth as it is in heaven!'" Now, choose to be obedient sons and daughters and participate in this becoming a reality experience in your lives and circumstances NOW! My Way is not the way of the soul, the flesh, and the world. The way of the Spirit and the way of unconditional love, which by the way, never fails to destroy the works of darkness, and establish My kingdom rule in your hearts, and is higher than your ways. I am calling you, "Come up higher! Will you come?' Do not continue to live below your 'means'! Remember Who your Father IS! And who you are and what Christ has accomplished for you! Remember where you are now positionally seated with ME in the heavenly realm! Hidden in Me. You are My house, My temple. I AM in the earth in you to establish My kingdom rule and destroy the works of darkness! My dwelling place is always glorious! My indwelling Presence will permeate and fill My house! My Spirit is working mightily within you, the veil of the 'soul' the 'flesh' is being rent, torn in this hour, and My glory and power is breaking forth from within and manifesting outwardly. You are a supernatural man! Purposed for supernatural works in the earth.

"Let go of all you are holding on to that you can't keep anyway, and lay hold of all I have for you, which you can never lose!

"Come now! Come walk with Me! I want to show you great and mighty things that you cannot imagine. For this is the time of My appearing in great glory. My manifested Presence upon and through My Family! What a day this is now! The darkness is but a backdrop for the light of My glory as it fills the earth through the people who know their Father is God!

"You must 'see' with the eyes of your spirit now and hear with your spiritual ears, and you must guard your tongue, that you speak words of life and not death. For you are My Ambassador. So keep My words before you, sit at My feet, lean upon My breast to hear my heartbeat and to hear My slightest whisper. I AM good! Do not lay to My charge that which is evil!

"And last, but very important: Do not be ignorant of your enemy's devices, his strategies, wicked plots. Learn to know his ways, recognize and discern spirits on assignment. Remember, you love the people, you hate the demons that harass and plot to inhabit and possess, influence and control humanity, to bring increase to satan's kingdom. I remind you, he is a practiced counterfeiter. Learn of his kingdom structure and do not be deceived. My armor is more than adequate, your weapons are powerful, your authority in My Name is unquestionable, and he is under My Feet, so yours as well. So move forward fearlessly, courageously, and do not cringe or fall back but press forward, forgetting the former things, and go forth and possess your land of promise! You are My glory!"

HIS EVER-UNFOLDING PLAN

The Holy Spirit had begun to give me 'hints' of change coming for me. The church was shifting smoothly along with the leadership change. Wonderful times in His Presence and at His table, feeding upon the word.

Max, Norma, others from the fellowship, and I were attending a conference in Dallas in the fall of '04. The morning before, I suddenly experienced an equilibrium problem, with weird symptoms that alarmed Max and Gene, so off we went to the ER! After they checked my heart, they decided it was an inner ear thing, and gave me an injection. It began to subside and I began to feel much better.

I have to share this 'happening' with you! While I was on the emergency table, so dizzy, everything whirling, stomach churning, pulse racing, just hanging in there, Max and Norma standing around me, praying, I began to have an open vision! I was looking at a baseball field, players on the field all dressed in uniforms, and someone called, 'batter up!' And I saw Norma, in a baseball uniform, with her cap turned to the back, looking very determined, step up to the plate and get into position to hit the ball! I began to laugh at the absurdity of me lying there and God the Holy Spirit giving me a vision concerning Norma! I began to share the vision and prophesy to Norma! We were shocked! He knew how to get our attention! About a month later, Norma was attending an event the Postal Service was having to recognize her service and soon retirement. She felt a little faint when they handed her a bronze plaque with a BASEBALL PLAYER holding the inscription, of all things!

I so love the Lord's sense of humor! He is alive and well within us, demonstrating we are spirit, we have a soul and we live in a body, and He is not limited by the weakness of the flesh or where we happen to be at the time!

I made the decision to go on to the conference. We were praying and I believed I would be just fine. Well, the next morning I could not get out of bed. Max was trying to find a pharmacy to get the prescription filled. I stayed on the medication, felt much better, and attended the meeting that evening. After the noon meeting the next day, I was walking with others down the hallway to the restrooms, when all of a sudden my head began to swim and I fell, hard, and landed on my shoulder. I tore a ligament and damaged the rotator cuff. I ended up having surgery in December, wearing a brace for six weeks, and driving to Abilene every day for physical therapy! It was a challenge for the family to take time from their work and drive from Corpus for a week at that time to take care of me. Lori was just recovering from surgery. I had just been to Corpus, staying a week with her the month before. During this time, Donny approached me concerning the family's desire for me to consider transitioning to Corpus. They felt it was time for me to sell the place and make the move while I was strong and in good health, to be with the family there. This brought more confirmation to what I had been sensing from the Lord and had not wanted to face.

Randy came in on Christmas Eve and we were having a snow-storm. Donny and Lori left, hating to leave the beautiful white Christmas scenery to return to Corpus, only to find a surprise when they arrived! Snowdrifts piled high on the island! A white Christmas on the coast!

Randy arranged for Gene to move in, take care of me, and drive me to Abilene for the next three weeks for therapy. My shoulder turned out great. Praise the Lord. It had been a tough two months.

I continued to pray and lean upon the Holy Spirit for timing and further instruction concerning transitioning to Corpus. There were such strong spiritual ties to the ministry and the family of LWM, as well as family roots in the soil. This home and property had been the Father's gift to us, all the miracles associated with it and the min-istry. Surely He had just the family that would honor and cherish it!

I had just not even considered that my journey would end anywhere else. At seventy-eight, I still had so much energy and vision I could not even consider not being in the middle of the 'river'! In one of my times in His Presence, He reminded me of His words in '03, when He was instructing me concerning the authority shift. He was extending my boundaries, and Billy prophesied, "The Lord says this is not demotion, it is not just this flock, you have inherited a golden heritage of His flock wherever you go."

Toward the end of the year of '05, I shared with Max the coming transition. He said one day as he was driving down the road in front of my gate, the Holy Spirit said, "Soon you will be driving by this gate and someone else will be living there." The Lord was preparing him.

The days following as I moved forward, to describe the tearing in my soul, would be difficult. There were times tears would be falling down my face, and at the same time in my innermost being I would be experiencing joy and anticipation. I knew that I knew this was His plan for me in this season, to serve and love on my sons and daughters and enjoy my grandchildren, and I also knew He would not let me fall behind in His move in the earth. He had a plan for me in His body in Corpus! Donny and Lori were staying in touch as they looked for property on which to build our home! One day a call came; they had purchased a wooded 1-1/2 acre lot in Flour Bluff and were working on plans! There would be a main house with a 'Granny flat' attached! I was to get busy and design it, and send it to them to give to the architect!

We worked to get the house and property ready to list by the first of the year. A wonderful couple from New Mexico, the Kilgos, called to see the house. She taught home economics, he had an agriculture degree. They fell in love with it and I fell in love with them. My heart was at peace. We closed in May. Possession was July first

Their love and appreciation of the house and property and all the plans they had for it brought so much comfort to me. I knew My blessed Lord was attending to every detail of this transition with tender love and care poured out upon me, and He had answered their prayers and provided a perfect blessing for them. How unspeakably good He is!

REGIONAL CONFERENCE, SEPTEMBER 2005

In the early part of the year, God the Holy Spirit began speaking to our hearts about a regional conference to be held in a neutral place that might encourage more to attend. More often than not, He directed us not to advertise. It would be by word of mouth and by His sending. But this time it was newspaper, radio and billboard! He dropped two words in my spirit: 'Fresh bread and fresh oil' to strengthen and anoint His people for the coming season! He brought this scripture to my mind:

Psalm 92:10, "But my horn [emblem of excessive strength and stately grace] You have exalted like that of a wild ox; I am anointed with fresh oil."

Renewing our strength, pouring upon us fresh oil that would break the yoke of weariness, discouragement and doubt. Bringing the righteousness, peace, joy, and power of the kingdom! He began to remind me of the third anointing of David, which set him in the chosen place of authority. He said: "My servants who will be speaking and ministering will not only serve fresh bread, not old and stale, but a pouring out of fresh oil upon the heads of key people in the region, to anoint them for the work ahead, spreading the good news of the kingdom with authority and manifestations. I Am reclaiming more territory, moving out tent pegs, establishing new boundaries. There will be a whole lot of 'stretching' going on within the 'shaking' of all that can be shaken!"

We rented the community center for a three-day conference. It had a large kitchen and serving area and we provided meals each day. The Lord had instructed us, no registration fees. This was 'on the house'!

Glenda, Jamie and the worship team would join us as well as Ministers Billy and Angie Nunez, Simon Purvis and Scott Beard.

The morning before the start of the conference that evening, I had just been in a time of prayer and began to go about preparing for the day, and suddenly, I began to have an open vision, looking into a vast area. What I saw in the Spirit, to the best of my ability I will try to describe.

He was raising up what looked like 'military camps,' 'outposts,' and 'operational headquarters' in this region. I was identifying this by the look of the different structures and the activity going on at each campsite. Maybe like something in the Civil War days. These camps were placed strategically by the Lord. We had been aware of some of the campfires, and had even warmed ourselves and fellow-shipped around some of them.

God intends to take in all of the territory between and around these camps, bringing them together under one 'tent, canopy' — He would use those two words interchangeably — forming a powerful army of worshippers, intercessors, a people of humility anointed to carry out the vision He had given them.

This 'tent, canopy' was being formed by cords of love and unity of purpose under the banner of the Kingdom of God, pronouncing Jesus Christ supreme Head of His body, the church! I saw fires burning at each campsite, each distinct, but the flames were at different levels, more visible and brighter than others, but all were under this tent. I thought about the tabernacle of David. I thought about the glory of the Lord increasing in His House.

As the different camps came under this tent, the smoke from the different campfires began to intermingle and merge, filling the tent and surrounding area, forming a canopy above and over all. The smoke seemed to form a layer of protection [I saw it as covering the heavens over the earth between the second and third heaven], and I was aware as I was viewing this, that the smoke had become a sign of the wrath of God against His enemies!

When the vision lifted, I immediately searched the scriptures for confirmation, and the Holy Spirit led me quickly to Isaiah 4:4-6! Wow! I could hardly contain the heat and rush of the Spirit through me as I read those words! I was glad I was sitting down!

"After the Lord has washed away the moral filth of the daughters of Zion [pride, vanity, haughtiness] and has purged the bloodstains of Jerusalem from the midst of it by the spirit and blast of judgment, and by the spirit and blast of burning and sifting. And the Lord will create over the whole site, over every dwelling place of Mount Zion and over her assemblies, a cloud and smoke by day, and the shining of a flaming fire by night; over all the glory shall be a canopy, a defense of divine love and protection! And there shall be a pavilion for shade in the daytime from the heat and for a place of refuge and a shelter from storm and from rain!" Psalm 18:11 " — His pavilion, canopy, round about Him were dark waters and thick clouds of the skies!" Revelation 8:14, smoke was incense created by the worship and prayers of the saints! Isaiah's vision in 6:4, " — the house was filled with smoke at the Presence of the Lord." At the Presence of the Lord upon Mount Sinai, the top of the mountain was covered in smoke.

I believe HE has revealed to us His vision for this region and this conference is a prophetic 'seed' sown that He intends to multiply to bring His vision to pass, as His people and leaders individually and corporately follow in obedience His leading in the coming days. The Church is an organism, not an organization, that God is re-structuring, out of man's structure and into His! He is the Lord God Sabbaoth, The Captain of the Host. His military agents are in the earth for the 'takeover'! And every kingdom of our hearts must be submitted to Him for training and discipline to be victorious. Not just submitted to him, but to one another, our comrades in arms.

Many came from all over the region. Truly fresh Bread, Oil and Wine were served to His people and there was great fellowship. We anticipated a harvest from the seeds sown in the fertile soil of the hearts of God's people, to the praise and honor of His glorious Name!

There were great churches represented, people who loved the Lord Jesus, called to serve Him through the anointing, gifts and vision they had been given. We were coming to understand the beautiful body of Christ, displaying His multifaceted beauty, nature, glory, power and love! We were coming to understand, even more, that it wasn't about the name above the door, the charter, and who we might be affiliated with. It was the Name by which we were called because of our being in Christ Jesus through our born again experience, His Spirit making us one together with Him! There is no elitism in His body. Every cell of His Body is important to the health of the whole body! It is through the revelation of our 'Oneness' in Christ through God the Holy Spirit, walls are crumbling! Love will triumph!

REVIEWING THE ARMOR
OF GOD

S atan, being the ancient serpent that he is, does a good job of covering up the fact he is the one attempting to overcome us, and we feel paralyzed to fight back. Many of us have not fully understood the nature of our archenemy. He is a master of psychology and will systematically work on breaking us down in such a way that we do not recognize who is behind this or what is taking place.

Have you ever tossed and turned on your bed under emotional burdens, your mind seemingly running loose and all sorts of imaginings and fears forming until you are emotionally distraught, depressed, oppressed? Pretty common for us all.

Demons on assignment will use those times of just before drifting off to sleep, or waking up in the middle of the night, or the semi-conscious state, or when our defenses are down and we are vulnerable, to indoctrinate us with insecurities, doubts and fears, to break us down emotionally and bring confusion and self-doubt. To move us from faith to fear, from truth to believing lies, from trust in God to blaming God. From repentance to pride. Leading us to destruction. He makes a determined effort to steal our peace, joy and fellowship with the Trinity, and steal our goods!

Most of us have caught on to his strategies and take some preventive measures: praying, worship, covering ourselves with the Word, binding, and loosing. There are times we just fall into bed without 'getting under the covers,' and we find ourselves in the 'throes' of turmoil and battle, and it's difficult to overcome. But we must! We are up against an enemy whose expertise is mind games.

Ephesians 6:10-18; "In conclusion, be strong in the Lord [be empowered through your union with Him]; draw your strength from Him. Put on God's whole armor [the armor of a heavy-armed soldier, which God supplies], that you may be able to successfully stand up against all the strategies and deceits of the devil. For we are not wrestling with flesh and blood [contending only with physical opponents], but against the despotisms, against the powers, against the master spirits who are the world rulers of this present darkness, against the spirit forces of wickedness in the heavenly supernatural sphere. Therefore, hold your ground, having tightened the belt of truth around your loins and having put on the breastplate of integrity and of moral rectitude and right standing with God, and having shod your feet in preparation to face the enemy with the firm-footed stability, the promptness, and the readiness produced by the good news of the Gospel of peace. Lift up over all the covering shield of saving faith, upon which you can quench all the flaming missiles of the wicked one! And take the helmet of salvation and the sword that the Spirit wields, which is the Word of God. Pray at all times, on every occasion, in every season in the Spirit, with all manner of prayer and entreaty. To that end keep alert and watch with strong purpose and perseverance, interceding in behalf of all saints."

Notice that it says in order for us to stand against the 'wiles' of the enemy, we must put on the whole armor of God. The word 'wiles' is defined as 'methods.' Meaning that the devil really has one method or inroad into our lives to defeat us with and that's through the carnal realms of the flesh, the deceptive, alluring call to appease the appetites of the flesh!

When Paul said, "we wrestle not against flesh and blood but against powers and principalities," he was saying that just as sure as one army pits itself against another, and one man against another, you and I are also striving against an army, only it is not one of flesh and blood, it is spirit powers and principalities. But this is just as real, although the weapons the devil uses are not guns, swords or spears but are imaginations, systems of thoughts, high things that exalt themselves against the Knowledge of God! 2 Corinthians 10:3-5 says the same thing.

What the devil is really after is our standing with God. He wants to destroy our relationship with Jesus Christ and ruin our testimony. He wants to seduce and deceive us until our prayers are no longer answered and we have lost fellowship with God the Holy Spirit!

You could be thrown in prison, reduced to poverty, even take your life, but none of these things would hurt our relationship with the Father. The devil would like our lives to offer infallible proof to the world that God does not exist, is not Omnipresent, Omniscient nor Omnipotent, even though we testify that HE IS!

The devil will go down through the generations fighting our children and fighting for our children!

Isn't it something, that God told us that in order to stand against a plotting, scheming murderer like satan and his host, we would have to put on the 'whole armor of God'? The Holy Spirit has His finger on these scriptures in this season to bring us up another 'notch' in awareness and preparedness! Like never before, I want us to know how to put on the whole armor of God so we will be standing in the Power of His Might!

The fact that the pieces of armor all represent or symbolize spiritual forces ought to tell us what the devil is really after! When Paul told us what to clothe ourselves in, he was really telling us what the devil is coming to take away!

Satan wants to wrestle away from us the whole armor of God piece by piece, because he knows God has given us power over all his power, and in order to defeat us, he has to destroy our relationship with God, which is symbolized by every piece of armor!

Notice that the first piece of armor the devil will wrestle you for is TRUTH! In fact, when Jesus instructed us to put off the old man and put on the new in Ephesians 4:24-25, the first instruction was to put off or put away 'lying'! It is interesting that the first piece of armor that we put on is the 'belt of TRUTH,' and when we put on the new man, the first thing we put away from ourselves is LYING!

We may have thought in the past that the 'truth' Paul was talking about here was strictly the revelation knowledge as set forth in His Word, but this is wrong. There is another piece of armor that makes strict reference to the use of revelation knowledge of His Word, and that is the Sword of the Spirit, which is the Word of God! But the truth he is talking about here is the same truth that Proverbs 12:22 is talking about. "Lying lips are an abomination to the Lord, but they that deal truly are His delight!" To gird up our loins with truth literally means to turn the Word inward and develop our character until we conform to the Word and not compromise truth!

Where the sword of the Spirit is an aggressive weapon is when we are confessing the Word, decreeing the word over circumstances, moving mountains, changing things around!

It does not matter how small or insignificant the compromise may seem to us, a 'little white lie,' or misrepresentation of the truth gives the devil authority in certain areas of our lives, because bottom line is, we have submitted ourselves to the 'father of lies,' and no matter how small the opening may be, he'll keep on hammering and pushing, trying to gain more ground! Jesus said in John 8:44, "The devil was a liar from the beginning and is the father of lies."

Now the arena for this wrestling match is the emotional realm of the soul! It is when the devil will use the lust of the flesh, pressure, torment or fear to coerce, seduce or deceive until he gets us into a place where we will lie just a little bit to keep the heat off, to save our 'skin.' We know when we do it. The real wrestling match takes place within ourselves when we resist with everything in us the temptation not to compromise the truth, no matter the consequence! Who we are really resisting is the devil, who wants to put a crack in our armor. He knows we literally have to give him authority in our lives.

We wonder at the fall of men and women, of those in great ministries, starting out so powerful and ending up so dead and defeated. Wiles of the enemy! Methodical military-like force, strategically planned to overcome the saints, especially where they can do the most damage to God's Name and His Kingdom! This is why Paul symbolized the spiritual forces that make up the armor of God after the military clothing of a Roman soldier. The Word stronghold [military fortresses] Paul uses to describe "casting down imaginations, and high things." Imaginations are elaborate systems of thought that become high things that exalt themselves against the knowledge of Christ, with the intention of removing him from lordship or influence. For instance, on a large scale example, such as the elaborate system of thought that makes up many of our large denominations who no longer preach the born again experience, Jesus the Christ being the only Way, the only door of salvation and eternal life. They no longer teach the infilling of the Holy Spirit or a holy lifestyle. Grace without law promotes lawlessness and death. In 2 Corinthians 10:15, Paul exhorts the people to bring every thought into captivity to the obedience of Christ!

Just the fact that there are thoughts that need to be captured and brought into the obedience to Christ ought to tell us that the devil has a way of planting certain thoughts into our minds. Now, he cannot read our minds, all he can do is make suggestions by planting thoughts, 'fiery darts' into our minds, and watch for some kind of response or reaction to see if they are having any effect upon us. But we do not have to accept his suggestions or his accusations. We must continually guard our minds, meditate upon the Word, and fellowship with God the Holy Spirit, growing in grace and in the knowledge of Him and casting down thoughts and imaginations, throwing them out immediately before they have time to germinate and bear fruit! And we begin to act out and speak out the lies we have believed!

If God were to open our eyes to the spirit realm of satan's kingdom, we would see ugly contorted demons, rulers of darkness of this world operating in earth's realm and among man, surrounded by a host of unclean spirits! The Father has gifted some with a level of discernment of spirits and He has opened their eyes to see into the dark realm. Those testimonies are available. When they do come around us, even though we cannot see them with our natural eyes or hear them, they will throw powerful suggestions and commands at us. Although we cannot hear them audibly, we can pick it up by our spiritual ear, and the suggestions and commands will manifest themselves in strong emotional feeling. These feelings give birth to anger, self-pity, fear, torment, unbelief, lust, unrestraint, etc.

The devil is trying to influence us to give place to him. Through intense emotional pressure, we react to the situation out of the carnal nature, the flesh. Thus, he has won that battle. And skirmish by skirmish, he intends to gain a foothold, and he rules our lives through unforgiveness, fear, torment, self-pity, self-exaltation, false belief system, filthiness of the flesh, addictions, etc. They become strongholds that defiantly take up residence and manifest through our personalities.

Let's talk about the pieces of the armor:

The breastplate of righteousness: When we were born again by the grace of God, we were made the righteousness of God in Christ! But the way we put on the breastplate of righteousness as a part of our protection from satan is when the nature of that right standing manifests itself in true holiness in our character and in our actions!

And our feet shod with the preparation of the gospel of peace: One of the most rugged pieces of the Roman soldier's equipment was his sandals. They would hold up for hundreds of miles in every kind of condition during their long forced marches. Paul was saying that in the same way, a Roman soldier would secure his sandals on his feet, the peace of God would enable you and I to stand sure-footed under any kind of circumstances or conditions! It is the peace of God that can make us virtually indestructible!

1 Peter 5:7-9; "Casting the whole of your care [all your anxieties, all your worries, all your concerns, once and for all] on Him, for He cares for you affectionately and cares about you watchfully! Be well balanced [temperate, sober of mind], be vigilant and cautious at all times; for that enemy of yours, the devil, roams around like a lion roaring, [in fierce hunger], seeking someone to seize upon and devour. Withstand him; be firm in faith against his onset — rooted, established, strong, immovable, and determined], knowing that the same identical sufferings are appointed to your brotherhood [the whole body of Christians] throughout the world. Lift up over all the covering shield of faith, upon which you can quench all the flaming missiles of the wicked one."

The best defense is to stop the devil before he can get to the other pieces of the armor! This is what the Roman shield was designed to do. When the alien army would approach, they would throw spears and shoot arrows. So when the demons are sent on assignment against us, he bombards us with imaginations, thoughts, and suggestions. The best way to take up the shield of faith is by meditating on God's Word until we are renewed in the spirit of our mind! For faith comes by hearing, and hearing by the Word of God, and when the fiery darts and missiles fly, they will bounce off the shield of faith and won't penetrate and cause a wound!

"And take the helmet of salvation and the sword that the Spirit wields, which is the Word of God and pray on every occasion, in every season, in the Spirit, with all manner of prayer and entreaty. To that end keep alert and watch with strong purpose and perseverance, interceding in behalf of all the saints."

These last three pieces of the armor go together. The only piece of the armor of a Roman soldier that was aggressive was his sword. It has been said that one of the most ferocious war machines ever assembled was the Roman army. It was relentless. The life of a Roman soldier depended on how well he could use his sword! They were so disciplined to follow the orders of their commander-in-chief that they would fight against any odds. They were fiercely loyal to one another, knowing their lives depended on it. No matter what the odds were, if they saw another soldier being overcome they would jump in and fight for him until he was back upon his feet! So this sword of the spirit is also an aggressive weapon on behalf of other saints.

Pray like Paul did in Galatians 4:19, when he made intercession for them when the devil used legalism to beat down their armor right down to the helmet of salvation! Paul cried, "My little children, I travail in birth again until Christ be formed in you!"

We all needed this 'review' and refresher course on the armor of God that has been supplied to us to wage and win this 'good' fight of faith! Amen?

THE HAMMER

Jeremiah 23:9; "Is not My Word like a fire that consumes all that cannot endure the test, says the Lord, like a HAMMER that breaks in pieces the rock of most stubborn resistance?"

The Holy Spirit has been like a hammer nailing certain truths securely to the wall of His House in this season, and it is bringing more stability to the whole house. He said to us during the time of the authority shift that He was dealing with us as 'sons,' those who have come to a level of maturity in the kingdom. How important it is for those of us in leadership to hear what the Spirit is saying to us in this season, this hour. He knows the revelation we need, that will continue to move us along in the maturing process. Obedience is gloriously difficult, but the discipline and training, the dethroning of the 'old' man [he only reigns positionally in Christ], and the 'crowning of the new man, the spiritual man,' in reality rules and reigns with Christ, for our ultimate blessing and His Honor! God will not shield us from the requirements and responsibilities of a son who has come from childhood to manhood! Childish things, carnal, spoiled undisciplined ways are no longer tolerated! Jesus said, "Come, follow me and become My disciple!" A disciplined one. A follower of the Pattern Son, to become as He is!

Max and I purposed that this flock of the Lord, that He has placed in our charge, is His for whatever purpose He desires and we will let Him pour us out wherever He wants to. Only He can prepare the menu, the meal that is needed to nurture, strengthen, heal and restore the 'cells' of His body. We all know it isn't about a 'good message,' a 'good sermon,' it is about what Father God desires to serve His people today, this hour from His recorded word [treasures from the old and treasure from the new] and 'fresh bread' warm from the oven of His ever-present Spirit! We are His, created in Christ Jesus unto good works that He has purposed!

Jesus came to reveal the Father! He said, "You have seen Me, you have seen the Father!"

Jesus as the Seed, the very Sperm of God planted into the womb of Mary — the time of developing in the womb, then the baby, the boy, the teenager, then the Son walking in His Father's footsteps, doing what He saw the Father doing, and saying what He heard His Father say! An obedient Son, full of grace, power and glory!

The same applies to us. I believe the Son is being revealed in the earth through the church. It is time for Him to be recognized as King of Kings and Lord of Lords, in His power and glory through the matured sons! Amen!

We should know by now that nurturing and raising babies up in the admonition of the Lord, discipling, ministry to the wounded and injured, helping the church move from babyhood to grown son, does not happen overnight! There must be commitment to follow through. A determination that will keep us pressing on as leaders, as led by His Spirit in all things. Fathering and mothering cannot happen unless the babies nurse at the breast of the 'mother,' and the child becomes obedient and submits to the 'father' for correction and discipline. Malachi 4:6; "And he shall turn and reconcile the hearts of the estranged fathers to the ungodly children, and the hearts of the rebellious children to the piety of their fathers."

Colossians 1:19 states that the fullness of the Godhead dwells bodily in Jesus. The full ministry of Jesus dwells in His body. It takes the gifts, anointing and ministry of the 'whole body' to bring wholeness, health and maturity. One will plant, one will water, one will harvest, but it is God who gives the increase and receives the glory! And we get to participate, enjoy and rejoice in it all! Can you see the importance of being in your place, functioning in your gifts, properly connected, enjoined and submitted to the Head and to one another?

We are the planting of the Lord, the trees in His field. But what if these 'trees' have grown crooked, twisted, bent because when planted they were not properly 'staked' or protected from the strong winds of adversity? Or perhaps the cords or ropes used to tie them to the stakes were left too long, and the cords began to damage the tree and the stakes held it back? Maybe their growth was stunted because of improper watering, feeding and cultivating. Maybe they were just left unattended. If someone cuts the cords, begins to properly water and feed and nurture it back to health, it over time begins to revive, put out new leaves and grow new branches. Although it may not become perfectly straight in the outward appearance, the bends, curves and scars produce a unique beauty, a one-of-a-kind tree that adds another dimension to the beauty of the field!

God's people are to become trees of righteousness, upright, straight and strong with inviting leafy branches for people to come under the shade of grace and eat of the fruit. There must be an ongoing relationship with a family of believers who will pray, and minister love, acceptance and encouragement! We will be known by our love, not by our gifts, talents or works. Only when the Word becomes a living Book, the Way of life, manifested in our lives through the power of the Holy Spirit, will we be living up to the name by which we are called: 'Christians.' Those like Christ.

We must remember that as a medical patient needs a time of recuperation, physical therapy and follow-up care, so do the casualties of satan's attacks and captivity. If they were to move too quickly into areas where they weren't strong enough or healed adequately to withstand the enemy's counterattacks, there would be danger to the whole body. God told the Israelites in Exodus 23 that He would not give them all the land in one year, lest the land become desolate and the beasts in the fields multiply against them. "But little by little, I will drive them out from before you until you be increased and inherit the land!"

All the exciting, awesome things God does for us and in our midst, the glory of His Presence, is so wonderful, we could just camp there! There is no test in that! The test is developing the character to walk out what God has spoken, to welcome the pressure, the situations and circumstances that have the potential to build that godly character and integrity, that we truly might be able to see others through His eyes, to love as He loves, to forgive as He has forgiven us, having arrived as matured sons, full of His goodness!

Let us worship Him in the Beauty of Holiness! Amen

CORPUS CHRISTI HERE WE COME!

2006 would be an unforgettable, life-changing, challenging, heart-wrenching, tear-jerking, humbling, blessed year!

The Art of Transition:

We must learn how to bend or we will break.
If we hold on to today, we will miss the glory of tomorrow and what lies ahead.
We must be weaned from yesterday, as Samuel had to be weaned from the breast of his mother before he could go forward into the fullness of his purpose.
Yesterday is in the tomb, the future is in the womb.
The best is ahead of us! The best is yet to come!

There were many ' Downys' (as in: the fabric softener) in this 'load' of transition! The Holy Spirit being, of course, the greatest! Donny, Lori, Lacey and of course the family of Living Water. Estate sale! Moving out of 3,000 square feet into an 800-square-foot apartment for a year, until our house was finished, then into my 1,200 square-foot 'granny flat'! Whew! Have you ever cleaned out an attic 60 feet long? Lacey drove down from Midland to facilitate. An organizer she is! "Granny, you sit in this comfortable chair and we will bring you boxes and we will decide what to keep." She was considerate and sweet, but no mercy. Nostalgia didn't equate, tears didn't move her, she got it done! And in record time! Donny and Lori were coming with the movers and he would take care of all the outside stuff and oversee the process. There was an anointing upon everyone to get this done, an outpouring of His grace! Shawn would be moving with us as well, since Corpus had been his home most of his life.

Sunday, July the 9th, was my last service with the family. A fullness of time had come. Parting was indeed a sweet sorrow! Reminiscing, marveling in all we had shared and experienced through the years. Tears, laughter, celebration and gifts! The honor they bestowed upon me was humbling. I was blessed beyond words. The seeds of honor, love and care they have sown into my life surely will be rewarded with blessings and a long life!

Max prophesied a book was forthcoming and the mantle of Caleb rested upon me, the Holy Spirit, the mighty Encourager! Don had prophesied I would be as 'Anna' in the temple for the next season.

The Lord had given us the time needed for me to be 'weaned' from the breast of the ministry and the congregation to be 'weaned' from 'mom's breast.' We were in covenant relationships, our hearts would always beat together, this would only be a physical separation according to the Lord's plan and purpose for each of our lives. Bless His holy Name forever!

I made my visit to the cemetery on Saturday to put out fresh flowers on the graves of T.W. and the family and visit a while.

On the weekend of July 4th, 2006, the movers arrived in their large van and Donny and Lori in another truck. Sunday morning by 9:00, we were packed and ready to 'move on'! Max, Norma, Gene, and Don and Cherri Crum were there to see us off. My faithful red healer, Lily, would be adopted by the Kilgos. Donny on the point, Shawn behind him, Lori and I next, then the big van. Donny stuck his head out the window and waved his cap and shouted, "Okay! Let's move 'em out. Corpus Christi, here we come!"

This was a huge shift, relocation, new identity, total change. As I waved goodbye, tears were flowing but there was a peace and joy, and exhilaration! For the next year, I would understand Don's word to me.

CORPUS CHRISTI, TEXAS

I never dreamed I would find myself living once again in Corpus! Do those words sound familiar? It seemed like an echo from down through the years! "I never thought I would be here, or go there or do that!" Who can know all that God has planned for those who love Him and trust Him? We just know His plans are GOOD, and He is TRUSTWORTHY! And He always does super-abundantly above all that we can think or ask! Once again, we experience the waters parting for us to cross over only when we walk by faith, not by sight. As we step into the 'Jordan at flood' stage, the wind of God's Spirit calms the sea and parts the waters and a way is made, a path is formed to pass through into the 'promises.'

Journal Entries from: July 24th to September 10th, 2006

My first night in my new temporary home. My familiar things around me made it warm, comfortable and certainly 'doable'! How gracious You are to me, Lord! My first morning, You 'christened' this place and me with Your Presence! How very precious was our time together for the purpose of establishing this day as the official day of this new season of my journey to 'parts unknown'! From glory to more glorious! I am in Your hands, Lord, and Your eye is upon me as even upon the sparrow! Even as you have clothed the lilies of the field, you have clothed me with Your robe and 'endued' me with power from on high! I am SO in awe of Your grace and mercy, the sense of security and peace that fills me.

The intercession with tongues, tears and travail with such faith and authority I knew was opening a way within me, as well as making a 'highway' for You! I had such a sense of 'reclaiming territory, clearing out the underbrush, setting boundaries and driving down stakes'!

Randy's visit was spirit to spirit, strengthening, encouraging, sobering, enlightening and challenging! Our flesh melts in Your Presence, and we are lifted up and out of the 'cares of this life' for a little while as we revel in Your Way with us! As we experience the new thing, the new place, "Behold! [stop, look, consider intently, be arrested by] I the Lord have done a new thing!" We embrace the 'new thing' for us, Lord!

July 29th:

My precious Donny and Lori were so sweet upon my heart this morning. Thank You, Father! They are such a beautiful blessing to me, so gracious, kind and loving. They have been the 'Downy' in this season of transition, softening each part of it. Reward them, Lord, according to Your Word! My heart continues to overflow with thoughts of Lacey. I give You praise. Out of the fiery furnace of her early years, You have brought forth 'gold' that I am sure will increase in purity and value as the years go by!

Thank You, Holy Spirit, for the ministry within my heart through this time. No regrets, fears or longings, only peace, joy and knowing I am in the center of Your will!

I began to sense Holy Spirit was leading me each day to revisit places we had lived in the past, and certain areas of the city that brought back hurtful, unpleasant memories. For several days, I drove the different neighborhoods and parts of the city, praying as He would lead me, worshiping and redeeming the land and the area. I was amazed at the effect it had upon me, the release it brought. I was so grateful to Him.

August 22:

The 'flesh' is so fickle, Lord! Thank You for the stability of Your Spirit! The unchangeableness of Your Nature. The steadfastness of Your Love! The grace that permeates our very lives! "Grace, Grace, Marvelous Grace! Grace that is greater than ALL our sins!" Faith Fact: My inner man is being changed into Your likeness, my new nature rules in the house of the Lord, whose house I am! Thank You, Lord, You will finish what You have begun! As David, I will encourage myself in the Lord!

While in prayer and intercession, I heard the word 'dermabrasion'! The outward appearance must accurately express the new inner grace, beauty, power and glory of the emerging body of Christ! The church has come to a new place and it must needs have a new face! After restructuring, a resurfacing! Surface dermabrasion is taking place to reveal the new face of the church! Uncovering the hidden beauty.

Dermabrasion in the natural removes dryness, flakiness, wrinkles, spots and blemishes! It is the Bride of Christ emerging! She will be without spot or wrinkle! Dermabrasion is 'friction' that causes a slight 'burn' of the outer layer of skin, like a deep 'sunburn'! The new skin emerges soft, pliable and glowing! Wow! Lord! That is good!

Father, thank You for keeping us 'abreast of things'! It helps to identify what is going on in our lives personally as well as with the church in this season! "These temporary light afflictions, the fiery trials are achieving for us an everlasting weight of glory, beyond all measure! A transcendent glory never to cease!" 1 Peter 1:7.

September 10:

Our human, natural way is to question, debate, and argue. We often think we can do this with the Lord as well. When He speaks to us out of His word, or face-to-face in our spirit man, or through others, however He communicates with us, there should be no discussion! We either receive it, respond appropriately, move on it, obey it OR not! It isn't open for discussion or debate!

If we receive it, embrace it, the Holy Spirit will then begin to work within our hearts, supply the grace and wisdom, and make a way when there seems to be no way, for the honor of His Name and our blessing!

Continuing on:

Only a few days of getting settled in and resting up, I find myself in a very important position of 'the go-fer' for Donny and helping with the house! He was the contractor on the house as well as doing much of the work himself. Lori was holding down the office and she and I were collaborating on the decorating. I prepared dinner for us almost every night during this time. The house was a large project, and sub-contractors were often not too dependable or available. It was very stressful and challenging for Donny, and at times for Lori as well. But it was exciting for us all and I was happy to be involved.

My apartment was on Oso Bay with a walk along the water's edge, which provided me a safe and beautiful place to take my morning walk, pray, and fellowship with the Lord. I did miss the hilly country road with Lily running up ahead to scout out any danger and chasing off the 'varmints'!

I returned to Cross Plains on November 14th to meet up with the group from LWM to attend the FMCI conference in Dallas. What a blessing!

I was so refreshed and strengthened from the worship, the prophetic ministry and fellowship! I was taking deep 'gulps' from the river I had swum in for years. Every church I had visited up to this point in Corpus felt as if I had stepped back in time ten or fifteen years! I was not being critical, they were a beautiful part of His body, serving where they had been planted with the vision they had been given. I just knew that was not the part of the body I felt I could connect to and flow with. I also knew it was not time yet.

I stayed a few days with Max and Norma before returning home, and slept in what had been my bedroom growing up! The essence of my mother and father still lingered, and it was very good, very peaceful.

Christmas was a wonderful family time. Not like Christmas at the farm, but it was good. The little adjustments all along the way.

The year flew by like a freight train! It was now January 2007. It looked like another six months before our house would be finished. Donny and Lori were searching the Internet to determine what breed of large dog they were going to adopt. They settled on a German Shepherd and looked at picture after picture, kennel after kennel! Finally! The Face! The Eyes! Pedigree a mile long! His name would be Levi! He arrived by plane in May at eight weeks old! He adopted us, as well as Muppy and Stormy, as a part of the 'pack' he was sent to love and protect! And he certainly took it seriously! He was a challenge for the' two little girls'!

In February, Jordan made his first missionary trip to the nations. It had quite an impact upon him. He had opportunity to experience the medical missionary, Dr. Dan Goodnight, and spent every moment with him that he could, hearing the stories of his life and experiences and challenges with political opposition. I was continually amazed at Jordan. At seventeen, he was wise far beyond his years, of impeccable character, considerate, God-centered, and most certainly a leader. I knew he was one of thousands of his generation all over the face of the earth who will indeed change the culture. World-changers, history-makers, bringing Your justice, not by might nor power but by Your Spirit, Lord Jesus, according to Your Word!

There was a conference at LWM in April, with Sam and Nancy Brassfield and the worship team from San Antonio! The Lord said go, to me and to Randy! An awesome time in His Presence. Encouragement, prophetic ministry and revelation from the prophets. Fellowship with Ronnie and Terri Jordan around the table of the Lord, bread and sweet wine of the Spirit served from golden vessels! He always knows just what we need in the season and place we are in, to keep us in the flow of His purpose and plan for our lives! Praise Him!

Jordan graduated in May and would be leaving in the fall for Texas A&M to earn an international business degree.

July 30, 2007:

We are in our new home! Challenges, not a few! But with the grace of heaven upon us and the wind of purpose at our backs, we are now in the middle of a dream come true! I feel very special, Lord! Highly favored and blessed. Wow! Private entrance to the 'the granny flat' joined to the main house. It is perfect, beautiful and comfortable! I step out the patio door from my bedroom into a huge patio area. Swimming pool, hot tub, the works! Totally shielded from the street or neighbors. Very private, trees, landscaping, tall fence! Doesn't even feel like you're in a city!

My Journal Entry Aug. 6/07:

I feel very loved by You, Lord, through my children and grand-children. It isn't really about what we have accomplished but how we have loved, right, Jesus? The seeds of caring, graciousness, thoughtfulness, hospitality that have been sown and continue to be sown in the soil of one another's lives is 'coming up roses'! Love does produce a 'lovely fragrance'! God's kind of love always brings its reward!

It has been one year since leaving the home You provided for me in Cross Plains. I believe that this provision is from You as well, for much more than I know at this point. You have been my shelter through the years and have always seen to it that I had a lovely home. I am keenly aware that it is a house of prayer, a place of ministry, where Your Presence is greatly desired and coveted. Ceilings of praise and walls of salvation, as a prophetic testimony of the Bible planted in the foundation, opened to Psalm 91: this family is established solidly upon THE ROCK!

I was so grateful and humbled, as You well know, as Your Presence filled this place and engulfed me in Your embrace this morning. I was reminded of the song I've sung through the years, "For I'm Sheltered in the Arms of God." What Your glory and Presence has touched becomes kingdom property! Yes, Lord!

The first week of November, I received an invitation from the Nunezes to visit a few days and attend a conference with them. It was a blessed time, and a surprise birthday celebration as well! I would travel on from there to Austin to meet the family at the FMCI conference.

My Journal Entry November 8/07:

Tears of thanksgiving pour from my eyes. My inner man presses to reach Your Heart and bring You joy and bless You! Thank You, Father God, for arranging this time with Angie, Billy and family. I miss being involved and in the middle of Your manifested Presence on a continual basis, and meeting with others of the body of Christ. On a personal note, Lord, how can I thank You for all your gifts and surprises this birthday week? I feel so honored and encouraged beyond words. I need to visit with You about this morning in our time together when You sent me to 1 Corinthians 1:26-31. What was that all about? I had no control over the flood of tears that kept pouring and pouring. Melting? Breaking? Cleansing? My seventy-ninth birthday! How can it be? I know, some time back I said to You, "Lord God, like Caleb I cry, Lord! Give me my mountain You promised! I am able Lord!" I don't really know what is ahead, what lies beyond, what I will find along the way higher up the mountain. I do not know what seventy-nine is supposed to feel like, but I feel young and strong! My body has certainly changed and I barely can make out 'me' when I look in the mirror!

Lord, you know my sitting down and my rising up, the challenges in my mind, the times when I consider my calendar years, and yet my inner man is 'chomping at the bit,' so to speak! It is hard to explain, I just don't feel old! I can't quit now, I might miss something! This is too exciting and glorious! Now, I know this doesn't compare to heaven, Lord, but I am very blessed. Okay, Lord? I am hearing You! The familiar scriptures this morning! Yes, You were doing some redeeming, delivering, and healing work in my heart for the upcoming season of my life! At any age, very young or very old, You still choose what in the world is foolish to put the wise to shame, and what the world calls weak to put the strong to shame! I will continue to be a testimony to, "the foolish thing that has its source in God is wiser than men and the weak thing that springs from God is stronger than men!" Yes, I am able, Lord, I shall keep running and not faint and mount up as the eagle! Oh! Yes!

November 18/07:

What a glorious two weeks! Times of refreshing from the Lord. "You brought me to Your banqueting table and Your banner over me was Love!" I know You were showering me with so many surprises and blessings, I am convinced You were 'buttering me up, softening me up' so I would 'slide' right into Your plans for me for the 'right around the corner' next season! Thank You, Gentle Shepherd! I am paying attention, listening, waiting. There is an unusual 'giddiness' within my spirit, a level of internal joy that is expressing itself in ways that I notice are attracting a little bit of attention! They are probably interpreting it as just a 'symptom of old age'! [Granny may be losing it a little bit!] They better be fastening their seat belts if they are going with me! Right, Lord? And I believe I am feeling Your joyful anticipation for the days ahead for Your flock, and Your justice sweeping the earth!

Randy is making time to come and get me in Austin, able to partake of a day of meetings and making connections. How beautiful are You in Your Body, Lord! How precious is their expression of You. Max is always so honoring of me. I praise You for the bountiful harvest You have prepared for him from the seeds he has sown, monetarily, prophetically and revelatory into my life. Your kingdom within me has been increased out of his love and integrity.

How awesome it was 'on the mountaintop'! I love the 'quality of air' and the ability to 'see afar'! I look forward to the next mountaintop experience, wrapped in Your Presence!

THE LION OF JUDAH IS ROARING!

T he writings of the Prophet Hosea represent God's yearning, unending love for His people. In Hosea 11, that love is expressed and the purpose is to stir the hearts of His people to return to Him in love!

"My people are bent on backsliding from Me. Though they call to the Most High, none at all exalt Him. My heart churns within Me; My sympathy is stirred. I will not execute the fierceness of My anger; I will not again destroy Ephraim. For I Am God and not man, the Holy One in your midst; and I will not come with terror! They shall walk after the Lord. He will roar like a Lion! When He roars, then His sons shall come trembling from the west; they shall come trembling like a bird from Egypt; like a dove from the land of Assyria. And I will let them dwell in their houses, says the Lord!"

The Lion roaring to call his young represents God calling His people out of captivity! They will come trembling! Which means with repentance, humbly, and with joy! They will come like a dove, noted for its swiftness.

Remember 2 Timothy 4:17? "But the Lord stood with me and strengthened me, and I was delivered out of the mouth of the lion." 1 Peter 5:8; 'Be sober, be vigilant because your adversary the devil, as a roaring lion walks about seeking someone he may devour whom resist steadfast in the faith. But the God of all grace who has called us into His eternal glory by Christ Jesus, after that you have suffered awhile, will Himself complete and make you what you ought to be, established and grounded securely and will strengthen and settle you!"

So! That old toothless lion is trying to imitate the True Lion of Judah! And intimidate the Church! But God will only allow the false, the evil, the imitation to operate so long until He roars and calls His people out of the mouth of that which is false and evil! The Church, no matter where she is, the warriors of the cross, true worshippers and intercessors are hearing the roar from within and without, calling His people to Himself as never before. It is His High Call! That is why we are experiencing such a hunger for the truth, the living God, and to drink only from His well! To encounter Him, experience Him.

Even as we individually have been changing and maturing and growing in the grace and knowledge of Him, being perfected through love, even so the Church as Christ's body has been coming into divine order — OR being exposed as dead, heretical or apostate! And the sheep must choose a true Shepherd. Not cling out of misguided loyalty to a denomination, a church, or to a person, or strange doctrines. But cling only to Christ and His Word, His teachings and doctrines. The Church's greatest hour is ahead of us! In spite of all the filth, shame, backsliding, and rebellion, we are headed for victory! The prodigals are returning home, the fatted calves are penned for the sacrifice of the great celebration! There is a mass exodus from the world, compromise, sin and deception! God's sons and daughters are moving into the Promised Land! The roar from the Great Lion of Judah is calling them home! The sons are returning home to the Father's house! Families are being reconciled! Don't give up yet! Don't give in yet! The greatest hour is upon the church! Our God is faithful! He will heal our backsliding. He will love us freely! He will be as the dew unto His Church and her roots will shoot downward and her branches shall spread outward and her beauty shall be as the olive tree and her fragrance as the Rose of Sharon and as the new wine! Oh! And all shall say, "What do I have to do anymore with idols? For the ways of the Lord are right and I shall walk in them!"

The Great Lion has sired many sons, and the righteous have become bold and strong as He, and a great roar is filling the earth and who can stand against it? So do not weep. For the Church of the Lion of the Tribe of Judah has overcome and conquered!

NEW BEGINNINGS

2008! Eight: the scriptural number of resurrection, regeneration, new beginnings and of super abounding!

In my life and the lives of our family, this would become a prophetic reality. And according to numberless other testimonies, this would prove to be a year of pronounced change, new life, new order and new beginnings! Entering through the new gate, to the beyond!

And we would discover anew that resurrection, new beginnings and super abounding can be totally concealed for a time in old grave clothes, adverse, earth-shaking circumstances and separations.

This would be the year of my eightieth birthday! 80 on November 8th of '08! 1928! Four eights! This is my eagle time! I knew this would be a huge beginning year marking the rest of my life!

On New Year's Eve, as I was in a prayer and seeking time, the Holy Spirit said: "The time of the changing of the guard!" I meditated upon it, and called Max to see if any understanding would unfold. We had a good visit and tossed some things around, but received no light on it. I was awakened early the next morning to pray and seek the Lord. I picked up the Word and was led to Judges. I was just kind of skipping over it and the Spirit arrested me at chapter six, I began to pray, reading slowly, when I got to verse 19. the words were highlighted off the page! "AT THE THIRD WATCH, AT THE CHANGING OF THE GUARDS AT THE GATE [I SAW ADDED TO IT THESE WORDS] "**OF HIS PRESENCE**!" Tears and tongues began to flow profusely. 2008 is a 'window' year, a time of the changing of the guards at the gate of His Presence. The

Church at large, time-wise, is stationed in the beginning of the third watch, just before the cock crows, just before daybreak at the GATE OF HIS PRESENCE. It was the Lord's desire that we not only go through this gate in '08, but far beyond and deep into spiritual territory and reclaim what had been stolen. A Gideon company has been prepared to do just that! To open the way into a dimension of His Presence, His Glory, and manifestations of His Kingdom we cannot imagine!

I was urged to keep reading further. After Gideon and his little company of sifted, tried, humbled, dedicated, committed and submitted warriors had broken through, entered in and staked their claim, Gideon began to rally the rest of Israel to enter in and press on! Once again, tears and tongues were flowing, travailing and intercession, scriptures coming to mind of when David challenged Goliath, and the army of Israel waited in fear and doubt a distance away. After David removed the 'head' of the usurper in Israel's territory, the rest of Israel joined David to participate in celebrating the victory! And Elisha as he had followed Elijah all the way through to receive his mantle, the double portion, the fifty prophets that had been standing 'afar off' observing,' when they saw that Elisha had indeed received the promise, they joined with him! The Lord so impressed upon me concerning the "Gideon companies" that would impact the nations. It is about harvesters for the harvest, taking cities and nations.

Right out of the womb of the year, a huge 'new beginning' for River City House of Prayer. Pastors Billy and Angie Nunez had become affiliated with Alamo City Fellowship as their worship leaders and RCHOP would be using their facilities. Their services would now be on Saturday nights. I was asked to be there for the weekend. I was still so 'pregnant' with the word of the Lord when Jamie came to pick me up. I would stay with her, so grateful for the opportunity to pray and support them. It became so evident this was all the Father's orchestration, the time with Jamie in the 'open portal,' engulfed in the Spirit, revelation, prophecy so much released into earth's atmosphere from heaven, so many things established. I shared with her the word the Lord had given me for the year. The Father's loving grace for the jolting shifts, throes of change and inner turmoil connected with this transitioning 'Lazarus experience.' "Grace like honey," thick and sweet, fragrant and sticky! A 'tonic' for the soul!

At the service on Sunday morning, the worship team was flowing in prophetic song and Jamie was under the 'influence' and was singing a new song of the Spirit, "Take us beyond the Gate of Your Presence!" People began to weep throughout the congregation. There was a holy hush upon us all. No doubt, God had His prophetic people all over the earth releasing His vision, His word for this season into the heavens, and angels hearkening to the voice of His word to see that it comes to pass! Halle!

The 'new thing' is out of the womb, it's been washed, the umbilical cord to the past season has been cut, salve is being applied to the eyes for clear vision to move ahead. Mucus is being removed from the throat for the new 'voice of authority'!

Lift up your heads, O ye gates. The King of Glory is coming through!

Lacey was moving to San Antonio, going to work for a branch of MHMR. Another new beginning! James would be joining her. It would be so good to have her so close!

Entry in my Journal. March of '08:

One year and nine months! And in one day You planted me in Your Garden of Victory South Coast Church! Connected me with the Pastor, David Bendett, intercessors and several of the young adults. The next Sunday morning was an 'extreme divine connection' with the assistant Pastor, a young woman, Sonya Martinez. Our hearts melded together, we both were weeping and she asked what was on the Lord's heart for this season. I said, the merging of the generations. Once again, clearly, only You, Holy Spirit, can make the true divine connections for the continuing fulfillment of the Father's plans for me as one of His building contractors! In the early years, the tools the Holy Spirit gave me were a sword in one hand and a hammer in the other hand! When I wrote the words, "the Garden of Victory," my spirit was so stirred, and You reminded me instantly of the words that came out of my mouth a few day ago, as

I was worshiping and singing spiritual songs, when suddenly, force-fully prophetically, I began to sing: "You're in the army now and you're behind a plow! And you'll be rich digging a ditch, you're in the army now!" I was singing it off and on all day. Knowing that was too unusual not to be YOU! So what You are saying to me is: "In this season, my tools of ministry will be a plow and a shovel"!? I am following the 'clues' here to see where we are going! Okay. At the women's Bible study on Tuesday, the theme was the merging generations. During ministry time, the Holy Spirit began to move within me and I began to have hard travailing contractions. At that time, I was asked to step up for prayer ministry. Linda began to prophesy over me that I was a mother and I would birth many more into the kingdom, as Sarah. Much travail in my soul. When I sat down, I heard You say, "The plowman shall overtake the reaper." The promise of Amos 9:13-15. Halle! What took place was a pro-phetic demonstration of this season on the earth in Your church! Then You spoke 2 Kings 3:16, "Dig ditches in this valley and I will fill them with water so all may drink"! Well Lord! So, the plow and the shovel! This should be an interesting season for me and the body of Christ! Lord! "I'm in the army now! And I'm behind a plow! I'll be rich digging a ditch! I'm in the army now!"

Lord, I am in such a different place. I am so accustomed to just moving and ministering, and it's hard because I don't have the lib-erty to move freely, I don't have a place. Trusting the gifts You have given me and the anointing will make the place and opportunity, the structure of the church. I feel I'm in a time warp! Holy Spirit, HELP!

Continuing on: June

Jordan had finished his first year of college, not without trials and tribulations! He spent the summer going on mission trips. The passion and fire continued to build. He participated in 'The Burn,' a harp and bowl ministry, as often as possible. In August, he and four-teen others rented a van and drove straight through to Washington to participate in "The Call." Then just before time for fall semester, off to California with friends for a week of surfing! Thank You, Lord, for the angels You have assigned to him to accompany him in all of his goings and comings! You are his shield and ark of safety, his strong tower! Thank You for the keeping power of Your Covenant Blood!

My relationship with Sonya and her family seemed to be for more reasons than I could see at the time. I knew I was sent to pray and encourage Pastor David and some other key people in the church, but there were great stirrings in the spirit concerning Sonya. I just could not connect to 'Victory Church,' but I was strongly connected to a core people. I became part of an intercessors team, and just available to the Lord.

June 28 through July 6:

Off to San Antonio and Cross Plains again! Thank You, Lord. I love these assignments. It is blessing to be with Jamie and Judy and the powerful intercession Saturday night. Blessed time with Pat and Martha, restful and refreshing. I felt that it was a strategic visit, because of the unexpected intercession that took place as I was having my morning time on the patio, much weeping, warfare and tongues, and knew it was for Pat. Maybe his health. The Holy Spirit didn't tell me.

I arrived in Cross Plains on July 2, and once again a memorable few days! Surprises and such blessings. I soaked in the love, graciousness, laughter, tears and joy. I reveled in the giftings and anointings, revelations and confirmations that swirled around us all. I was experiencing such supernatural joy that continually bubbled forth. My inner man was so energized. It had been several years since I had seen Amber, Miranda and Penny, and to hear their testimonies of the Lord's delivering, transforming grace and the powerful work of the Holy Spirit in their lives, was glorious! The fruit of the Spirit was sweet and precious! And all the children! How beautiful are Tina and Rodney's, Glenda and Jeremy's children! Always so good to be with Franke. I do not know what I would do without her! And Gene! A loving, servant heart. I miss them all so much! What an awesome July Fourth celebration! Rodney had seen to the fireworks at the lake and the weather was perfect. One to be remembered! Bless them richly, Father. I know they will be good stewards of what You pour out and a humble host of Your Presence.

As I was traveling to Cross Plains, I kept hearing in my spirit the word 'stakes.' I was puzzled. In the services Sunday morning in Max's opening prayer, he used the word 'stakes.' It jumped out at me, and after the prayer I began to prophesy the word of the Lord over the body of Christ. "The throes' of change, the jolting shifts and inner rumblings of turmoil. Precious and of great worth are My arrows, My weapons I have been honing and sharpening as 'stakes' being driven deep into the ground of My Kingdom! Staking off My territories, staking My claim on My gold mines, to extract My treasure! Mining out of the 'earth,' the gold, silver and precious gems, to display before the world! I have 'staked' My claim to the earth, I will have what is mine! It is the time of the changing of the guard. Go through! Go through the gate! The enemy will flee before you! Continue to move forward, Go beyond! Go beyond! I am opening the way! For you are a gate many will come through and experience the broad place of brooks, fountains and springs. Break through! Break through! For I have already broken through before you!"

On my return, I received an invitation in the mail to my birthday party! This was going to be lavish and BIG! Robert and his new wife, Cindy, were coming from Arkansas. We were going to have members of the 'Sojourners' of the 70s, and the band! With Lori and Lacey in charge, I was so blessed and excited! Could hardly wait for The Day! Everyone was invited!

Then the news: our baby girl, Lacey, and James were expecting a baby! Oh Jesus, draw Lacey to Yourself and protect this precious gift that You have chosen to be born at this time, to become a mighty champion of the faith and powerfully anointed for the work of Your kingdom. May he totally reject the ways of the world and fully embrace the Way of God, the One True God, and Lord of all Lords! James and Lacey's lives would seem to be a prophetic picture of this being a year of new beginnings and super abounding. This child will be so special! His name would be Noah! How prophetic is that? My great-grandson!

I went on my first missionary trip to Mexico, with a team from Victory Church headed up by Sonya! The passion and hearts of the young adults was awesome. A large feeding and distribution of clothing took place at the city dump. The presence of God was there in a special way. We had a wonderful ministry time with the pastors and people. God moved powerfully in our midst, loving on His precious ones. The children at the orphanage were so beautiful and precious. One little girl just took to me and clung to me the whole time! It was very emotional for me to leave her. It was an experience I won't soon forget.

Prophecy to Pastors and Key Leaders, 10/22/08:

"Let not your hearts faint within you. Let no fear or intimidation reign for even a moment. For you are indeed at the threshold of a dimension of glory that will envelope all of you and all I have called you to! A glory you have only tasted up to this hour, but you shall indeed not only see the glory manifested around you, but you will be a part of the glory that others will run into and be healed and restored!

"Yes, I come! But not as some suppose at this time, but I AM come suddenly to My temple prepared for Me, consecrated to Me, and I Myself will fill it with the fullness of My Spirit! It is imperative that you keep Me upon the throne of your heart through your worship and praise, as well as being committed to Me in intimacy, acknowledging My Lordship over your lives. I desire to keep My scepter extended over you with a continual release of anointing and authority, as well as blessing and provision!

"Practice until you perfect praise, until your hearts pour forth continual thanksgiving, that any and all things that would hinder you or keep you from moving forward in your purpose and destiny, or prevent you from entering and pressing into My Presence, are broken off! This is the unity first and foremost that must be accomplished, making a symphony unto Me! Only then as you lift your hands and you lift your hearts and through the intense pressure of desire within you; your body, soul and spirit come into unity and you become an instrument of praise unto Me! I AM conducting this orchestra and a sound is being released into the atmosphere that is shaking earth and opening portals!

"This is indeed a time to rejoice! It is always good to rejoice! In every season, rejoice! Sing! Sing a new song! Dance! Dance a new dance! Declare, decree and prophesy! Submit your bodies and all your faculties to My Spirit and let us rejoice together on earth as it is in heaven!

"Sound the trumpet in Zion and stir up the people! Stir! Stir! Stir! Call the troops to order! The command of the Captain of the Host is: 'Forward March!'"

My Journal November 9:

The Big Day! The Big 80! Unbelievable! How good to see Robert as well as Cindy. My heart could not help but miss Lois. It is amazing what You worked in my heart toward Cindy. It feels so good to just love, with Your pure love! I dearly love her! Gary and his sons, reconnecting by Your Spirit. I loved it! Pat and Martha, thank You, Lord, for their hearts. What fun, how precious 'our jivin' fun dance! I think it surprised him, I was 'up to it' even more than he was! The MUSIC, the FOOD, the CAKE, the FLOWERS, FAMILY, FRIENDS, WEATHER, the LOVE, the JOY! What can I say, Your blessing was upon it all! I felt Your Presence embellishing and enhancing everything the whole time! You always loved feasts and celebrations!

Lacey is one special young lady! James one special young man! Lori, Donny, Randy, Betty and Jordan, blessings! Singing with the team again, so blessed by the gifts and talents You have given them. Surely that won't be the last time? Only You know, dearest Lord, the blessing all of that was to my heart. It will all forever be a memorable event in my life and an expression of love and honor to me from my family and friends and from You!

How can I say thanks for the things You have done for me? Things so underserved that You did to prove Your love for me! The voices of a million angels cannot express my gratitude. All that I am or ever hope to be, I owe it all to Thee! (Andre Crouch, *My Tribute*, copyright 1971. Bad John Song Inc., EMI Christian Music.)

Heading out for Cross Plains to meet up with the family there to attend the FMCI conference and meet up with another precious part of the family of God. Thank You for all the hearts You have intertwined and lives You have woven together through the years. I eat the bread and partake of the wine from the fruit of their lives and become strengthened and 'intoxicated'! After the great surprise disappointing election outcome. To hear what You are saying to the church in this hour.

November 15th Journal:

I was amazed at the 'pall' that hung over the conference because of the election results. Dutch Sheets, being the intercessor and prophet to the nations that he is, was absolutely inconsolable. I did not know if the internal giddiness, the joy that I was experiencing, was a left over thing from my birthday celebration or not. Or if what I was feeling, which was certainly inappropriate in that atmosphere, was YOUR feelings and assessment of what had taken place! In my discussing this with Max, he seemed to confirm it was the latter! I became concerned at my joy spilling out on those I came in contact with, not wanting to be misunderstood. As I sought Him on the matter, this is what God the Holy Spirit shared with me. We were riding the 'wave,' surfing in the waters of reformation! This 'wave' threw us, slammed us upon the Rock, and we were stunned, shocked, trying to stem the fear. It felt like an earthquake, so much lost. We were trying to get our 'bearings'! All the while, our 'heads' were swimming, our emotions running wild! But deep within was an unexplainable calm, a deep stillness, a JOY! Halle! The light began to dawn! We were BEACHED upon THE ROCK! We were 'slammed' against THE ROCK! Now we had our BEARING! We are back on course, in the SHIP, not on a surfboard, of reformation! This 'SHIP' was not the TITANIC. It was UNSINKABLE!

The CHURCH must change the culture, must infiltrate all realms of society with excellence and integrity. We must abide vitally united to the VINE and LOOKING unto JESUS! Not to the government, the world systems, only God can change a heart, and that will bring a cultural change that will bring His kingdom rule upon the earth. In spite of all the 'bad news,' it is a glorious day for the church of Jesus Christ and the spreading of the gospel of His Kingdom!

At the second night of the conference, Apostle Jim was introducing the worship team, of which Glenda and Jeremy were a part. In his introduction, he said, "From Living Water Ministries in Cross Plains founded by Apostle Colleen Anderson." 'Apostle' went through me like the voice of the Lord! I was trembling under the impact of it. I knew this was a 'sign.' I shared with Max concerning my strong reaction. Max said he felt the spiritual impact of that himself and sensed strongly God was confirming the apostolic office through Apostle Jim because of his level of apostolic authority! It would become needful for me to walk in another dimension of authority in the Spirit. It was certainly a part of the 'picture' of the Father's ever-unfolding plans for my life that I did not have a clue about, as well as being acutely aware the process of preparing me to step into that role from where I was might be very challenging!

A first cousin, Jo Riddle, a close friend of mine since childhood, had the most awesome new beginning of us all! She passed from earth to Glory on the nineteenth. I had visited her on the fifteenth and left crying out to the Lord not to let this go any further. "She is in such need of Your grace and mercy, she loves You so, take her home quickly!" I received a call from Sherrie just as I had arrived back in Corpus Christi — a massive heart attack took her instantly! Jo was safe and sound and experiencing the joys of heaven and the rewards of her salvation! Oh, the mercies of our God! I was to meet Pat on Friday in San Antonio to attend the memorial services on Saturday, in Hamlin, TX. She had asked Pat and me to minister in song and for me to share.

Entry in my Journal 11/23/08:

What a trip, Lord! I suppose 'things just happen,' but somehow I just don't believe that! Pat decided for us to travel in his new Corvette, and the route to West Texas would take us through a very long stretch of road, barren land and no towns for miles. A blow out! The good news, the 'Vette had tires you could drive another fifty miles before they went flat, if you drove under sixty! This was Saturday, the closest town was Ballinger, not a very big place to find a tire for a Corvette! Services were at two o'clock, two hours away from Balinger. Time was tight. The only place open for service did not have a tire! We began to make calls to surrounding cities, located a tire, and they would have to go pick it up! No way we could make the service! No rental car place. The owner of the place only had one large flatbed truck and agreed under the circumstances that he would rent it to Pat! We would have to be back before they closed at five-thirty! We were grateful and laughing as Pat helped me up into the truck. We started out in a Corvette and ended up arriving barely on time in a big flatbed truck! We attracted a lot of attention as we stepped out, all dressed up for the services! Of course, with Pat's sense of humor, he made the most of it. What laughter and fun we shared, how You, Lord, lifted our spirits in the midst of all the hassle! Thank You for the sweetness of Pat's and my relationship. What a comfort and blessing the fun, foolishness and joy were, and your grace that gets us through and over!

2009: The year of the Vine!
Journal 1/3/09:

"And if the Vine, then the Branches, and if the Branches then the Fruit and if the Fruit, then the Wine! Come and Dine! The Master Calleth! He is the Vine, we are the branches. He who abides in Me shall bear much fruit. I would that you bear much fruit, more than thirty-fold, more than sixty-fold, but a hundredfold! As the fruit produced from the indwelling Spirit increases, so do the works of the kingdom increase! Why do you marvel at the things you see ME do? Greater works than these you will do! The wine is pressed from the fruit in the wine press! I will extract some of My best wine in this time!"

"Faith and Patience. Love and Grace. Fruit and Works. Communion and Community. Partners in the Kingdom. You can't have one without the other. Align! Align! Align!"

My prayer: Lord, I come boldly to Your throne of grace and build an altar of worship! I present the whole burnt offering, Lord. I present my whole self to You, having been made a holy and acceptable sacrifice through Your sacrifice at Calvary. I plead that Blood, Father God, the redeeming power of the Blood of the New Covenant over myself and my seed. As for me and my house, we shall serve You! We will worship You! We will follow You wherever You lead us. AWAKE! AWAKE! Family of God! AWAKE, sons of the Living God. I say AWAKE out of your slumber, come up, come out, come into position! Put on your coat of many colors Your Father has made for you! Dreams! Visions! Angelic encounters! Holy Visitations! The Lion of Judah within you is restless, He is beginning to roar! He will not be held back any longer! The hour will not allow it!

So be it! Yes! Father!

This word came from Holy Spirit on January 9:

"Yes, this is indeed the year of the Vine. When hasn't it been the 'year of the Vine'? And if the year of the Vine, then the branches as well and if the branches then the fruit, and if the fruit then the wine, and if the wine then the new wineskins! The beginning of the hundredfold and the glorious works of the Kingdom!

"I Am doing two things simultaneously, two works of the Spirit happening at the same time! To prepare the new wineskins for the new wine! I Am causing to come to birth and I Am pruning. In order for the release of My works of the kingdom, there must needs be an increase of the fruit produced by My Spirit! There are promises, prophecies, visions, dreams that have been in the womb of the spirit that have now come to full term, to a fullness of time! I have called for the midwives, it is time for the birthing! The body is beginning to turn, the 'head' is under pressure, the passageway is narrow. Suddenly! In a moment, breakthrough! Out of darkness into the light, out of the old place into the new, out of the constraints and constrictions and familiarity, into new levels of faith, love and authority. And you will face the giants with confidence and courage and you will see 'heads' roll!

"At the same time of causing to come to birth, I Am pruning away the wilted, dead, unproductive branches and snipping cords here and cutting away there! This pruning will produce an increase of precious fruit that will bring great pleasure to the Father, and

open the storehouses of heaven and blessing will be poured out in abundance! Great strides will be made by the church and mighty demonstrations of My power, beyond your present ability to imagine! My glory will continue to rise upon you and you will indeed shine as stars in the darkness!"

Thank You, Father.

This year and the next would prove to be awesome, exciting and fast-moving! Very satisfying and fulfilling! I was not only experiencing a blessed harvest, I was sowing into the lives of those around me and experiencing the wind of the Spirit swirling all around. Truly, the plowman was overtaking the reaper. Randy was in a good place spiritually; restoration and activation. We had heart connections to the same people, increase in dreams, visions, and the prophetic in all of those around me, within the 'troop' the Holy Spirit had set me in! I was energized and challenged! The relationship with Sonya was an honor. I was so blessed that the Father had chosen me to be one of those in her life to encourage her, pray and fan the flame of passion that was upon her. The vision and call God had imparted to her, and continued to explode within her and around her, was a large part of my assignment for however long. The way my heart had been melded to hers, I foresaw that to be unending!

Interesting: in March, she called to come and visit. We had begun to meet one day each week. I would fix us lunch and she would share her heart and the Holy Spirit would minister to her and she would challenge me! But this day, in her time with the Lord, He had instructed her to ask me to become the Apostolic oversight for her and the ministry the Lord had called her to form. The Holy Spirit had recently confirmed it would be called 'Blue Nations'! The Lord had already set a team of young adults around her and Charles with the same vision!

The downloads, visions and encounters began as a Joseph's company to feed the poor, and then advocating against slave trafficking. A continuing, unfolding vision including Israel! She had begun to have such a heart for Israel and felt she had Jewish roots. Light came as to the 'happening' at the conference last year, when Apostle Jim

Hodges set that in place with the level of authority in the spirit, for me to assume that position.

Amazing! Our continuing journey together would become even more exciting, challenging and awesome!

February 12th through April 16th Journal Entries:

I feel the need to journal this in detail, if possible! Such a continual flood of tears and tongues for so long. An unusual manifestation of Your Presence with me and in me! I began to feel such a tender loving sense of Your Presence upon me, such holy emotion, indescribable, a 'oneness,' more than I could hardly bear. I was immersed in a realm of the Spirit that enveloped past relationships and You were communicating to me that my experiences in those marriages grieved Your heart for me and had not been forgotten, and at this time You wanted me to experience the blessing and to know what You intended for Your man and woman in a godly relationship. A pure love, in a true supernatural, earthly relationship, which expressed Your love to the man and to the woman out of Your spirit within! Wow! This cannot be adequately expressed! During all of this, the deep in me was released, a dam burst, my soul was freed! Then You said You were betrothing me to a wealthy Jewish man, Jew and Gentile, and this would be an end-time prophetic sign! This became overwhelming. I was literally undone.

You have continued to remind me that You chose to use me as a prophetic sign from the beginning. My very life has been a prophetic 'seed.' My journey with You, your direction and instruction, the connections; my life has been displayed like a revelation of things to come, road signs. My God! Where is THIS going, PAPA? This is unreal. Holy Lord, protect me, shield me, keep me, I am Yours! I trust You! I do. But this is more than I can deal with. But know that I know You are behaving toward me as a Bridegroom. Is this about me crying out to You, Father, that I must needs be more in love with my Bridegroom? You know the place You put me in the Spirit, enveloped in Your love. I could only cry out 'Yes!' to any plans You have for me. I have been so content. You have filled every need, surrounded by family, comfortable and comforted. Don't let me misrepresent You by my words or my life.

The unfolding of this is going to be VERY interesting! No wonder the supernatural laughter that happened during part of all the weeping. And I thought about Sarah when You told her she was pregnant and she laughed! Lord, You have to admit, from a human standpoint, this is pretty awesome!

February 21st:

Lord, I have never been here before, as You well know! In the midst of a world in turmoil like I have never experienced in my eighty years! I feel as though I am being carried or moved gently along by the 'current' of a river of divine purpose!

These precious ones You have joined me to, that You have given such assignments for these 'end-times,' You are bringing out of 'hidden' places and networking together. It is so plainly, unmistakably Your doing, Your word unfolding before our eyes in a panoramic revelation! I am 'struck dumb'! I see myself with others in a hidden part of a river, flowing quietly; a gentle current moving us slowly but surely along. I feel so quiet and peaceful within. You have taken everything out of my hands and placed me with others who are a part of more than I can wrap my mind around! It is all gloriously, absolutely impossible for man to conceive or accomplish! Holy! Awesome! I am definitely in 'over my head in this river'! [Again! I may be drowning!] The dreams, visions, encounters, directions You are giving to all of them were and are SO supernatural! Their boldness and courage, the call and anointings You have placed upon their lives! And Jordan is one of them. Such visionaries! I am stretched! To say the least! I am aware of the magnitude of Your hand upon us all in this hour!

There is a humility that comes from seeing from where we have come, but the greater measure of humility comes from seeing our future! What is before us is impossible without the Power of Your grace, Your strength, Your wisdom and Your guidance! On a personal level, I must reach another level of faith! Lord, give me the gift of faith! Of healing! The perfected gift of love and discernment! I need to be fearless and bold!

Oh! Papa! You are SO good to those I love. Lord, bless me, cause Your face to shine upon me. Thank You for seeing to the increase upon the generations and the restorations upon your family! Lord, hold on to us!

I am significant!
I am known to God!
He knows who I am!
He knows me by my name!
He is always present with me!

March 19th:

I was in San Antonio for the birth of Noah Maxwell Bennett. Once again, Lacey was remarkable, James was a trooper and proud father! Beautiful, perfect baby. 8 lb., 4oz, 22 inches long! Thank You, Father, for the gift of this child to our family, purposed in Your appointed time, another righteous seed now in the earth for Your kingdom purpose!

April 16th:

This has been a season of stirrings, pressures, frustration, 'groping,' restlessness, AND AWE in Your Presence! 'Sparklers' of light, breakouts and breakthroughs! Revelation and illumination! I marvel at the 'shakings' and the revelation and freedom they produce! Who can explain or interpret the ways and the works of the Spirit in our innermost being and our lives? I am becoming a believer who believes! I am a lover who is learning to love! And to know Who love is! I am a seeker of truth and I am coming to know Him who is truth!

I have loved the light, and when the Revelator entered my life, illumination began! One day I will know even as I am known! For He will have shaken all that can be shaken and all that will be left is

the Kingdom of God. My understanding will be fully enlightened!
Amen!

The revelation that 'exploded' in my spirit this morning: I am
an ISRAELITE! Somehow my true identity was revealed supernaturally, unexpectedly to my understanding, into the core of my
being and I KNOW what I had only knowledge of, but obviously
no revelation of. I felt a 'shockwave of light' within my very being
that brought an alignment, as truth exploded into the darkness of
my understanding! This is AMAZING! After all these years of my
relationship with Christ, of believing the word, I thought I KNEW
I was of the seed of Abraham, that I had been grafted into the Vine.
No longer "male or female, bond or free, Jew or Gentile but all one
in Christ." No longer an 'outsider' without covenant.

This revelation did not come from the outside in, but what I had
believed in my heart, my 'inner man,' 'my spirit man' knew full
well, exploded through the separating veil up into my understanding
and flooded my being with 'light.' I am a true ISRAELITE! And
Holy Spirit said, "From the Tribe of Benjamin!" Interesting, concerning Benjamin. Jacob [God changed his name to Israel] called
him the son of his right hand. The Benjamites were left-handed and
mighty warriors. Rachel had two sons, Joseph and Benjamin, whom
she died giving birth to. Joseph is a prophetic picture of Jesus, and
Benjamin a prophetic picture of the church. Benjamin was found
with Joseph's cup, and whoever had the cup became his servant.
The portion of land allotted to Benjamin was between Judah and
Ephraim. The full significance of all of this is still hidden. Thank
You for the promise that things hidden shall be revealed! Selah.

In a few holy moments, I knew my identity and the tribe I was a
part of! Emotion engulfed me. I was undone! I had been exposed to
this through Annelori, but there was always a 'block.' I 'heard' but
never 'got it'! Then years ago, I was always drawn to Sister Gwen
Shaw's ministry and teaching concerning our Jewish roots. Then
there was Chuck Pierce's revelation and continuing to draw the
church toward 'oneness' with Israel. Then last year, Sonya, Linda
and some of the group began to talk about the different tribes and
trying to determine what tribe they were a part of. I listened, entered

into some discussions, but always felt a little uncomfortable or concerned of perhaps the danger of getting into Judaism.

I have had a strong desire for the word, of course, to search out the scriptures for further revelation. I would be stirred and my spirit quickened as I would read of the light, or see the word 'illumination.' Often reading, and water would be pouring from my eyes so that I could hardly see to read. I knew the Lord was sovereignly bringing revelation, revealing mysteries of the kingdom. The shakings were opening us up to be able to receive the 'light'! Through this time, the Holy Spirit strongly led me to a book, *End-time Delusions.* I would read and study just a few pages and start weeping and praying in tongues, stop and read a few more pages, and the same thing happened. This went on through the entire book! I had very little understanding at the time what the Holy Spirit was working in me. I felt in some sort of a 'shock'! The book emphasized the difference between natural Israel and spiritual Israel in interpreting the scriptures. Then this morning, as I was reading in the book of Revelation in describing the Holy City with the names of the twelve Tribes, the Holy Spirit engulfed me, no mistaking His Voice: "You are an Israelite of the tribe of Benjamin!" I was melted and poured out for quite a long time. What a huge breakthrough! I began a search for information concerning the tribe of Benjamin. I could not believe it! In the 'stash of books and files and boxes' from years back, I reached in and pulled out a binder I had received from Gwen Shaw years ago, and had never really studied. It was a complete study, with diagrams and pictures of the twelve tribes of Israel! Obviously, seeds planted in my heart along the way had seemingly sprung up overnight! Season, timing, hour! I pray the light that has dawned will become brighter and brighter! As always, Father, I am in Awe of You, and trembling!

I received a very exciting email from Bob Long. A pastor friend had sent him an email; he had a dream concerning 'staking' off cities and counties! He and Bob talked and prayed and they felt it was the Lord's plan. They sent out a rally call, organized intercessors, and on a designated day they would go to the highest point on the county lines and drive a stake, reclaiming the territory, decreeing and prophesying over the cities and land! One of the intercessors I was connected with in Corpus Christi did just that! This took place all over the state and nation. After the word I had released at LWM concerning the stakes in '08, I was very excited!

May 17th:

These first few months of the year have been awesome and now a 'lull.' I am somewhat overwhelmed. I trust the Holy Spirit is 'working behind the scenes.' I am sure, somewhere along the way I will be able to 'see,' after You have opened up the way and have me prepared to walk in it.

What a wonderful blessing to have some time with baby Noah! And to hear talk of their moving to Corpus! I am ecstatic! And even talk of Andreas, Lori's son, moving to Corpus after he graduates! A truckload of blessings for our family, Lord. Thank You!

July through August 14th:

A glorious month in Cross Plains! I love the way You order my steps, Lord! It always brings me such joy and makes the path much brighter, so I can see further and run faster!

Such a blessing that You purposed Sonya and Abby to go with me, for many obvious reasons! So much more that unfolded in Your Presence and among Your anointed and called ones that defies description! They were so blessed and were such a blessing! Blessed is not the word — they experienced a real move of the Spirit and ministry that blew them away and impacted them eternally!

I was in my 'melted and poured out' state for all three days of the conference! Don and Cherrie Crum, Sam and Nancy Brassfield, and the Merrells. Apostle and prophets who carry the glory, powerful 'equippers'! Elijahs, Pauls, Deborahs and Esthers! The minstrel prophets took us to a 'place' that released powerful decrees and legislation acted out prophetically and released God's will and word over America, Israel and the nations! I have never experienced such a 'governmental' anointing upon His chosen for divine Kingdom purpose at His precise timing that 'shook' up the second heaven and released some powerful things 'on earth as it is in heaven'! Glory to His Name! This was not a conference. This was a 'convening' of the chosen for legislation!

Sonya, Abby, and I stayed at the lake cabin and of course, Max, Norma, and Tina went out of their way to make us comfortable and keep us well-fed. There was not much time for showing them around. Before services on Sunday, I drove them by the even more beautiful than when I left it home the Lord had given us to enjoy and host His people, as He sent them to encourage us and to receive refreshing and ministry themselves! They were in awe of the place and the testimony of God's goodness and provision. [Precious memories.]

Almost the entire time I was undone, tears flowed and gratitude flooded my soul! One of the things the Holy Spirit spoke to me: "Many things coming to full circle. Visions and prophecies had come to a fullness of time. He was recycling, and at each cycle it was spiraling upward at a higher level. It was a 'harvest time' of seeds sown. He had prepared a table before me, a feast, in the presence of the enemy who had failed to prevent or destroy what God had ordained. He had seated me as guest of honor at the King's table, to flaunt me as a testimony to His great grace and power and the YES of His Word! My labor of love had not been in vain." Jesus! Lover of my soul! Worthy of more praise than this mortal body can express!

Barbara prophesied over me: "I was as Simeon, who had waited in the temple for the promised Messiah, rounded a corner and held the promise in his arms!" That could not have described the emotion and awe I was experiencing any better!

A part of the 'recycling spiral': Glenda and Jeremy returned 'home.' Jamie returned just recently after being on another assignment for a few years!

No way to tell of all the 'downloads' from the Holy Spirit all through the years. The visions, encounters and prophecies concerning LWM, Max, the team, and me. And to be in the middle of and a part of such holy happenings is more humbling than I can describe. As well as it being like receiving a panoramic view of the fulfillment of so much.

Sunday morning was like a heavenly scene. We were encased in a cloud of glory. The authority level upon the ministers was incredible! The 'crowning of Max' was a new kingly anointing for this time and move of God, a level of authority that would enable him to carry out new assignments and keep the 'command post' operating for the increase that was coming, and other awesome things for the worship team and many others.

Powerful words were released over Sonya and Abby and me. The Spirit had instructed Brother Don to use the ram's horn that the minister of Israel had used to anoint him with, symbolic of the one used to anoint King David, was poured out upon Max and all of us. The word and ministry from Brother Sam was under an anointing so powerful and released the word of the Lord for 2010. Barbara, Nancy, all a convening of the Lord, impacted all of us in that room, but we all knew the impact in the heavenlies was more than we could comprehend. It was indeed a marked day in the earth, by Father God's design!

Sonya and Abby left for Corpus after the service. The next two weeks were spent with the Evanses and the family, continuing to fellowship around the table of the Lord. I had planned to stay for the conference with Simon and Mary Alice Purvis.

I am thankful there were two weeks between conferences. We had barely arrived back down to earth, and then three days with Simon Purvis! I had the blessing of staying with them out at the Jordans' and it was 'wild'! After the governmental prophetic conference, there was no doubt this was all perfectly orchestrated by God Himself! Revelation! Alignment! Order! I went from melted and poured out to passionate and violent! As the revelatory word shot like an arrow, it brought confirmation that settled some things forever! Then from righteous anger to a river of tears of thanksgiving because of the needed, longed-for alignment! My God! My God! Great is Your faithfulness to Your people! Oh! How beautiful upon the mountains are the feet of those who bring the Good News!

October 20th:

Max called. During a time in prayer and fellowship with the Lord, the Holy Spirit instructed him to go to the farthest tip of the state of Texas, NESW, and 'Drive a Stake and Open The Gate'! This was a commission [I am sure only the first] after the 'crowning' and a new level of authority in July! He was to accomplish this before the first of the year! How can we doubt the Spirit of the Living God is hovering over the chaos on this earth, over Texas and over our United States! Prophets were prophesying that Texas will be the light of the nation! How can we not be filled with hope and expectancy for the coming days? Whose report shall we believe?!

Remember, He commissioned Dutch Sheets and Chuck Pierce a few years ago to go to every state, to historical landmarks and cities. Many prophetic acts were carried out, intercession, decrees and declarations all over this nation! The devil will once again be brought to an open shame and the Name of Jesus will be glorified! Our God has established His throne in the heavens and He rules over all! And His Kingdom will be established on earth as it is in Heaven!

Jesus! Jesus! My mind cannot take it in! How magnificent are Your ways! How big is our God! As I was penning those words, within my being I felt an anointing of strength, an expansion within. A feeling of importance in a very good, holy way! Your people are Your hands, feet, mouth, voice! Your body! You are the Head, we are the body, the government is upon the shoulders of the church! Oh! Dearest, awesome, holy Lord! Release upon us everything we must have to carry out Your will and to be carriers of Your Glory! Cause Your Spirit of wisdom and revelation to rest upon us and fill us, envelop us! Take Your seat upon the throne of every heart and rule over Your creation as our triumphant king! Blessed be the Name of the Lord Jesus the Christ! King of Kings, Lord of Glory!

Max and Norma completed their assignment before the first of the year, rather covertly! The boundaries were staked. It was 'Takeover Time'!

THREE DREAMS OF EVIL

November 2nd, 4th and 9th of 2009:

*W*hile I lay sleeping, an evil presence stood over me. I began to suffocate, unable to move, to breath. It is hard to describe the effect upon my body and faculties. I was struggling to move, to cry out the Name of Jesus, the Blood, but there was no air to push it out, such pressure upon my chest! I kept 'mouthing' Jesus! The Blood, the Blood! The presence was enveloping me, the darkness, smothering sensation was indescribable. All the while, I 'knew' I was not helpless, although I experienced fear and almost panic. Then a strength began to rise from deep within, when it seemed I was about to be 'swallowed' up by the evil presence. I awoke sitting up in bed shouting, "Jesus! In the name of Jesus! The Blood The Blood! Satan, go! Leave this room and this house, these premises NOW!"

I got up out of bed to pray, record and 'ponder' the experience. I knew I was being shown the effects of a strong spirit on assignment against the body of Christ, in this hour. Something we have not experienced at this level.

Of course, the obvious came to mind, Python, Jezebel, Belial.

They attempt to 'choke' out the Spirit, paralyze the prophetic, manipulate and bring death.

Then on the 4th, another dream.

I was in a large facility. It seemed to be a conference or gathering of some sort, obviously religious. I was sitting in a room as *if waiting, and an older woman, rather businesslike, gray hair, matronly, approached me about going with her to another area where a meeting was taking place. She had a Bible in her hand and I had my Bible with me and a handbag. I followed her. She opened a door leading to the area and as I started to walk through, I was startled to see there were no steps, just a long, narrow passageway that sloped downward to a basement room. I wondered if I would be able to walk it without falling. But I did. In the large room there were several women, looking very much like the woman who brought me. All of them dressed in rather tailored clothing. I began to feel uncomfortable. It seemed rather exclusive. They began to talk or have discussions. I do not remember what they were saying. I began to be aware their Bibles did not appear to be the same as mine. I began to experience intimidation, uneasiness, helplessness. How did I find myself here? The first woman came and stood in front of me and opened a very large Bible, and on the page the first line were very large, printed words, then the next two lines were graduated in size to smaller print. I could not make out the words. I began to 'fumble' through my Bible and couldn't concentrate, felt disoriented, confused and a little fearful. Then they began to lead me through other parts of the building, the facility? It felt cold, rather dark, the floor was stone, some narrow passageways. The walls were rock or stone. Suddenly I awakened, greatly alarmed!*

I stayed up a while to pray, record it and consider the significance of the two dreams. Once again, I knew I was being shown the influence and effect of other evil spirits upon the church right now.

Through the dreams, it all seemed colorless, all areas of dim light, as hidden, false doctrines, the 'gray' area between right and wrong.

This is obviously the spirit of Babylon. Humanistic agenda. Anti-Christ spirit. A form of godliness, but denying the power thereof. Idolatry.

The large facility/building could mean large organization/ denominations. It could be one's own church. I believe it is a picture of the present structure of much of the church.

The first large room was colorless, rather unimpressive, formal. There was no life of the Spirit. Kind of businesslike, or serious.

Doors have to do with choices and change. Passageways have to do with change and transition. I felt the other women may have represented religious spirits, and the situation with the large Bible, with the doctrines of men and not the 'full' gospel, or the gospel of the kingdom.

The stone floors and rock walls were the construction of the area in the basement [basement has to do with the carnal nature, depression, something hidden; also the dungeon spirit of Babylon].

I was 'heavy' concerning the dreams, then on the 9th, another dream of evil!

What I recall:

It was almost sundown, I think maybe 'twilight.' I was alone in an outdoor area, kind of rough terrain, rocky, kind of barren; once again rather colorless and lifeless. I was enveloped in trying to clean something up. I became aware of a large domestic cat sitting up kind of high on an outcropping of rock, just watching me. After a bit, innocently I reached and picked it up to pet it and it was very dirty. It rubbed against me like cats do and it got my jacket very dirty. [I was dressed in a business suit, pants and jacket.] I quickly put it down and began to feel uncomfortable and a little fearful. I walked away and the cat followed me and grabbed hold of my arm. I turned to look back to shake it off and it had turned into a distorted, ugly, dirty man demon! From that moment I was trying to free myself. It just held on rather 'sneeringly' and determined. I jerked my arm free and somehow fell. Then I was crawling on the ground, trying to get away and he was holding to my foot or ankle. I kept moving forward and looking back at him and demanding he go. He was dressed in a suit, a wool-looking, dirty sport coat and a dirty wool felt hat. His face was dark, fat with fatty scrolls, misshapen. While this was going on, in the dream I knew I was being shown another evil spirit on assignment against the body of Christ. I knew if I didn't give in or give up, he had no power over me, so I persistently kept moving forward, using the authority I knew was mine, and broke free and was suddenly awake!

Once again I was alarmed and disturbed but not in fear. I just had a peace, knowing the Lord's faithfulness and goodness and purpose for all things are good!

There were just so many details in the dreams, so real, and I felt a little overwhelmed at the prospect of interpreting them and His purpose. So I did feel strongly I needed to share with a few prophetic people for insight. And now I share with you so as to be forewarned of the enemies we face as believers as we move forward, the effect they have upon the mind, soul and spirit, affecting our decisions and circumstances. I remind you this is a spiritual battle.

I also knew that having the dreams before the new year of 2010, as well as three in sequence, was Holy Spirit's exclamation point, to listen and pay attention. Ten is a corporate number, the ending of one cycle and the beginning of another. New territory, new devils!

Cat: Predator, unclean spirit, bewitching, charmer, crafty, deceptive. Sitting high upon a rock. This is a witchcraft spirit operating in those who are in elevated positions, presenting themselves deceptively as being trustworthy. A spirit of divination. In the dream I 'innocently' picked it up and was defiled by it! And the defilement gave it a right to pursue and attempt to bring me down. It was somewhat of a battle to get free! Once again, "Resist the devil at the onset and he will flee!" Become wiser than our enemy!

He pursued me and caught my arm, which has to do with strength. The enemy was at work, coming against my life and purpose. Then as I pulled away and fell, he caught the ankle and foot, which has to do with faith and call or assignment, authority to tread on the head of the enemy!

The clothing must be significant because it was detailed. A hat has to do with 'covering,' opinions, attitude, thoughts. Filthy clothes have to do with uncleanness, unrighteousness, or self-righteousness. The hat and coat were of 'wool,' that is humanism, men's works, striving. The priests were required to only wear linen. There was to be no 'sweat' in the Holy Place.

I know these are significant. I don't have dreams like this, certainly not these kinds of dreams, and three in a row, on the same theme. And in each dream I knew God was letting me experience the effect of the works of darkness and the evil spirits involved. A day or two later, I came across a word from Chuck Pierce dated November 2 that 'blew me away'! I knew these were important for all of us.

Quote: 'The season of 'Ayin' or 'the eye' when God opens your eyes to the demonic realm in a greater dimension!' We must 'see' beyond the dark structure that we have discerned and view the realm of God. The Lord is showing you the demonic so you will know what is resisting you or that which will attempt to block or discourage you. When you see these foes, do not be overwhelmed. Remember, Elijah saw the 'word and the demon gods' that Jezebel was aligned with and ran from his position and authority. This postponed the Lord's plan to change the government of Israel. The Spirit of God is giving you the prophetic revelation before you need it!

Kim Clement: "You're coming out of a season of suffocation! Throughout this nation a spirit of divination has rested upon My people. The spirit which is python that suffocates and strangles you. It has taken the breath and life away from My people. Enough! says the Lord! You are coming out of a season of suffocation! This python has come close to My people and your energy has been lifted, your faith has been suffocated, your finances stolen. I have brought this beast to a place where it can no longer operate! Great revivals, movements, families have been suffocated. God said, 'Do not fear for 'I AM' breathing on the land that has been plowed by praise. I AM breathing upon the dry places and My Breath is going to revive you in a way you have never seen or felt before!'"
Thank You, Father God, for Your prophets!

The first dream: Python, Jezebel.
Second dream: Religious spirits, confusion, deception, spirit of Babylon.
Third dream: Divination, manipulation.

I feel there are 'details' that need to be revealed, sense there is something else the Lord wants us to 'see' besides the 'obvious.' So you give this some thought.

Three or four weeks prior to the dreams, I felt strongly the Holy Spirit instructed me to memorize, hide the words in my heart: Psalm 121, 37, 191 and 23. I poured over those scriptures and meditated on them night and day. And many of the scriptures in those particular Psalms have been emphasized by the Spirit to many. Anyway, I just thought this was connected to the above.

Max called on the 27th of January: "The Lord told me to call you. I don't know exactly why, so I'm just going to start sharing what is on my heart and what I believe the Lord is saying and showing me." Wow! The Lord is SO GOOD! [This is what I can remember.] He began talking about the religious 'systems.' The systems we are caught up in, humanism, seeker-friendly, self-promotion, and the idolatry of it! Then he said, "I believe the dreams the Lord gave you are the principalities, rulers, demon spirits that are involved in the 'system.' And this is what we will be dealing with and 'contending' with as we attempt to move forward, breaking with the 'system' leading people into true freedom in Christ, out of the natural into the supernatural, out of idolatry into true worship. Out of the 'rote' into the new, into God's flow! Loving and obeying the Father first, being more loyal to God than the 'system' and the ways of man and tradition, the pressure of produce, produce, produce! Being truly led by the Spirit, following the voice of the Shepherd wherever He leads. Truly putting our trust in God and not in the church where we gather, or in all the learned ways of the system."

We have been doing man's works so long, we don't even know it! That will make leadership very uncomfortable. It will look like rebellion, desertion, betrayal, how are we going to pay our bills? etc. But it isn't! It will expose what and WHO we really trust in! There are people who can't help themselves. The well within is 'springing' up. It's the heart and passion of the Lord moving them toward purpose and destiny! They want to hear God for themselves. They want to hear the prophets with the proceeding word of the Lord, and loving the recorded historical word and drawing closer to Christ through the understanding and light He brings. They want to experience for themselves everything He has made available to His people. It is God on the inside of them stirring, fanning the flame, igniting their hearts to have Him, to experience Him, to apprehend all the richness in Christ so they can do the works of Jesus! We all must be released to follow where 'He' leads. Everything must flow out of fellowship with Christ Jesus. Leadership must find creative ways to release people to obey God! We must help them and release them to become more accountable to God rather then the system, more faithful to God than to the church.

Example: If a leg is 'broken,' it's put in a cast until the bone is mended. If it's left in the cast too long, it will atrophy; it will grow weaker, not stronger. The 'cast' has been on too long in most cases. The church is certainly important and must continue in its journey of enlightenment, community, and creative ways of leading the people to Christ, who came to set His people free and to heal all who come to Him. This is the day of 'the saints'!

1 Corinthians 3:13-15; "The work of each one will become plainly, openly known, shown for what it is; for the day of Christ will disclose and declare it, because it will be revealed with fire, and the fire will test and critically appraise the character and worth of the work each person has done."

What works will be burned up? Those created through men's minds, which are consequences of reasoning. Is Spirit life breathed into it? Did you pay a price, did you yield to your own initiative? He purposes to dethrone us from the center of our lives. The power of flesh does more to hinder the work of God than any evil spirit. Our toughest battle is with the flesh! The devil doesn't work through power, he works through deception. What we need is more 'light.' When light comes, darkness flees!

January 16th, 2010:

On the way to church, just praying and worshipping, I began to cry out loudly: "I present myself to You, Lord, and all of my faculties, having been made holy and acceptable in Your sight through the precious Blood of Christ Jesus, as a living sacrifice, which is just my reasonable service." I was weeping and worshipping and heard the Holy Spirit say, "I want you to 'shift' to the other side of the sanctuary, as a prophetic act that I Am shifting you forward out of the familiar and comfortable once again into the new and unfamiliar and not so comfortable. You will do this as a prophetic sign of what I Am doing in My Church in this hour!"

I sought out Sonya for a few minutes and she shared a revelation the Lord had given her that the 'body' was experiencing an attack upon the 'immune system'! There was a 'systemic' problem, affecting the entire body! She had met with Mary the day before and she had been hearing the word 'systemic' as well!

Systematism: Adherence to a system or 'method.'
Systematize: To arrange according to a system, or reduce to a system or order.
Systemic: Pertaining to or affecting the entire body as a whole.

The Holy Spirit had also spoken 'broken cisterns' to her. Hector had been in prayer and had shared with her he had seen 'cracked clay pots'!

After I shared with the congregation about 'the shift,' and after prayer ministry time, I took the communion bread at the altar and walked back to my seat, toasting the Lord. I began to feel a stirring in my spirit and felt very alarmed that our wineskins would not be able to hold or accommodate the new wine that had been pressed from the fruit of the vine in '09 that He wanted to pour out upon us! Some pots would break and the wine would be spilt. The broken cisterns would not be prepared at all. I began to weep and earnestly plea for the Lord to prepare us to receive all that He desired and purposed for us! Standing in the gap, surrendering to Him to work within us and in our midst, presenting ourselves as living sacrifices unto Him, praying again Romans 12. Wineskins, vessels and cisterns have to do with spiritual structures.

Then I heard Cody behind me, in tongues and laughter, prophetically releasing the Lord's heart. I felt led to go back and engage with him, join in agreement with the manifest word of the Lord! "He sits in the heaven and rules over all and laughs at the plans of the enemy as well as man's!" Psalm 2, and 37:13, and later Job 8:32.

I meditated on all of these things. Certainly God was shedding light upon the dreams and confirming the prophet's words.

Jeremiah 2:13; "For My people have committed two evils; they have forsaken Me, the Fountain of Living Water, and have hewn out for themselves cisterns, broken cisterns which cannot hold water!"

Jeremiah 18:1-6; "Arise and go down to the potter's house, and behold, he was working at the wheel. And the vessel that he was making from clay was spoiled in the hand of the potter; so he made it over, reworking it into another vessel as it seemed good to the potter to make it."

Jeremiah 22:28; King Coniah was called a 'cracked pot,' a man who shall not prosper in his days and would be childless.

Fasting the following week, a word came from the Lord during prayer: "Oh, daughter! Is there anything too hard for Me? Have I ever failed you? Failed to deliver and enlarge your boundaries? Have I not said and shall I not do it! My! My! My! How far you have come! How far you still have left to go! An eternity more than I can tell you or show you or you can experience on this earth! Every desire that I have given you, I will fulfill and you must trust that this is so. Continue to trust Me, lean upon Me! What can you really do without Me? I AM the only Way, the Truth and the Life! I never change, but you and yours, My people who are called by My Name are continually being changed, being conformed into My image. What can you really do but what I show you or lead you to do? That will remain? The ways of man will fail, but those who consistently walk and conduct their lives according to My way will never really fail or fall, although it may appear so in the natural because of the many challenges and satanic attacks along the way and the lack of spiritual perspective. But for those My children who have a lifestyle of charity, grace and kindness, and continually seek My Face, they never fail and I always deliver and bring victory! And you are lifted up and I receive all the glory!"
Thank You, Father.

I was so honored to be in the lives of Sonya and the family of 'Blue.' There was such a Presence of the Lord upon Sonya, so many encounters, visions, challenges, and fire! God the Holy Spirit was moving at an accelerated pace. My head was swimming. They would be going to Africa at the end of the year, to build The Beautiful Dream Center for the rescue of those involved in slave trafficking in Lesoto, South Africa. One day you will read the account of her, Charles, Maya, and their family's life and journey from pastors, missionaries, to advocating against slave trafficking. Ministering to the downtrodden and leading the people to the Promised Land! And also the story of those young adults God positioned by their side as they made their way through the jungle of roaring lions to cross over into God's vision and call upon their lives.

MOVING TOWARD THE
FINISH LINE

We are almost there! 2010 did feel like a year of a runner drawing upon every ounce of his training and stamina to reach the finish line!

We are on the last chapter of the book! It is February of 2011, and by the end of the month we will be entering the process of getting published! This has been a challenge, but another assignment that has been SO rewarding, in so many ways! I am excited for those who will read and will be enlightened and encouraged, and even perhaps be entertained and challenged! But much more for those who will be drawn into a place of intimacy and communion with God the Holy Spirit, and will become zealous for the Word and to know Him, Jesus! The Anointed One Who is the Living Word!

Let us finish up 2010! What an awesome year! Things were 'popping' the whole year!

In a time of intercession at the beginning of the year, I began to see myself in the center of a very calm, beautifully clear, still atmosphere. The Holy Spirit said, "You are in the eye of a spiritual storm!" I have been so blessed and feel so privileged to have been a part of three 'outpourings.' I cannot find the words to describe the wonders of all the manifestations of God the Holy Spirit upon all of those who were touched, caught up, radically changed and never the same, the revelations of Christ Jesus to our hearts that set us aflame. There was a 'spiritual earthquake' that created a great 'chasm' between religion and the religious system and the Kingdom of God, and brought about separations, for the separating unto God and His Christ! This 'latter day' storm has been brewing for years. There have been different velocities of wind, significant 'downpours' through the years, building up to a day purposed of God when a deluge would come. A perfect storm. We have experienced only 'previews' of a 'big one.' I only benefited from the testimonies of the Azusa outpouring, but I experienced the 60s and 70s renewal rain that covered America and some of the nations. I was in the middle, swimming and splashing around in the downpours of the 90s! But the greatest spiritual storm is yet to come. It is close, in fact all around us if we are in the 'eye'! The eye gives us time to prepare, make changes, lay in store, and come out of the Babylonian system. In this deluge, the Kingdom of God on earth and the Kingdom of Heaven will merge. His Glory will fill the valleys and cover the mountaintops!

Oh, the Glory of Your Presence! We Your people give You Reverence! So arise to Your rest and be blessed by our praise as Your Presence, Power and Glory are manifest!

Randy was experiencing some debilitating health problems that were going to require surgery. 2010 was a challenging year for him; two major surgeries before the year was over, and a long recovery. But recover he did! Praise God for His grace upon all situations and answered prayer!

Our household felt like a nest of bees buzzing 'every which away,' Donny and Lori being the 'top buzzers'! Lacy and James moved into their new, beautiful home, both of them settling into their new jobs and being the most loving, determined, perfect parents for Noah any child ever had! Andreas for certain is moving to Corpus in June and will be here with us! My life is as full as my family, God and the church family can possibly 'stuff in,' and that being a glorious amount!

Journal Entry April 20th, 2010:

PAPA! How do I break out of these 'restraints'? I realize I am under an attack, probably because I am committed to pray, intercede, be on watch for my family and be available to Sonya and the Blue team. As well as 'stuff' going on in the church family, and the mandate to get the book finished! It is impossible to articulate what I am experiencing within my mind and soul! I remind myself that You know every thought and every word before it even comes out of my mouth and that Your Eye is ever upon us! I know I do not have to describe it to You, but it just helps to talk about it, to gain some clarity and hopefully some release! Not only am I feeling restrained, but feeling lethargic in 'contending,' going through the motions but no 'unction'! Just not my usual self! How do I get from where I am to where I need to be? I never like these places, Lord! I wonder, being God Almighty and yet our Father, how You handle it emotionally, hearing us crying out the same things when we are in one of these times of having to be reminded how powerless and inefficient we are without Your manifest Presence! No matter how far along the journey we have come, having to navigate life without the sense of Your Presence and the unction of Your Spirit, how can we not cry out in desperation?! I am trying, Lord, to carry on, to rest, wait and trust. But I am experiencing fear that I will let You, Sonya and the beautiful dream team down! Or myself! Or my family! In this 'state' I do not 'feel' I can be efficient, duly focused, and be a 'joint' that functions smoothly or a part of the joint that supplies what is needed to move! I can't bear to be a 'cog' in the wheel that slows it down, or a broken spoke that weakens it. I was swept into this as You are well aware! I haven't navigated in this part of the river before. Yes, Father! I hear You! What do my 'feelings' have to do with Your plans and will being fulfilled? I just keep doing what I know to do, just staying in Your lap, holding to the wheel! You are still in the driver's seat with Your hands upon everyone and everything!

Dearest Lord, I recognize You through divine connections, out of the mouths of Your prophets and anointed ones. The circumstances, the evidence of Your involvement and orchestrations, this is Your vision, Your plan to bring justice in the earth and these are Your called out ones. My inner man knows it is time! You are moving with a vengeance against the enemy to rescue Your precious ones. It is the beginning of the fullness of time! When I wrote those words, suddenly I saw in the spirit every mantle that had been given and placed upon man or woman historically recorded, every manifestation of Your glory, life and power through Your people. All that earth has experienced of heaven up to this time, it is being released and poured out accumulative as well as with what, "the eye has not seen nor the ear heard, or that has entered into the heart of man!" The Voice of the Mighty One of Israel is resounding and echoing all around the universe! The 'crowning' is taking place. "They shall be Kings and Priest unto their God! The Captain of the host is leading the charge! There will be only one kingdom standing! Dominion mandate! Angels awaiting their orders!

Lord! Thank You! That is awesome and I know it is happening! I hate to bother You, but back to 'me'! I am desperate! Minister of the Interior, Sir! I am depending upon You. Prayerfully and hopefully I 'will be coming up out of this stretch of the wilderness leaning heavily upon Your arm, forever changed'! With a new mantle for increased strength, perseverance and whatever it is that I need for the days ahead. Thank You, Father!

Entry 5/2:

Night vision. I think the Holy Spirit is opening my 'eye' to see through the 'veil'! Lately when I have lain down to sleep, before drifting off, with eyes closed, I 'see,' not distinct, as in a mist or haze or cloud, the faces of people. They look alive, non-threatening, men and women. Very pleasant, peaceful expressions, yet expressionless. I would question the Lord what this is about. Who are these people? No answer, but I sensed He was bringing or introducing me to a new dimension of the spirit realm. Then one night, after getting up from leg cramps, I lay back down, closed my eyes and just before drifting off, an 'opening' came in the veil! I first began to see a very bright yellow gold beam of light. Like a curtain, it began to fracture, creating an opening! There was a scene being played out within the opening. I was standing, just saw my back, with a large 'wolf' by my side. There was a large ferocious 'wolf' coming towards me, threateningly. The wolf by my side took a stance and growled loudly, and the other wolf ran swiftly, fearfully, and passed by me! As he ran by me, I saw he had very thick, matted, goat-like fur!

Two things came immediately to mind: "And the wolf shall dwell with the lamb and the wolf shall feed with the lamb. And they shall not hurt or destroy on all My Holy Mountain." Isaiah 11 and 65:29. Then Ezekiel 22:27; "Her priests in the midst of her are like devouring wolves, rending and devouring, shedding innocent blood and devouring her to get dishonest gain." Matthew 7:15; "Beware of false prophets who come to you dressed as sheep, they are devouring wolves!" My mind also went to the visions given to Linda Fortune in 2004, concerning the end-times, false prophets, and the coming 'falling away.'

Interesting and awesome experience. Thank You, Dearest Lord, for a continuing 'rending of the veil' that enables me to look beyond and see into another dimension and be instructed and warned!

Prophecy 5/10:

"I Am on a housecleaning spree, sweeping out the cobwebs, dust and debris! And nothing will stop Me! You think you are free, but when I finish cleaning house, you will be free indeed!

Take courage now and face the days ahead with your eyes upon Me. This is going to be a bumpy ride, but I will be right by your side! This will require great resolve not to turn back, but keep moving forward. I promise there will be no lack! The revelations and the mysteries of the kingdom I am releasing now will flood the nations! It will confront your flesh and assault your mind and jar your senses before the glory explodes around you and upon you and through you! The glory of My Kingdom will have its full expression!"

There had been stirrings in my spirit and much intercession concerning the need for the prophetic voice in our church and in Corpus Christi. Many of the people around me were traveling to other cities and conferences to hear the 'now' word of the Lord, and to just be in a corporate anointing and move of the Spirit under prophetic minstrels. To hear and receive from the prophets. I was sensing strongly that I was to host such a meeting or meetings. I was also sensing strongly the Father was wanting to minister and release especially over Sonya, Charles and the team that would be going to Africa.

I began to receive conformation. I shared some with Max. The first of July I received a call from him that he had heard the Lord two different times that he was to come to Corpus Christi! We began to pray, fast and make plans. We set a date for August the fourth and Jamie would come and lead the worship. Donny and Lori were going out of town that weekend and would allow us to use the whole house for sleeping accommodations, as well as the place of gathering.

We had our meetings on Saturday evening and Sunday morning, with a covered dish fellowship afterward. At least thirty or more people came, and half of them were young adults! Such an anointing, such a powerful Presence of the Lord! It was indeed a 'gourmet' table prepared for His people. He opened the springs for the thirsty and prepared a feast for the hungry. So much was released over the church, the city and region, the Spirit of prophecy flowed like a river! We were all very blessed!

Off and on during Saturday night, the Holy Spirit was speaking to me about kings and priests. He said, "I am revealing and releasing the kings and priests in the earth! It is time for kings to go to war, driving out the inhabitants of the land, cleansing the land of idols and establishing kingdom culture! It is time for the priests to weep before the altar, releasing holy incense before the throne and by the sprinkling of the Blood cleanse their 'houses,' build an altar and offer up the sacrifice of the sweet fragrance of burning flesh! Oh, how sweet and fragrant is the smoke from the altar upon which the sacrifice of flesh has been placed!"

I knew He would be placing a 'kingly' and a 'priestly' anointing on individuals, bringing a people to a maturity level as kings and priests in this hour.

The meeting on Sunday began with His Presence so heavy upon us. Powerful worship and release. Holy, profound revelation and release from the prophets. Max, moving under the anointing, began to place mantles, setting things in order in the spirit, bringing align-ment. There was commissioning, impartations, and releasing the sure Word of the Lord! The Holy Spirit's word to me during the night was being played out before my eyes!

Afterward, I shared the Word of the Lord, upon which was an awesome anointing to confirm and seal it in the hearts of those who were there! Also, making them aware of the prophetic significance of what was happening in our midst. It was a 'seed' Father God would continue to multiply in the earth! A 'preview of coming attractions' from the Great Director! It is now a 'fullness of a time' for the sons of God to step up into their 'kingship and priesthood' and rule over their allotted portion! It is the time for kings to go to war and not stay at home ' lollygagging' and gazing out the window at Bath Sheba! Instead, they should be engaging the enemy, removing the trespassing kings and their idols out of the land! Building altars, opening portals, presenting ourselves as the sacrifice upon His altar of love, allowing the consuming fire of His passion to consume the flesh. And He promises to give us beauty for ashes! I speak over you as Paul over Timothy, "inspired and aided by and through the prophetic words and ministry released over you that you will be able to wage the needed good warfare!"

For the past month I was hearing the word 'measure.' The Holy Spirit is measuring out a greater measure! This reminded me of Ruth as she lay at Boaz's feet on the threshing floor. We are being drawn to the threshing floor. And our Boaz will send us away with much more than we came with! More than enough for ourselves, so that we have more to give to others! We are leaving today with much more than we came with, and a fuller measure of the revelation of His love, a fuller measure of His anointing, and a clearer vision of where He is taking us and what He requires of us. And the awesome assurance that He who has called us to Himself, and anointed us, will enable us to do it!

Let me give you these scriptures: Revelation 1:6; "He has formed us into a royal race of priests unto His God and Father." Revelation 5:10; "You have made them [the redeemed] a kingdom, a royal race and priests to our God and they shall reign as kings over the earth!" And Revelation 17:14 declares that He is KING of 'kings,' LORD of 'lords'! Isaiah 61:6; "But you shall be called the priest of the Lord; people will speak of you as ministers of our God! You shall eat the wealth of the nations, and the glory, once that of your captors, will be yours!" YES!

There was no doubt in any of our minds that the Holy Spirit Himself had commissioned this gathering, and this would not be the last. About two weeks later, I received a call from Sam Brassfield.

WE ARE ALMOST THERE!

S am Brassfield was under the anointing when he called. I quickly grabbed pen and notebook, praying for an anointing as well, to be able to record at least the outline of what he was saying! He had been very stirred in his spirit concerning Corpus Christi and the coast! He said the Holy Spirit had begun to speak to him that morning. The following is what I was able to record [by my own hand! I was wishing I had a recorder!], and what I can recall:

"New song, sound coming forth! Opening new spiritual gates, releasing a breaker anointing to break through the gate that had fenced some in and fenced others out. This new gate leads to new, greener pastures! The church has to force its way through! This season is about breaking through the gate, breaking down the door! [If you know Sam you will understand my saying he was becoming filled with righteous indignation and becoming violent! I was not having a problem hearing him, I was just having a problem writing fast enough and trying to listen with my spirit and not my head!] This is a brand new thing! You haven't seen this before nor experienced anything like this before! This is new wine! No way the old wineskin can hold this or contain it! It's all about His Presence, the manifestation of the glory! There will be visitations and breaking out of organized religion like we have never seen! It's the remnant, the church within the church! The Lord says I'm calling out and releasing new mantles and assignments for the equipping!"

He stopped for a moment and said, "This for you from the Lord! New venues coming, new assignment, hosting His Presence, hosting the equippers. My gift to My body for the healing of My Church! This will be a one, two, three punch!"

He then began to talk about the Latino people, of Mexican, Indian and Spanish descent! "They are a people of humble hearts and My grace is abundantly poured out upon them in this hour! There is a bonus blessing for all those laboring or pouring into those of Latino descent. Revival will sweep Mexico and the coast! The glory will sweep away the young and old, the youth, college and career, capturing a generation for Myself!"

These scriptures are prominent in the Spirit at this time: Isaiah 42:8-23, Micah 2, and Amos 2:10-16, 9:11-13.

The Lord spoke: *"The closer my second coming, the greater manifestation of My Glory." He then gave him a vision of a house and the family waiting for the son to arrive, and watching as the first sign of headlights of the car as it came up the road toward the house became brighter and brighter. "There will be a continual increase of light and glory until I return."*

The reality of His Presence transforms us into worshippers. Worship is the evidence of a transformed life. True worship deepens and matures as we walk on with God. He will transform all that we are, and in the process, we become true worshippers, loving Him with all our hearts, with all our souls, and all our minds!

Isaiah 63: God desires to rend the heavens! Whatever is blocking us in this season from fully trusting Him, He wants to destroy. He is speaking into our specific needs in the form of 'breakthroughs,' as well as exposing those strongholds that are blocking those breakthroughs, and He is also speaking new strategies for defeating our enemy! It is breakout and breakthrough time! This is a time of awakening of a Remnant Company who will be great champions for God. The Lord Christ will release power and kingdom virtue through obscure champions.

This generation is emerging with an Isaiah 22:22 commission, a governmental people like King David who were worshipers and warriors!

He knew he was to come to Corpus Christi. We set up a meeting of the gathering of the remnant for September!

We had two days of gatherings and we believed there was a gathering of angels as well, as they would be sent forth to see that the Word of the Lord came to pass! I am totally out of 'words' for describing these events and happenings that were so awesome, holy and were so strategically timed of the Lord. The Father's voice through Sam brought many to attention and set them on course, and brought clarity and vision. Many of the young adults who were there had specific ministry, as well as many others. I believe the great words and ministry to Pastor David are still resounding loudly in his ears!

At the closing, Nancy had been walking the floor, praying over what she was hearing the Lord say, somewhat fearful to release it! She came to me for agreement and permission to release it. It was all quite profound. Briefly: a huge wave was approaching the coast, a tsunami that would cover this area. Its waters would be as the sea and as far as you could see! This is a spiritual wave and I believe it is time for Corpus and the entire coast to experience the harvest of seeds sown into this soil and released into this area from years ago. So many prayers, decrees, prayer walks and drives! There is an awesome body of Christ on the coast; the heavens are being bombarded with sounds of worship, praise and the testimonies of the people of God. One ministry sent by God to this area years ago, Shammah Ministries, has been faithful warriors for Christ in this area for years. I am blessed to be here and to be a part of and to experience the coming WAVE!

I received an email from Jamie, a very detailed dream. The scene was in Corpus Christi and here at our home, where we had held the first gathering when she had been present. She was central in the dream, but others were present, with several young adults. She had not been told anything concerning the later meetings with Sam and Nancy. The dream was very detailed, and real.

Briefly: A storm, waves of water hitting against the bank of glass windows on the north side of the house, until all that could be seen was an ocean of water engulfing everything as far as you could see. It was all pretty threatening. Then the water receded and the terrain looked bleak, red like red clay, almost desert-like, a lot of sand and pebbles. At that point, suddenly she was lifted up and over the area and was looking down upon it and it looked like the Garden of Eden! Plush, green and tropical! Many more details.

Just a few clues to what the Holy Spirit is saying over Corpus Christi and this region:

Donny's house and the large room: There is a remnant, a group of believers in this area that have a large influence in the heavenlies!

Jamie is a prophetic minstrel: Represents the sound of worship and praise that is rising up in this area and impacting the atmosphere!

The bank of windows: There are four large glass windows. Four is a finishing number, completed revelation, four seasons, global implication.

Windows: All things revealed and open to those who believe! Revelatory gifts, illumination, opportunity! What is coming will bring a 'tsunami' of revealed truth and revelation! He is the Spirit of Wisdom and Revelation!

Taken up to reveal the devastation: Desert, red clay, sand and pebbles; a difficult time period. The flood revealed the flesh, carnality, religiosity, and frailty of man.

The voice of Holy Spirit, the prophetic calling you 'up higher' to see from a 'heavenly perspective' the true realty, to see what God sees. What was seen through spiritual eyes was the Garden of Eden, restoration, lush foliage, green trees of righteousness, true life of the Spirit. Fellowship with the Father!

We continued to receive more confirmation. Sonya called then emailed a dream she had received: Same location. She and I in our swimsuits were sitting out by the pool. A crocodile was in the pool and would raise its head above the water and swim toward us. There were three birds flying around, they were tropical-looking. Suddenly she began to see waves of water coming from the west. [We were on an acre-and-a-half, and on the west there were three vacant lots covered in trees and brush.] The water rose, wave after wave until it engulfed the swimming pool area. We just sat and watched as it all happened and the waters receded and carried the crocodile with it! That old ancient Leviathan spirit! We were in our swimsuits; obviously this would be water over our 'heads.' We will not be able to understand from our natural reasoning. Only the spiritual man that Paul speaks of in 1 Corinthians 2:10-16.

Corpus Christi, the region and the coast is breaking through and going 'beyond.' Three angels are watching over us!

I made the trip back to Cross Plains with Max and Norma for my yearly visit home!

It wraps its arms around me like a mother's love! Memories surrounded me as I sat on the porch and looked across the fields, across the little valley, and scanned the hills of the Callahan County Divide. *And in my mind's eye, I saw Pat with his dog and one of us running after him to keep him close to home and out of the barbed wire fences! My grandparents, aunts and uncles, cousins and friends, Dad and Mom, Pat and me. Either visiting around the dinner table, working in the fields and going about the numerous chores! Cooking huge meals for the family. Mom catching two or three chickens for frying, wringing off their heads and skinning off the feathers! Mixing up the biscuits, mashed potatoes, opening up a jar of beans from out of the cellar, cutting up some fresh tomatoes, peppers and cantaloupe from the garden! She had already been up early that morning making a cake or cobbler, because there always had to be a dessert or Dad would 'fuss'!*

The old peanut thresher kicking up a whirlwind of dust and me with a hat on and a bandana tied around my face so I could breathe without inhaling the dust as I sewed up the sacks of peanuts as they came out of the thresher!

As you were reading, I know you were almost 'overcome with emotions.' Ha! Nostalgia almost made you cry, then your mouth began watering over the scrumptious meal! [Amazing, we were all very strong and healthy!] And as you were grimacing over the chicken scene, you found yourself indignant and gasping at the last!

An old song came to mind: "Wouldn't take nothing for my journey now!"

The wave made up of the Martinezes, Abby, Cristen, Nathan and Richard hit the shores of Lesoto, Africa in December! Difficult for us, but a blessing for the community there. And the first big wave of slave trafficking awareness in Corpus Christi was launched the following week, headed up by the Blue Nations team. GOD things are happening in this city!

2011 came out of the gate like a bucking bronco! I believe this is the year of the Horse! I see the warhorse described in the scriptures, chomping at the bit for the rider to let him run, mane flying in the wind, tail up in the air.

Max had called: Two days with Alimu Beeftu in January, to finish what God had sent to release in December. He felt certain Randy and I were to be there. If Randy did not feel led to bring me, then he would come after me or fly me! I called Randy and asked him to pray. He called me the next day, definitely I was to go. The Lord, through Pastor Beeftu, has something for me as well as for you! Off we went on Thursday to go by Pat and Martha's new place, and up early the next morning to drive into Cross Plains for the ten o'clock meeting on Saturday. We arrived close to eleven because of the weather. From that point until noon on Sunday would impact Randy as well as myself profoundly! Every word from Apostle Alimu's mouth out of the book of Ruth was so revelatory, powerfully prophetic and timely! Veils were rent, walls crumbled, ungodly cords severed, lies dismantled and the way made clear!

Randy was absolutely 'undone awakened and energized' to move forward. We all were. You know how it is, we felt like this meeting had been purposed of God just for Randy and me at this time. We were in awe and so very blessed! The Holy Spirit had spoken to Alimu in December and told him he was not to deliver this message until January fifteenth, for the church would not be ready to hear and receive until then! Everyone that was supposed to be there was there to hear the word of the Lord for the hour for each of us. And for Living Water corporately.

I will leave you with a cliffhanger, just in case the next years will necessitate another book for the finale, that you would certainly want to read!

It became necessary for Randy to find a house for him to move into. The loan was a miracle. As he was looking with our realtor friend Brian, Randy suddenly began to have thoughts, 'This is large enough for Mother and me to live together.' Within himself he just prayed a little prayer, 'Lord, I've been so lonely, and I would really enjoy having Mom live with me and for us to have a place fitting for meetings.' About thirty minutes later, he received a call from Donny. "Hey, Bro, what's going on?" Randy replies, they talk, Donny shares with him his and Lori's desire to liquidate, downsize and buy a piece of land, but just were hesitant, not knowing what would be the best thing for Mom. They thought of trying to buy me a little house, but not wanting me to live by myself. Randy, of course, was elated! Donny would be freed up to move forward! Randy called later, so excited, telling me the conversation. My heart leapt. I knew the Father was moving on the behalf of this family in this season! Donny, Lori and I spoke later, reassuring one another that this was indeed the Lord!

This was all my wonderful Lord's doing! I am acquainted with His Ways and His watchful care over me and those I love! I am filled with joy and expectation for the coming days! My faith is increased, I am hope-filled and so very blessed. The perfect house became available, and the loan will close in March, with a little hard place and a few challenges in between. These four years with Donny, Lori and the canine family have been so precious, I have been so comfortable and content. I have learned not to hold on too tightly to anything. Every blessing has come from My Father and I make every transition with joy as all things are working according to His plan and, 'Father Always Knows What Is Best For Me and Mine!

I leave you with these parting words spoken by Paul as he was saying goodbye to the Corinthians (2 Corinthians 13:11-14):

"Finally my brethren, farewell, rejoice! Be strengthened, perfected and completed, made what you ought to be; be encouraged and consoled and comforted; be of the same agreeable mind with one another; live in peace, and then the God of Love, Who is the Source of affection, goodwill, love and benevolence toward men; and the Author, Promoter of Peace will be with you!

"Greet one another with a holy kiss. I salute you!

"And may the grace, favor and spiritual blessings of our Lord Jesus Christ and the love of God and the Presence and fellowship, the communion and sharing together and participation in the Holy Spirit be with you all! Amen."

Colleen Anderson

A WORD FROM THE
LORD FOR 2011

January 6, 2011

I had been in prayer and just sitting before the Lord, wondering if
He had a word for me and the church for this year. I heard 'the
church is between the hard place and the Rock'! That surprised me!
What are You saying, Lord? He started at 2008, taking me on a little
revelatory journey.

2008 was a season of resurrection, the wind of new life, new beginnings was blowing upon My church. There was a 'changing of the
guard' at the gate in '08. And a part of the church began to lift up
their heads, looking unto Jesus only, for the King of Glory to come
through! Other kingdoms began to topple, satan lost his hold and
grip on many, and King Jesus began in earnest the restructuring of
the church and administering dermabrasion upon the face of the
church, removing wrinkles, spots and blemishes, to match the new
inner beauty that would be revealed.

2009: The year of the vine. And if the vine, then the branches; and
if the branches, then the fruit; and if the fruit, then the wine. '09 was
a season of the 'press' to extract the New Wine from the fruit of the
branches who had consistently been abiding in the Vine, that their
lives might express the nature of Christ, the Anointed One in all of
His power and glory.

2010: The year and season of a completed cycle. A new level of maturity and authority had come to a people who had stayed in the river, paid the price, made the sacrifice, and have now moved supernaturally into a place and position of maturity and authority in the Spirit for further alignment and governmental order, positioning them in rank and file to be able to move forward in an orderly fashion for the 'crossing over'! The year of the 'double portion' anointing upon the apostolic and prophetic.

2011: Year of transition as well as a fuller measure. A greater revelation of His love and a greater revelation and release of the immeasurable, unlimited and surpassing greatness of His power in and for us who believe! Now the Holy Spirit said, "We are 'between' the hard place and the Rock!" 2011 is a 'hinge point year.' The year between 10 and 12, as we transition from 2011 to 2012. I believe He was emphasizing the importance of our absolutely being led by His Spirit and the standard of His Word. This year of transitioning forward will determine our being in the right place at the right time, doing the right thing according to His direction to be victorious in the coming days! We have been in a 'hard place,' but this is an 'open heaven time' to transition out of the 'hard place' and up to the ROCK! He said, "Many believers will be securely established upon THE ROCK! Some will still be lagging behind, watching from afar, out on a 'limb' of indecision, deception, self-indulgence, under control of religious spirits, refusing to hear, refusing to 'see'! Still blinded by the God of this world! Those who find themselves established upon The ROCK of the truth of His Word and His law of Love, walking in obedience, compelled by the revelation of that Love, will indeed do mighty exploits in His Name, as there will be a marked increase in the transitioning year of 2011 of apostolic authority for signs and wonders that are beyond what man can imagine, dream or envision! For 2011 is indeed a season of open heavens by My great Grace for an ingathering that will confound many! A flood of Grace upon the earth from the Spirit of Grace! The message from My messengers will not be in lofty words of eloquence of human philosophy and wisdom, with persuasive words of wisdom, but they will be in demonstration of the power of the Holy

Spirit and power of God operating upon them! Imparting a higher wisdom once hidden from man's understanding, but now decreed by God Almighty to be released to lift you into the Glory of His Presence for your glorification!"

Transitioning out of the Superfluous, Superficial, Substitutionary gospel and religious system into the glories of His Kingdom! WOW! Lord, how awesome is that!

The Rock:

Genesis 49:24, Deuteronomy 32:13, Psalm 18:2, 19:4, 61:2, 144:1, Isaiah 26:4, Matthew 7:24, 16:18, 1 Corinthians 10:4.

Just a few scriptures for you to read.

THERE'S A GREAT WAVE BUILDING
Written by Donny Anderson

Dm   Am
There's a big move coming Can't you feel it in your soul?

     C   Dm
When things build up against ya Rejoice The Lord is close!

                  Am
The devil's come to steal your word he knows the end draws near

     C   Dm Am   Dm
His last stand against us The final fight is here!

                Am
satan's called up his spirits from the dark where they abide

     C   Dm
They're coming up against us with the devil at their side!

                Am
The battle cry has sounded satan's made his final move

     C   Dm   Am   Dm
When off in the distance a storm begins to brew!

                Am
There's a great wave building It's heading for the shore!

     C   Dm
The Army of The Lord They're moving into war!

                                        Am
They're armed with the word of God that cuts like a knife!

        C   Dm   AM   DM
They're moving into battle with the Angels by their side!

                                        Am
There's a great Light behind them it's the power from The Lord!

        C   Dm
They're pushing back the evil one as The Wave hits the shore

        C   AM
They're sweeping out the demons! Satan's gonna fall!

        C   DM   AM   DM
It's Jesus riding on the crest with the army of the LORD

Chorus:

Rejoice! Rejoice! Let Your Praises Ring!

satan's Been Defeated and The Battle Has Been Won!

Lucifer We've Won The War You'll Bind Me Down No More!

You've Got No Power Over Me God's Wave Has Hit The Shore

Rejoice! Rejoice! Let Your Praises Ring!

satan's Been Defeated And The B-A-TT-L-E Has Been Won!

CPSIA information can be obtained at www.ICGtesting.com
Printed in the USA
242543LV00002B/3/P